Just The facts101

Textbook Key Facts

Rwanda Mineral & Mining Sector Investment and Business Guide

by Cram101

Table of Contents

Index: Answers

Just The Facts101

Exam Prep for

Rwanda Mineral & Mining Sector
Investment and Business Guide

Just The Facts101 Exam Prep is your link from
the textbook and lecture to your exams.

**Just The Facts101 Exam Preps are unauthorized and comprehensive reviews
of your textbooks.**

Just The Facts101 Exam Prep

eAIN 449245

Foundations of Business

A business, also known as an enterprise, agency or a firm, is an entity involved in the provision of goods and/or services to consumers. Businesses are prevalent in capitalist economies, where most of them are privately owned and provide goods and services to customers in exchange for other goods, services, or money.

:: Management ::

_____ is the identification, evaluation, and prioritization of risks followed by coordinated and economical application of resources to minimize, monitor, and control the probability or impact of unfortunate events or to maximize the realization of opportunities.

Exam Probability: **Medium**

1. *Answer choices:*

(see index for correct answer)

- a. Risk management
- b. Cross ownership
- c. Preventive action
- d. Productive efficiency

Guidance: level 1

:: Credit cards ::

A _____ is a payment card issued to users to enable the cardholder to pay a merchant for goods and services based on the cardholder's promise to the card issuer to pay them for the amounts plus the other agreed charges. The card issuer creates a revolving account and grants a line of credit to the cardholder, from which the cardholder can borrow money for payment to a merchant or as a cash advance.

Exam Probability: **High**

2. Answer choices:

(see index for correct answer)

- a. Credit card
- b. CardIt
- c. HSBC
- d. Payoneer

Guidance: level 1

:: Statistical terminology ::

_____ es can be learned implicitly within cultural contexts. People may develop _____ es toward or against an individual, an ethnic group, a sexual or gender identity, a nation, a religion, a social class, a political party, theoretical paradigms and ideologies within academic domains, or a species. _____ ed means one-sided, lacking a neutral viewpoint, or not having an open mind. _____ can come in many forms and is related to prejudice and intuition.

Exam Probability: **Medium**

3. Answer choices:

(see index for correct answer)

- a. Innovations vector
- b. Core damage frequency
- c. Fisher consistency

- d. Bias

:: ::

_____ is the collection of mechanisms, processes and relations by which corporations are controlled and operated. Governance structures and principles identify the distribution of rights and responsibilities among different participants in the corporation and include the rules and procedures for making decisions in corporate affairs. _____ is necessary because of the possibility of conflicts of interests between stakeholders, primarily between shareholders and upper management or among shareholders.

Exam Probability: **Medium**

4. *Answer choices:*

(see index for correct answer)

- a. Sarbanes-Oxley act of 2002
- b. information systems assessment
- c. process perspective
- d. Corporate governance

:: Business ::

_____ is the activity of making one's living or making money by producing or buying and selling products . Simply put, it is "any activity or enterprise entered into for profit. It does not mean it is a company, a corporation, partnership, or have any such formal organization, but it can range from a street peddler to General Motors."

Exam Probability: **High**

5. *Answer choices:*

(see index for correct answer)

- a. Business
- b. Mavis Amankwah
- c. Westnile Distilling Company Limited
- d. Hellenic Australian Business Council

Guidance: level 1

:: Private equity ::

_____ is a type of private equity, a form of financing that is provided by firms or funds to small, early-stage, emerging firms that are deemed to have high growth potential, or which have demonstrated high growth . _____ firms or funds invest in these early-stage companies in exchange for equity, or an ownership stake, in the companies they invest in. _____ ists take on the risk of financing risky start-ups in the hopes that some of the firms they support will become successful. Because startups face high uncertainty, VC investments do have high rates of failure. The start-ups are usually based on an innovative technology or business model and they are usually from the high technology industries, such as information technology , clean technology or biotechnology.

Exam Probability: **Medium**

6. *Answer choices:*

(see index for correct answer)

- a. Private equity in the 1980s
- b. Magix
- c. Venture capital
- d. Special purpose private equity fund

Guidance: level 1

:: Television commercials ::

_____ is a characteristic that distinguishes physical entities that have biological processes, such as signaling and self-sustaining processes, from those that do not, either because such functions have ceased , or because they never had such functions and are classified as inanimate. Various forms of _____ exist, such as plants, animals, fungi, protists, archaea, and bacteria. The criteria can at times be ambiguous and may or may not define viruses, viroids, or potential synthetic _____ as "living". Biology is the science concerned with the study of _____ .

Exam Probability: **High**

7. *Answer choices:*

(see index for correct answer)

- a. Gay Mountain
- b. Second Generation
- c. ZADZADZ
- d. Yeh Dil Maange More!

Guidance: level 1

:: Management ::

A _____ is a method or technique that has been generally accepted as superior to any alternatives because it produces results that are superior to those achieved by other means or because it has become a standard way of doing things, e.g., a standard way of complying with legal or ethical requirements.

Exam Probability: **High**

8. *Answer choices:*

(see index for correct answer)

- a. Best current practice
- b. Project cost management
- c. Management styles
- d. Best practice

Guidance: level 1

:: Human resource management ::

_____ encompasses values and behaviors that contribute to the unique social and psychological environment of a business. The _____ influences the way people interact, the context within which knowledge is created, the resistance they will have towards certain changes, and ultimately the way they share knowledge. _____ represents the collective values, beliefs and principles of organizational members and is a product of factors such as history, product, market, technology, strategy, type of employees, management style, and national culture; culture includes the organization's vision, values, norms, systems, symbols, language, assumptions, environment, location, beliefs and habits.

Exam Probability: **Low**

9. *Answer choices:*

(see index for correct answer)

- a. Organizational culture
- b. Contractor management
- c. Human relations movement
- d. Talent supply chain management

Guidance: level 1

:: Human resource management ::

_____ is the corporate management term for the act of reorganizing the legal, ownership, operational, or other structures of a company for the purpose of making it more profitable, or better organized for its present needs. Other reasons for _____ include a change of ownership or ownership structure, demerger, or a response to a crisis or major change in the business such as bankruptcy, repositioning, or buyout. _____ may also be described as corporate _____ , debt _____ and financial _____ .

Exam Probability: **Low**

10. *Answer choices:*
(see index for correct answer)

- a. Management by objectives
- b. The war for talent
- c. Internal communications
- d. E-HRM

Guidance: level 1

:: Meetings ::

A _____ is a body of one or more persons that is subordinate to a deliberative assembly. Usually, the assembly sends matters into a _____ as a way to explore them more fully than would be possible if the assembly itself were considering them. _____ s may have different functions and their type of work differ depending on the type of the organization and its needs.

Exam Probability: **Low**

11. *Answer choices:*

(see index for correct answer)

- a. Committee
- b. Mighty Men Conference
- c. Audience
- d. Awayday

Guidance: level 1

:: Euthenics ::

_____ is an ethical framework and suggests that an entity, be it an organization or individual, has an obligation to act for the benefit of society at large. _____ is a duty every individual has to perform so as to maintain a balance between the economy and the ecosystems. A trade-off may exist between economic development, in the material sense, and the welfare of the society and environment, though this has been challenged by many reports over the past decade. _____ means sustaining the equilibrium between the two. It pertains not only to business organizations but also to everyone whose any action impacts the environment. This responsibility can be passive, by avoiding engaging in socially harmful acts, or active, by performing activities that directly advance social goals. _____ must be intergenerational since the actions of one generation have consequences on those following.

Exam Probability: **Medium**

12. *Answer choices:*

(see index for correct answer)

- a. Social responsibility
- b. Minnie Cumnock Blodgett
- c. Family and consumer science
- d. Home economics

Guidance: level 1

:: Management ::

_____ is a process by which entities review the quality of all factors involved in production. ISO 9000 defines _____ as "A part of quality management focused on fulfilling quality requirements".

Exam Probability: **Low**

13. *Answer choices:*

(see index for correct answer)

- a. Identity formation
- b. Management entrenchment
- c. Meeting system
- d. Professional performances

Guidance: level 1

:: Management ::

_____ is the practice of initiating, planning, executing, controlling, and closing the work of a team to achieve specific goals and meet specific success criteria at the specified time.

Exam Probability: **Medium**

14. *Answer choices:*

(see index for correct answer)

- a. Manager Tools Podcast
- b. Continuous-flow manufacturing
- c. Law practice management
- d. Project management

Guidance: level 1

:: Stochastic processes ::

_____ is a system of rules that are created and enforced through social or governmental institutions to regulate behavior. It has been defined both as "the Science of Justice" and "the Art of Justice". _____ is a system that regulates and ensures that individuals or a community adhere to the will of the state. State-enforced _____ s can be made by a collective legislature or by a single legislator, resulting in statutes, by the executive through decrees and regulations, or established by judges through precedent, normally in common _____ jurisdictions. Private individuals can create legally binding contracts, including arbitration agreements that may elect to accept alternative arbitration to the normal court process. The formation of _____ s themselves may be influenced by a constitution, written or tacit, and the rights encoded therein. The _____ shapes politics, economics, history and society in various ways and serves as a mediator of relations between people.

Exam Probability: **High**

15. *Answer choices:*

(see index for correct answer)

- a. Fractional Poisson process

- b. Polynomial chaos
- c. Law
- d. BCMP network

Guidance: level 1

:: Non-profit technology ::

Instituto del Tercer Mundo is a Non-Governmental Organization that performs information, communication and education activities. _____ , which was established in 1989, shares the same secretariat and coordinating personnel as Social Watch and is based in Montevideo, Uruguay.

Exam Probability: **High**

16. *Answer choices:*
(see index for correct answer)

- a. ITeM
- b. World Information Society Day
- c. The Malian Foundation
- d. Wau Holland Foundation

Guidance: level 1

:: Business models ::

A _____ , _____ company or daughter company is a company that is owned or controlled by another company, which is called the parent company, parent, or holding company. The _____ can be a company, corporation, or limited liability company. In some cases it is a government or state-owned enterprise. In some cases, particularly in the music and book publishing industries, subsidiaries are referred to as imprints.

Exam Probability: **Medium**

17. *Answer choices:*

(see index for correct answer)

- a. Parent company
- b. Interactive contract manufacturing
- c. Subsidiary
- d. Microfranchising

Guidance: level 1

:: Business law ::

A _____ is a business entity created by two or more parties, generally characterized by shared ownership, shared returns and risks, and shared governance. Companies typically pursue _____ s for one of four reasons: to access a new market, particularly emerging markets; to gain scale efficiencies by combining assets and operations; to share risk for major investments or projects; or to access skills and capabilities.

18. *Answer choices:*

(see index for correct answer)

- a. Secret rebate
- b. Limited liability limited partnership
- c. Single business enterprise
- d. Wrongful trading

Guidance: level 1

:: Workplace ::

_____ is asystematic determination of a subject's merit, worth and significance, using criteria governed by a set of standards. It can assist an organization, program, design, project or any other intervention or initiative to assess any aim, realisable concept/proposal, or any alternative, to help in decision-making; or to ascertain the degree of achievement or value in regard to the aim and objectives and results of any such action that has been completed. The primary purpose of _____ , in addition to gaining insight into prior or existing initiatives, is to enable reflection and assist in the identification of future change.

Exam Probability: **Low**

19. *Answer choices:*

(see index for correct answer)

- a. Open allocation
- b. Workplace romance
- c. Workplace relationships
- d. Evaluation

Guidance: level 1

:: Business ::

_____ is a trade policy that does not restrict imports or exports; it can also be understood as the free market idea applied to international trade. In government, _____ is predominantly advocated by political parties that hold liberal economic positions while economically left-wing and nationalist political parties generally support protectionism, the opposite of _____ .

Exam Probability: **Low**

20. *Answer choices:*

(see index for correct answer)

- a. For-profit charity
- b. Student@Home
- c. Free trade
- d. Architecture of Interoperable Information Systems

Guidance: level 1

:: Information systems ::

_____ are formal, sociotechnical, organizational systems designed to collect, process, store, and distribute information. In a sociotechnical perspective, _____ are composed by four components: task, people, structure , and technology.

Exam Probability: **High**

21. *Answer choices:*

(see index for correct answer)

- a. Strategic information system
- b. Reason maintenance
- c. Shadow IT
- d. Information systems

Guidance: level 1

:: International trade ::

In finance, an _____ is the rate at which one currency will be exchanged for another. It is also regarded as the value of one country's currency in relation to another currency. For example, an interbank _____ of 114 Japanese yen to the United States dollar means that ¥114 will be exchanged for each US$1 or that US$1 will be exchanged for each ¥114. In this case it is said that the price of a dollar in relation to yen is ¥114, or equivalently that the price of a yen in relation to dollars is $1/114.

22. *Answer choices:*

(see index for correct answer)

- a. Silk Road
- b. Global financial system
- c. Market price support
- d. Exchange rate

Guidance: level 1

:: ::

_____ is the production of products for use or sale using labour and machines, tools, chemical and biological processing, or formulation. The term may refer to a range of human activity, from handicraft to high tech, but is most commonly applied to industrial design, in which raw materials are transformed into finished goods on a large scale. Such finished goods may be sold to other manufacturers for the production of other, more complex products, such as aircraft, household appliances, furniture, sports equipment or automobiles, or sold to wholesalers, who in turn sell them to retailers, who then sell them to end users and consumers.

Exam Probability: **Medium**

23. *Answer choices:*

(see index for correct answer)

- a. cultural
- b. similarity-attraction theory
- c. personal values
- d. Manufacturing

Guidance: level 1

:: Strategic alliances ::

A _____ is an agreement between two or more parties to pursue a set of agreed upon objectives needed while remaining independent organizations. A _____ will usually fall short of a legal partnership entity, agency, or corporate affiliate relationship. Typically, two companies form a _____ when each possesses one or more business assets or have expertise that will help the other by enhancing their businesses. _____ s can develop in outsourcing relationships where the parties desire to achieve long-term win-win benefits and innovation based on mutually desired outcomes.

Exam Probability: **Medium**

24. *Answer choices:*

(see index for correct answer)

- a. Defensive termination
- b. Management contract
- c. Cross-licensing
- d. Strategic alliance

:: Generally Accepted Accounting Principles ::

An _____ or profit and loss account is one of the financial statements of a company and shows the company's revenues and expenses during a particular period.

Exam Probability: **Medium**

25. *Answer choices:*
(see index for correct answer)

- a. Trial balance
- b. Petty cash
- c. Long-term liabilities
- d. Normal balance

:: Business law ::

A _____ is an arrangement where parties, known as partners, agree to cooperate to advance their mutual interests. The partners in a _____ may be individuals, businesses, interest-based organizations, schools, governments or combinations. Organizations may partner to increase the likelihood of each achieving their mission and to amplify their reach. A _____ may result in issuing and holding equity or may be only governed by a contract.

Exam Probability: **Medium**

26. *Answer choices:*

(see index for correct answer)

- a. Forward-looking statement
- b. Partnership
- c. Closed shop
- d. Ordinary course of business

Guidance: level 1

:: Information science ::

A _____ is a written, drawn, presented, or memorialized representation of thought. a _____ is a form, or written piece that trains a line of thought or as in history, a significant event. The word originates from the Latin _____ um, which denotes a "teaching" or "lesson": the verb doceo denotes "to teach". In the past, the word was usually used to denote a written proof useful as evidence of a truth or fact. In the computer age, "_____" usually denotes a primarily textual computer file, including its structure and format, e.g. fonts, colors, and images. Contemporarily, "_____" is not defined by its transmission medium, e.g., paper, given the existence of electronic _____ s. "_____ ation" is distinct because it has more denotations than "_____". _____ s are also distinguished from "realia", which are three-dimensional objects that would otherwise satisfy the definition of "_____" because they memorialize or represent thought; _____ s are considered more as 2 dimensional representations. While _____ s are able to have large varieties of customization, all _____ s are able to be shared freely, and have the right to do so, creativity can be represented by _____ s, also. History, events, examples, opinion, etc. all can be expressed in _____ s.

Exam Probability: **Medium**

27. *Answer choices:*

(see index for correct answer)

- a. Digital artifact
- b. Scientific literature
- c. Document
- d. Data drilling

Guidance: level 1

:: Infographics ::

A _____ is a graphical representation of data, in which "the data is represented by symbols, such as bars in a bar _____ , lines in a line _____ , or slices in a pie _____ ". A _____ can represent tabular numeric data, functions or some kinds of qualitative structure and provides different info.

Exam Probability: **Low**

28. *Answer choices:*

(see index for correct answer)

- a. State diagram
- b. Chart
- c. Rhizome Navigation
- d. Four Square Writing Method

Guidance: level 1

:: Financial markets ::

A _____ is a financial market in which long-term debt or equity-backed securities are bought and sold. _____ s channel the wealth of savers to those who can put it to long-term productive use, such as companies or governments making long-term investments. Financial regulators like the Bank of England and the U.S. Securities and Exchange Commission oversee _____ s to protect investors against fraud, among other duties.

29. *Answer choices:*

(see index for correct answer)

- a. Market distortion
- b. Risk arbitrage
- c. Market depth
- d. Index cohesive force

Guidance: level 1

:: Marketing ::

_____ is based on a marketing concept which can be adopted by an organization as a strategy for business expansion. Where implemented, a franchisor licenses its know-how, procedures, intellectual property, use of its business model, brand, and rights to sell its branded products and services to a franchisee. In return the franchisee pays certain fees and agrees to comply with certain obligations, typically set out in a Franchise Agreement.

Exam Probability: **Medium**

30. *Answer choices:*

(see index for correct answer)

- a. Target market
- b. Franchising

- c. Marketing brochure
- d. Exploratory research

Guidance: level 1

:: Generally Accepted Accounting Principles ::

Expenditure is an outflow of money to another person or group to pay for an item or service, or for a category of costs. For a tenant, rent is an _____ . For students or parents, tuition is an _____ . Buying food, clothing, furniture or an automobile is often referred to as an _____ . An _____ is a cost that is "paid" or "remitted", usually in exchange for something of value. Something that seems to cost a great deal is "expensive". Something that seems to cost little is "inexpensive". " _____ s of the table" are _____ s of dining, refreshments, a feast, etc.

Exam Probability: **Low**

31. *Answer choices:*

(see index for correct answer)

- a. Insurance asset management
- b. Expense
- c. Net profit
- d. Management accounting principles

Guidance: level 1

:: Stock market ::

A _____ , equity market or share market is the aggregation of buyers and
sellers of stocks , which represent ownership claims on businesses; these may
include securities listed on a public stock exchange, as well as stock that is
only traded privately. Examples of the latter include shares of private
companies which are sold to investors through equity crowdfunding platforms.
Stock exchanges list shares of common equity as well as other security types,
e.g. corporate bonds and convertible bonds.

Exam Probability: **High**

32. *Answer choices:*

(see index for correct answer)

- a. Stockjobber
- b. Stock market
- c. Trader
- d. Matchbook FX

Guidance: level 1

:: Decision theory ::

A _____ is a deliberate system of principles to guide decisions and achieve rational outcomes. A _____ is a statement of intent, and is implemented as a procedure or protocol. Policies are generally adopted by a governance body within an organization. Policies can assist in both subjective and objective decision making. Policies to assist in subjective decision making usually assist senior management with decisions that must be based on the relative merits of a number of factors, and as a result are often hard to test objectively, e.g. work-life balance _____ . In contrast policies to assist in objective decision making are usually operational in nature and can be objectively tested, e.g. password _____ .

Exam Probability: **High**

33. *Answer choices:*

(see index for correct answer)

- a. Policy
- b. Distinction bias
- c. Belief structure
- d. Choquet integral

Guidance: level 1

:: ::

_____ is the means to see, hear, or become aware of something or someone through our fundamental senses. The term _____ derives from the Latin word perceptio, and is the organization, identification, and interpretation of sensory information in order to represent and understand the presented information, or the environment.

Exam Probability: **Low**

34. *Answer choices:*

(see index for correct answer)

- a. empathy
- b. interpersonal communication
- c. Perception
- d. co-culture

Guidance: level 1

:: International trade ::

_____ involves the transfer of goods or services from one person or entity to another, often in exchange for money. A system or network that allows _____ is called a market.

Exam Probability: **Low**

35. *Answer choices:*

- a. Trade
- b. Poundage quota
- c. Harberger-Laursen-Metzler effect
- d. financial account

Guidance: level 1

:: Semiconductor companies ::

_____ Corporation is a Japanese multinational conglomerate corporation headquartered in Konan, Minato, Tokyo. Its diversified business includes consumer and professional electronics, gaming, entertainment and financial services. The company owns the largest music entertainment business in the world, the largest video game console business and one of the largest video game publishing businesses, and is one of the leading manufacturers of electronic products for the consumer and professional markets, and a leading player in the film and television entertainment industry. _____ was ranked 97th on the 2018 Fortune Global 500 list.

Exam Probability: **High**

36. *Answer choices:*

- a. Sony
- b. Reading Works
- c. GainSpan

- d. Entropic Communications

Guidance: level 1

:: Consumer theory ::

A _____ is a technical term in psychology, economics and philosophy usually used in relation to choosing between alternatives. For example, someone prefers A over B if they would rather choose A than B.

Exam Probability: **Low**

37. *Answer choices:*

(see index for correct answer)

- a. Consumer service
- b. Elasticity of substitution
- c. Autonomous consumption
- d. Preference

Guidance: level 1

:: Commerce ::

_____ relates to "the exchange of goods and services, especially on a large scale". It includes legal, economic, political, social, cultural and technological systems that operate in a country or in international trade.

Exam Probability: **High**

38. *Answer choices:*

(see index for correct answer)

- a. V-commerce
- b. Issuing bank
- c. E-receipt
- d. Commerce

Guidance: level 1

:: Business ::

The seller, or the provider of the goods or services, completes a sale in response to an acquisition, appropriation, requisition or a direct interaction with the buyer at the point of sale. There is a passing of title of the item, and the settlement of a price, in which agreement is reached on a price for which transfer of ownership of the item will occur. The seller, not the purchaser typically executes the sale and it may be completed prior to the obligation of payment. In the case of indirect interaction, a person who sells goods or service on behalf of the owner is known as a _____ man or _____ woman or _____ person, but this often refers to someone selling goods in a store/shop, in which case other terms are also common, including _____ clerk, shop assistant, and retail clerk.

Exam Probability: **Medium**

39. *Answer choices:*

(see index for correct answer)

- a. Values scales
- b. Corporate social media
- c. Corporate housing
- d. Sales

Guidance: level 1

:: National accounts ::

_____ is a monetary measure of the market value of all the final goods and services produced in a period of time, often annually. GDP per capita does not, however, reflect differences in the cost of living and the inflation rates of the countries; therefore using a basis of GDP per capita at purchasing power parity is arguably more useful when comparing differences in living standards between nations.

Exam Probability: **Medium**

40. *Answer choices:*

(see index for correct answer)

- a. National Income
- b. Gross domestic product

- c. capital formation

Guidance: level 1

:: Data collection ::

A _____ is an utterance which typically functions as a request for information. _____ s can thus be understood as a kind of illocutionary act in the field of pragmatics or as special kinds of propositions in frameworks of formal semantics such as alternative semantics or inquisitive semantics. The information requested is expected to be provided in the form of an answer. _____ s are often conflated with interrogatives, which are the grammatical forms typically used to achieve them. Rhetorical _____ s, for example, are interrogative in form but may not be considered true _____ s as they are not expected to be answered. Conversely, non-interrogative grammatical structures may be considered _____ s as in the case of the imperative sentence "tell me your name".

Exam Probability: **Low**

41. *Answer choices:*
(see index for correct answer)

- a. Human-based computation game
- b. Interpellation
- c. PISCES
- d. Question

Guidance: level 1

:: Summary statistics ::

_____ is the number of occurrences of a repeating event per unit of time. It is also referred to as temporal _____ , which emphasizes the contrast to spatial _____ and angular _____ . The period is the duration of time of one cycle in a repeating event, so the period is the reciprocal of the _____ . For example: if a newborn baby's heart beats at a _____ of 120 times a minute, its period—the time interval between beats—is half a second . _____ is an important parameter used in science and engineering to specify the rate of oscillatory and vibratory phenomena, such as mechanical vibrations, audio signals , radio waves, and light.

Exam Probability: **Medium**

42. *Answer choices:*

(see index for correct answer)

- a. Frequency
- b. Pareto index
- c. Quantile
- d. Mean percentage error

Guidance: level 1

:: Stochastic processes ::

_____ in its modern meaning is a "new idea, creative thoughts, new imaginations in form of device or method". _____ is often also viewed as the application of better solutions that meet new requirements, unarticulated needs, or existing market needs. Such _____ takes place through the provision of more-effective products, processes, services, technologies, or business models that are made available to markets, governments and society. An _____ is something original and more effective and, as a consequence, new, that "breaks into" the market or society. _____ is related to, but not the same as, invention, as _____ is more apt to involve the practical implementation of an invention to make a meaningful impact in the market or society, and not all _____ s require an invention. _____ often manifests itself via the engineering process, when the problem being solved is of a technical or scientific nature. The opposite of _____ is exnovation.

Exam Probability: **Medium**

43. *Answer choices:*

(see index for correct answer)

- a. Vasicek model
- b. Loop-erased random walk
- c. Affine term structure model
- d. M/G/1 queue

Guidance: level 1

:: Poker strategy ::

_____ is any measure taken to guard a thing against damage caused by outside forces. _____ can be provided to physical objects, including organisms, to systems, and to intangible things like civil and political rights. Although the mechanisms for providing _____ vary widely, the basic meaning of the term remains the same. This is illustrated by an explanation found in a manual on electrical wiring.

Exam Probability: **High**

44. *Answer choices:*

(see index for correct answer)

- a. Protection
- b. M-ratio
- c. Bluff
- d. Check-raise

Guidance: level 1

:: Property ::

The right to property or right to own property is often classified as a human right for natural persons regarding their possessions. A general recognition of a right to private property is found more rarely and is typically heavily constrained insofar as property is owned by legal persons and where it is used for production rather than consumption.

Exam Probability: **Low**

45. *Answer choices:*

(see index for correct answer)

- a. Property rights
- b. Lockean proviso
- c. Intermediate rent
- d. Gross annual value

Guidance: level 1

:: Stock market ::

_____ is freedom from, or resilience against, potential harm caused by others. Beneficiaries of _____ may be of persons and social groups, objects and institutions, ecosystems or any other entity or phenomenon vulnerable to unwanted change by its environment.

Exam Probability: **Medium**

46. *Answer choices:*

(see index for correct answer)

- a. Accelerated Return Note
- b. Security
- c. Profit warning
- d. Split share corporation

:: Employment ::

_____ is a relationship between two parties, usually based on a contract where work is paid for, where one party, which may be a corporation, for profit, not-for-profit organization, co-operative or other entity is the employer and the other is the employee. Employees work in return for payment, which may be in the form of an hourly wage, by piecework or an annual salary, depending on the type of work an employee does or which sector she or he is working in. Employees in some fields or sectors may receive gratuities, bonus payment or stock options. In some types of _____ , employees may receive benefits in addition to payment. Benefits can include health insurance, housing, disability insurance or use of a gym. _____ is typically governed by _____ laws, regulations or legal contracts.

Exam Probability: **Low**

47. *Answer choices:*

(see index for correct answer)

- a. Supernumerary
- b. Holland Codes
- c. Employment
- d. Occupational sexism

:: Evaluation ::

_____ is the practice of being honest and showing a consistent and uncompromising adherence to strong moral and ethical principles and values. In ethics, _____ is regarded as the honesty and truthfulness or accuracy of one's actions. _____ can stand in opposition to hypocrisy, in that judging with the standards of _____ involves regarding internal consistency as a virtue, and suggests that parties holding within themselves apparently conflicting values should account for the discrepancy or alter their beliefs. The word _____ evolved from the Latin adjective integer, meaning whole or complete. In this context, _____ is the inner sense of "wholeness" deriving from qualities such as honesty and consistency of character. As such, one may judge that others "have _____ " to the extent that they act according to the values, beliefs and principles they claim to hold.

Exam Probability: **Low**

48. *Answer choices:*

(see index for correct answer)

- a. Commercial Product Assurance
- b. XTS-400
- c. Transferable skills analysis
- d. Integrity

Guidance: level 1

:: Shareholders ::

A _____ is a payment made by a corporation to its shareholders, usually as a distribution of profits. When a corporation earns a profit or surplus, the corporation is able to re-invest the profit in the business and pay a proportion of the profit as a _____ to shareholders. Distribution to shareholders may be in cash or, if the corporation has a _____ reinvestment plan, the amount can be paid by the issue of further shares or share repurchase. When _____ s are paid, shareholders typically must pay income taxes, and the corporation does not receive a corporate income tax deduction for the _____ payments.

Exam Probability: **Medium**

49. *Answer choices:*

(see index for correct answer)

- a. Shareholder primacy
- b. Poison pill
- c. Dividend
- d. Proxy statement

Guidance: level 1

:: Free trade agreements ::

A _____ is a wide-ranging taxes, tariff and trade treaty that often includes investment guarantees. It exists when two or more countries agree on terms that helps them trade with each other. The most common _____ s are of the preferential and free trade types are concluded in order to reduce tariffs, quotas and other trade restrictions on items traded between the signatories.

Exam Probability: **Low**

50. *Answer choices:*

(see index for correct answer)

- a. South Asia Free Trade Agreement
- b. New West Partnership
- c. European Union Central American Association Agreement
- d. South Asian Free Trade Area

Guidance: level 1

:: ::

In regulatory jurisdictions that provide for it, _____ is a group of laws and organizations designed to ensure the rights of consumers as well as fair trade, competition and accurate information in the marketplace. The laws are designed to prevent the businesses that engage in fraud or specified unfair practices from gaining an advantage over competitors. They may also provides additional protection for those most vulnerable in society. _____ laws are a form of government regulation that aim to protect the rights of consumers. For example, a government may require businesses to disclose detailed information about products—particularly in areas where safety or public health is an issue, such as food.

Exam Probability: **Medium**

51. *Answer choices:*

(see index for correct answer)

- a. similarity-attraction theory
- b. corporate values
- c. Consumer Protection
- d. hierarchical perspective

Guidance: level 1

:: Training ::

_____ is teaching, or developing in oneself or others, any skills and knowledge that relate to specific useful competencies. _____ has specific goals of improving one's capability, capacity, productivity and performance. It forms the core of apprenticeships and provides the backbone of content at institutes of technology . In addition to the basic _____ required for a trade, occupation or profession, observers of the labor-market recognize as of 2008 the need to continue _____ beyond initial qualifications: to maintain, upgrade and update skills throughout working life. People within many professions and occupations may refer to this sort of _____ as professional development.

Exam Probability: **Low**

52. *Answer choices:*

(see index for correct answer)

- a. Officer training
- b. Makers Academy
- c. Training
- d. human resource development

Guidance: level 1

:: Financial risk ::

_____ is a type of risk faced by investors, corporations, and governments that political decisions, events, or conditions will significantly affect the profitability of a business actor or the expected value of a given economic action. _____ can be understood and managed with reasoned foresight and investment.

Exam Probability: **High**

53. *Answer choices:*

(see index for correct answer)

- a. Over-the-counter
- b. Political risk
- c. Downside risk
- d. Basis risk

Guidance: level 1

:: Globalization-related theories ::

_____ is an economic system based on the private ownership of the means of production and their operation for profit. Characteristics central to _____ include private property, capital accumulation, wage labor, voluntary exchange, a price system, and competitive markets. In a capitalist market economy, decision-making and investment are determined by every owner of wealth, property or production ability in financial and capital markets, whereas prices and the distribution of goods and services are mainly determined by competition in goods and services markets.

54. *Answer choices:*

(see index for correct answer)

- a. Capitalism
- b. postmodernism
- c. Economic Development

Guidance: level 1

:: Organizational theory ::

_____ is the process of groups of organisms working or acting together for common, mutual, or some underlying benefit, as opposed to working in competition for selfish benefit. Many animal and plant species cooperate both with other members of their own species and with members of other species .

55. *Answer choices:*

(see index for correct answer)

- a. Cooperation
- b. The three circles model
- c. Organizational effectiveness
- d. Conflict

:: Stock market ::

A shareholder is an individual or institution that legally owns one or more shares of stock in a public or private corporation. _____ may be referred to as members of a corporation. Legally, a person is not a shareholder in a corporation until their name and other details are entered in the corporation's register of _____ or members.

Exam Probability: **Medium**

56. *Answer choices:*

(see index for correct answer)

- a. S chip
- b. Alternative display facility
- c. Stock certificate
- d. Sell side

:: ::

A _____ is any person who contracts to acquire an asset in return for some form of consideration.

Exam Probability: **High**

57. *Answer choices:*

(see index for correct answer)

- a. cultural
- b. process perspective
- c. Buyer
- d. similarity-attraction theory

Guidance: level 1

:: Derivatives (finance) ::

_____ is any bodily activity that enhances or maintains physical fitness and overall health and wellness. It is performed for various reasons, to aid growth and improve strength, preventing aging, developing muscles and the cardiovascular system, honing athletic skills, weight loss or maintenance, improving health and also for enjoyment. Many individuals choose to _____ outdoors where they can congregate in groups, socialize, and enhance well-being.

Exam Probability: **Low**

58. *Answer choices:*

(see index for correct answer)

- a. Equity swap
- b. Callable bullbear contract
- c. Financial future
- d. Swap

Guidance: level 1

:: Monopoly (economics) ::

A _____ is a form of intellectual property that gives its owner the legal right to exclude others from making, using, selling, and importing an invention for a limited period of years, in exchange for publishing an enabling public disclosure of the invention. In most countries _____ rights fall under civil law and the _____ holder needs to sue someone infringing the _____ in order to enforce his or her rights. In some industries _____ s are an essential form of competitive advantage; in others they are irrelevant.

Exam Probability: **High**

59. *Answer choices:*

(see index for correct answer)

- a. Economies of scope
- b. Patent portfolio

- c. Patent
- d. Wartime Law on Industrial Property

Guidance: level 1

Management

Management is the administration of an organization, whether it is a business, a not-for-profit organization, or government body. Management includes the activities of setting the strategy of an organization and coordinating the efforts of its employees (or of volunteers) to accomplish its objectives through the application of available resources, such as financial, natural, technological, and human resources.

:: Management accounting ::

In economics, _____ s, indirect costs or overheads are business expenses that are not dependent on the level of goods or services produced by the business. They tend to be time-related, such as interest or rents being paid per month, and are often referred to as overhead costs. This is in contrast to variable costs, which are volume-related and unknown at the beginning of the accounting year. For a simple example, such as a bakery, the monthly rent for the baking facilities, and the monthly payments for the security system and basic phone line are _____ s, as they do not change according to how much bread the bakery produces and sells. On the other hand, the wage costs of the bakery are variable, as the bakery will have to hire more workers if the production of bread increases. Economists reckon _____ as a entry barrier for new entrepreneurs.

Exam Probability: **High**

1. *Answer choices:*

(see index for correct answer)

- a. Direct material total variance
- b. Fixed cost
- c. Management control system
- d. Certified Management Accountants of Canada

Guidance: level 1

:: Classification systems ::

_____ is the practice of comparing business processes and performance metrics to industry bests and best practices from other companies. Dimensions typically measured are quality, time and cost.

Exam Probability: **Medium**

2. *Answer choices:*

(see index for correct answer)

- a. Benchmarking
- b. Biological dark matter
- c. Mini-international neuropsychiatric interview
- d. Fach

Guidance: level 1

:: Critical thinking ::

An _____ is someone who has a prolonged or intense experience through practice and education in a particular field. Informally, an _____ is someone widely recognized as a reliable source of technique or skill whose faculty for judging or deciding rightly, justly, or wisely is accorded authority and status by peers or the public in a specific well-distinguished domain. An _____ , more generally, is a person with extensive knowledge or ability based on research, experience, or occupation and in a particular area of study. _____ s are called in for advice on their respective subject, but they do not always agree on the particulars of a field of study. An _____ can be believed, by virtue of credential, training, education, profession, publication or experience, to have special knowledge of a subject beyond that of the average person, sufficient that others may officially rely upon the individual's opinion. Historically, an _____ was referred to as a sage . The individual was usually a profound thinker distinguished for wisdom and sound judgment.

Exam Probability: **Low**

3. *Answer choices:*

(see index for correct answer)

- a. Expert
- b. False equivalence
- c. Succinctness
- d. Center for Critical Thinking

Guidance: level 1

:: ::

A _____ is a problem offering two possibilities, neither of which is unambiguously acceptable or preferable. The possibilities are termed the horns of the _____ , a clichéd usage, but distinguishing the _____ from other kinds of predicament as a matter of usage.

Exam Probability: **Low**

4. *Answer choices:*

(see index for correct answer)

- a. hierarchical
- b. personal values
- c. interpersonal communication
- d. similarity-attraction theory

Guidance: level 1

:: Statistical terminology ::

_____ is the magnitude or dimensions of a thing. _____ can be measured as length, width, height, diameter, perimeter, area, volume, or mass.

Exam Probability: **Low**

5. *Answer choices:*

(see index for correct answer)

- a. Neutral vector
- b. Endogeneity
- c. Degrees of freedom
- d. Fair coin

Guidance: level 1

:: Production economics ::

_____ is the creation of a whole that is greater than the simple sum of its parts. The term _____ comes from the Attic Greek word sea synergia from synergos, , meaning "working together".

Exam Probability: **Medium**

6. *Answer choices:*

(see index for correct answer)

- a. HMI quality
- b. Post-Fordism
- c. Ramp up
- d. Product pipeline

Guidance: level 1

:: Decision theory ::

Within economics the concept of _____ is used to model worth or value, but its usage has evolved significantly over time. The term was introduced initially as a measure of pleasure or satisfaction within the theory of utilitarianism by moral philosophers such as Jeremy Bentham and John Stuart Mill. But the term has been adapted and reapplied within neoclassical economics, which dominates modern economic theory, as a _____ function that represents a consumer's preference ordering over a choice set. As such, it is devoid of its original interpretation as a measurement of the pleasure or satisfaction obtained by the consumer from that choice.

Exam Probability: **High**

7. *Answer choices:*

(see index for correct answer)

- a. Choquet integral
- b. VIKOR method
- c. TOPSIS
- d. Utility

Guidance: level 1

:: ::

_____ , in its broadest context, includes both the attainment of that which is just and the philosophical discussion of that which is just. The concept of _____ is based on numerous fields, and many differing viewpoints and perspectives including the concepts of moral correctness based on ethics, rationality, law, religion, equity and fairness. Often, the general discussion of _____ is divided into the realm of social _____ as found in philosophy, theology and religion, and, procedural _____ as found in the study and application of the law.

Exam Probability: **Low**

8. *Answer choices:*

(see index for correct answer)

- a. deep-level diversity
- b. levels of analysis
- c. hierarchical
- d. Justice

Guidance: level 1

:: Information science ::

_____ is the resolution of uncertainty; it is that which answers the question of "what an entity is" and thus defines both its essence and nature of its characteristics. _____ relates to both data and knowledge, as data is meaningful _____ representing values attributed to parameters, and knowledge signifies understanding of a concept. _____ is uncoupled from an observer, which is an entity that can access _____ and thus discern what it specifies; _____ exists beyond an event horizon for example. In the case of knowledge, the _____ itself requires a cognitive observer to be obtained.

Exam Probability: **Low**

9. *Answer choices:*

(see index for correct answer)

- a. Information space analysis
- b. Web Feature Service
- c. Datafication
- d. American Documentation Institute

Guidance: level 1

:: Evaluation methods ::

In social psychology, _____ is the process of looking at oneself in order to assess aspects that are important to one's identity. It is one of the motives that drive self-evaluation, along with self-verification and self-enhancement. Sedikides suggests that the _____ motive will prompt people to seek information to confirm their uncertain self-concept rather than their certain self-concept and at the same time people use _____ to enhance their certainty of their own self-knowledge. However, the _____ motive could be seen as quite different from the other two self-evaluation motives. Unlike the other two motives through _____ people are interested in the accuracy of their current self view, rather than improving their self-view. This makes _____ the only self-evaluative motive that may cause a person's self-esteem to be damaged.

Exam Probability: **High**

10. *Answer choices:*

(see index for correct answer)

- a. Business excellence
- b. Qualitative research
- c. Self-assessment
- d. Question-focused dataset

Guidance: level 1

:: ::

_____ is the consumption and saving opportunity gained by an entity within a specified timeframe, which is generally expressed in monetary terms. For households and individuals, " _____ is the sum of all the wages, salaries, profits, interest payments, rents, and other forms of earnings received in a given period of time."

Exam Probability: **High**

11. *Answer choices:*

(see index for correct answer)

- a. corporate values
- b. Income
- c. process perspective
- d. co-culture

Guidance: level 1

:: Scientific method ::

In the social sciences and life sciences, a _____ is a research method involving an up-close, in-depth, and detailed examination of a subject of study , as well as its related contextual conditions.

Exam Probability: **High**

12. *Answer choices:*

(see index for correct answer)

- a. Preference test
- b. Case study
- c. Causal research
- d. pilot project

Guidance: level 1

:: Data collection ::

A _____ is an utterance which typically functions as a request for information. _____ s can thus be understood as a kind of illocutionary act in the field of pragmatics or as special kinds of propositions in frameworks of formal semantics such as alternative semantics or inquisitive semantics. The information requested is expected to be provided in the form of an answer. _____ s are often conflated with interrogatives, which are the grammatical forms typically used to achieve them. Rhetorical _____ s, for example, are interrogative in form but may not be considered true _____ s as they are not expected to be answered. Conversely, non-interrogative grammatical structures may be considered _____ s as in the case of the imperative sentence "tell me your name".

Exam Probability: **Medium**

13. *Answer choices:*

(see index for correct answer)

- a. Question

- b. Pop-up satellite archival tag
- c. Provenance
- d. Datalogix

Guidance: level 1

:: Marketing ::

_____ comes from the Latin neg and otsia referring to businessmen who, unlike the patricians, had no leisure time in their industriousness; it held the meaning of business until the 17th century when it took on the diplomatic connotation as a dialogue between two or more people or parties intended to reach a beneficial outcome over one or more issues where a conflict exists with respect to at least one of these issues. Thus, _____ is a process of combining divergent positions into a joint agreement under a decision rule of unanimity.

Exam Probability: **High**

14. *Answer choices:*

(see index for correct answer)

- a. Negotiation
- b. Inbound marketing automation
- c. Disruptive innovation
- d. Processing fluency

Guidance: level 1

_____ involves the development of an action plan designed to motivate and guide a person or group toward a goal. _____ can be guided by goal-setting criteria such as SMART criteria. _____ is a major component of personal-development and management literature.

Exam Probability: **Low**

15. *Answer choices:*

(see index for correct answer)

- a. levels of analysis
- b. Goal setting
- c. open system
- d. co-culture

Guidance: level 1

:: Project management ::

Some scenarios associate "this kind of planning" with learning "life skills". _____ s are necessary, or at least useful, in situations where individuals need to know what time they must be at a specific location to receive a specific service, and where people need to accomplish a set of goals within a set time period.

16. *Answer choices:*

(see index for correct answer)

- a. Drag cost
- b. Project
- c. Sunk costs
- d. Schedule

Guidance: level 1

:: Project management ::

A _____ is a source or supply from which a benefit is produced and it has some utility. _____ s can broadly be classified upon their availability—they are classified into renewable and non-renewable _____ s.Examples of non renewable _____ s are coal ,crude oil natural gas nuclear energy etc. Examples of renewable _____ s are air,water,wind,solar energy etc. They can also be classified as actual and potential on the basis of level of development and use, on the basis of origin they can be classified as biotic and abiotic, and on the basis of their distribution, as ubiquitous and localized . An item becomes a _____ with time and developing technology. Typically, _____ s are materials, energy, services, staff, knowledge, or other assets that are transformed to produce benefit and in the process may be consumed or made unavailable. Benefits of _____ utilization may include increased wealth, proper functioning of a system, or enhanced well-being. From a human perspective a natural _____ is anything obtained from the environment to satisfy human needs and wants. From a broader biological or ecological perspective a _____ satisfies the needs of a living organism .

17. *Answer choices:*

(see index for correct answer)

- a. Project workforce management
- b. Resource
- c. Participatory impact pathways analysis
- d. Market requirements document

Guidance: level 1

:: Organizational structure ::

An _____ defines how activities such as task allocation, coordination, and supervision are directed toward the achievement of organizational aims.

Exam Probability: **Low**

18. *Answer choices:*

(see index for correct answer)

- a. Automated Bureaucracy
- b. Unorganisation
- c. Organizational structure
- d. Followership

:: Project management ::

Contemporary business and science treat as a _____ any undertaking, carried out individually or collaboratively and possibly involving research or design, that is carefully planned to achieve a particular aim.

Exam Probability: **Low**

19. *Answer choices:*

(see index for correct answer)

- a. Participatory impact pathways analysis
- b. Mandated lead arranger
- c. Student syndrome
- d. Design structure matrix

:: Analysis ::

_____ is the process of breaking a complex topic or substance into smaller parts in order to gain a better understanding of it. The technique has been applied in the study of mathematics and logic since before Aristotle , though _____ as a formal concept is a relatively recent development.

Exam Probability: **Low**

20. *Answer choices:*

(see index for correct answer)

- a. Divergent question
- b. Paradox of analysis
- c. Analysis
- d. Deviation analysis

Guidance: level 1

:: Management ::

A _____ describes the rationale of how an organization creates, delivers, and captures value, in economic, social, cultural or other contexts. The process of _____ construction and modification is also called _____ innovation and forms a part of business strategy.

Exam Probability: **Medium**

21. *Answer choices:*

- a. Process management
- b. Business model
- c. Radical transparency
- d. Business workflow analysis

Guidance: level 1

:: Management ::

_____ is a technique used by some employers to rotate their employees' assigned jobs throughout their employment. Employers practice this technique for a number of reasons. It was designed to promote flexibility of employees and to keep employees interested into staying with the company/organization which employs them. There is also research that shows how _____ s help relieve the stress of employees who work in a job that requires manual labor.

Exam Probability: **Medium**

22. *Answer choices:*

- a. Risk management
- b. Job rotation
- c. Value proposition
- d. Communications management

:: ::

A _____ or sample _____ is a single measure of some attribute of a sample . It is calculated by applying a function to the values of the items of the sample, which are known together as a set of data.

Exam Probability: **High**

23. *Answer choices:*

(see index for correct answer)

- a. deep-level diversity
- b. Statistic
- c. levels of analysis
- d. similarity-attraction theory

:: Evaluation ::

_____ solving consists of using generic or ad hoc methods in an orderly manner to find solutions to _____ s. Some of the _____ -solving techniques developed and used in philosophy, artificial intelligence, computer science, engineering, mathematics, or medicine are related to mental _____ -solving techniques studied in psychology.

Exam Probability: **Low**

24. *Answer choices:*

(see index for correct answer)

- a. Problem
- b. Common Criteria Testing Laboratory
- c. Impact assessment
- d. Knowledge survey

Guidance: level 1

:: Organizational behavior ::

_____ is the state or fact of exclusive rights and control over property, which may be an object, land/real estate or intellectual property. _____ involves multiple rights, collectively referred to as title, which may be separated and held by different parties.

Exam Probability: **Medium**

25. *Answer choices:*

- a. Managerial grid model
- b. Satisficing
- c. Self-policing
- d. Civic virtue

Guidance: level 1

:: Packaging ::

In work place, _____ or job _____ means good ranking with the hypothesized conception of requirements of a role. There are two types of job _____ s: contextual and task. Task _____ is related to cognitive ability while contextual _____ is dependent upon personality. Task _____ are behavioral roles that are recognized in job descriptions and by remuneration systems, they are directly related to organizational _____ , whereas, contextual _____ are value based and additional behavioral roles that are not recognized in job descriptions and covered by compensation; they are extra roles that are indirectly related to organizational _____ .
Citizenship _____ like contextual _____ means a set of individual activity/contribution that supports the organizational culture.

Exam Probability: **Low**

26. *Answer choices:*

- a. Communication design
- b. Paper sack
- c. Punnet
- d. Performance

Guidance: level 1

:: Industrial Revolution ::

The _____ , now also known as the First _____ , was the transition to new manufacturing processes in Europe and the US, in the period from about 1760 to sometime between 1820 and 1840. This transition included going from hand production methods to machines, new chemical manufacturing and iron production processes, the increasing use of steam power and water power, the development of machine tools and the rise of the mechanized factory system. The _____ also led to an unprecedented rise in the rate of population growth.

Exam Probability: **Low**

27. *Answer choices:*

(see index for correct answer)

- a. James Henry Northrop
- b. Leawood Pump House
- c. Tredegar Iron and Coal Company
- d. Industrial Revolution

Guidance: level 1

:: Leadership ::

_____ /Management is a part of a style of leadership that focuses on supervision, organization, and performance; it is an integral part of the Full Range Leadership Model. _____ is a style of leadership in which leaders promote compliance by followers through both rewards and punishments. Through a rewards and punishments system, transactional leaders are able to keep followers motivated for the short-term. Unlike transformational leaders, those using the transactional approach are not looking to change the future, they look to keep things the same. Leaders using _____ as a model pay attention to followers` work in order to find faults and deviations.

Exam Probability: **Low**

28. *Answer choices:*

(see index for correct answer)

- a. Transactional leadership
- b. Three levels of leadership model
- c. Complex adaptive leadership
- d. Situational leadership theory

Guidance: level 1

:: Reputation management ::

_____ or image of a social entity is an opinion about that entity, typically as a result of social evaluation on a set of criteria.

Exam Probability: **Medium**

29. *Answer choices:*

(see index for correct answer)

- a. Reputation
- b. Reputation system
- c. Lithium Technologies
- d. Raph Levien

Guidance: level 1

:: Training ::

_____ is teaching, or developing in oneself or others, any skills and knowledge that relate to specific useful competencies. _____ has specific goals of improving one's capability, capacity, productivity and performance. It forms the core of apprenticeships and provides the backbone of content at institutes of technology . In addition to the basic _____ required for a trade, occupation or profession, observers of the labor-market recognize as of 2008 the need to continue _____ beyond initial qualifications: to maintain, upgrade and update skills throughout working life. People within many professions and occupations may refer to this sort of _____ as professional development.

30. *Answer choices:*

(see index for correct answer)

- a. American Council on Exercise
- b. Arts Party
- c. Training workshop
- d. Training

Guidance: level 1

:: Financial risk ::

_____ is a type of risk faced by investors, corporations, and governments that political decisions, events, or conditions will significantly affect the profitability of a business actor or the expected value of a given economic action. _____ can be understood and managed with reasoned foresight and investment.

Exam Probability: **Low**

31. *Answer choices:*

(see index for correct answer)

- a. Active risk
- b. Basis risk

- c. Institute of Operational Risk
- d. Acceptance set

Guidance: level 1

:: Business ethics ::

_____ is a type of harassment technique that relates to a sexual nature and the unwelcome or inappropriate promise of rewards in exchange for sexual favors. _____ includes a range of actions from mild transgressions to sexual abuse or assault. Harassment can occur in many different social settings such as the workplace, the home, school, churches, etc. Harassers or victims may be of any gender.

Exam Probability: **Medium**

32. *Answer choices:*
(see index for correct answer)

- a. Sexual harassment
- b. Minority business enterprise
- c. Linda Peeno
- d. Philosophy of business

Guidance: level 1

:: Human resource management ::

_____ is the corporate management term for the act of reorganizing the legal, ownership, operational, or other structures of a company for the purpose of making it more profitable, or better organized for its present needs. Other reasons for _____ include a change of ownership or ownership structure, demerger, or a response to a crisis or major change in the business such as bankruptcy, repositioning, or buyout. _____ may also be described as corporate _____ , debt _____ and financial _____ .

Exam Probability: **Medium**

33. *Answer choices:*

(see index for correct answer)

- a. Restructuring
- b. Recruitment process outsourcing
- c. Job knowledge
- d. Sham peer review

Guidance: level 1

:: Business law ::

A _____ is a group of people who jointly supervise the activities of an organization, which can be either a for-profit business, nonprofit organization, or a government agency. Such a board's powers, duties, and responsibilities are determined by government regulations and the organization's own constitution and bylaws. These authorities may specify the number of members of the board, how they are to be chosen, and how often they are to meet.

34. *Answer choices:*

(see index for correct answer)

- a. Commercial law
- b. Perfection
- c. Ordinary resolution
- d. Chattel mortgage

Guidance: level 1

:: Management ::

A _____ is a method or technique that has been generally accepted as superior to any alternatives because it produces results that are superior to those achieved by other means or because it has become a standard way of doing things, e.g., a standard way of complying with legal or ethical requirements.

Exam Probability: **Low**

35. *Answer choices:*

(see index for correct answer)

- a. Dominant design
- b. Design leadership
- c. Logistics management

- d. Goals Breakdown Structure

Guidance: level 1

:: ::

_____ is the means to see, hear, or become aware of something or someone through our fundamental senses. The term _____ derives from the Latin word perceptio, and is the organization, identification, and interpretation of sensory information in order to represent and understand the presented information, or the environment.

Exam Probability: **Medium**

36. *Answer choices:*

(see index for correct answer)

- a. imperative
- b. cultural
- c. co-culture
- d. Perception

Guidance: level 1

:: Management ::

_____ is a process by which entities review the quality of all factors involved in production. ISO 9000 defines _____ as "A part of quality management focused on fulfilling quality requirements".

Exam Probability: **High**

37. *Answer choices:*

(see index for correct answer)

- a. Managerial Psychology
- b. Quality control
- c. Integrative thinking
- d. Earned schedule

Guidance: level 1

:: Time management ::

_____ is the process of planning and exercising conscious control of time spent on specific activities, especially to increase effectiveness, efficiency, and productivity. It involves a juggling act of various demands upon a person relating to work, social life, family, hobbies, personal interests and commitments with the finiteness of time. Using time effectively gives the person "choice" on spending/managing activities at their own time and expediency.

Exam Probability: **High**

38. *Answer choices:*

(see index for correct answer)

- a. Time management
- b. Getting Things Done
- c. Time perception
- d. waiting room

Guidance: level 1

:: Discrimination ::

In social psychology, a _____ is an over-generalized belief about a particular category of people. _____ s are generalized because one assumes that the _____ is true for each individual person in the category. While such generalizations may be useful when making quick decisions, they may be erroneous when applied to particular individuals. _____ s encourage prejudice and may arise for a number of reasons.

Exam Probability: **Low**

39. *Answer choices:*

(see index for correct answer)

- a. Stereotype
- b. Economic discrimination
- c. Elitism

:: Information systems ::

_____ is the process of creating, sharing, using and managing the knowledge and information of an organisation. It refers to a multidisciplinary approach to achieving organisational objectives by making the best use of knowledge.

Exam Probability: **Low**

40. *Answer choices:*

(see index for correct answer)

- a. Manufacturing execution system
- b. Payroll automation
- c. Electronic Case Filing System
- d. Accounting information system

:: ::

An _____ is a process where candidates are examined to determine their suitability for specific types of employment, especially management or military command. The candidates' personality and aptitudes are determined by techniques including interviews, group exercises, presentations, examinations and psychometric testing.

Exam Probability: **High**

41. *Answer choices:*

(see index for correct answer)

- a. similarity-attraction theory
- b. Assessment center
- c. imperative
- d. personal values

Guidance: level 1

:: Marketing ::

_____ is the percentage of a market accounted for by a specific entity. In a survey of nearly 200 senior marketing managers, 67% responded that they found the revenue- "dollar _____ " metric very useful, while 61% found "unit _____ " very useful.

Exam Probability: **Low**

42. *Answer choices:*

- a. Digital brand engagement
- b. Merchandise Mart
- c. Mandatory labelling
- d. Licensing International Expo

Guidance: level 1

:: Industrial agreements ::

_____ is a process of negotiation between employers and a group of employees aimed at agreements to regulate working salaries, working conditions, benefits, and other aspects of workers' compensation and rights for workers. The interests of the employees are commonly presented by representatives of a trade union to which the employees belong. The collective agreements reached by these negotiations usually set out wage scales, working hours, training, health and safety, overtime, grievance mechanisms, and rights to participate in workplace or company affairs.

Exam Probability: **High**

43. *Answer choices:*

- a. Enterprise bargaining agreement
- b. In Place of Strife

- c. Collective bargaining
- d. Ex parte H.V. McKay

Guidance: level 1

:: ::

In mathematics, a _____ is a relationship between two numbers indicating how many times the first number contains the second. For example, if a bowl of fruit contains eight oranges and six lemons, then the _____ of oranges to lemons is eight to six . Similarly, the _____ of lemons to oranges is 6:8 and the _____ of oranges to the total amount of fruit is 8:14 .

Exam Probability: **High**

44. *Answer choices:*

(see index for correct answer)

- a. similarity-attraction theory
- b. deep-level diversity
- c. corporate values
- d. Sarbanes-Oxley act of 2002

Guidance: level 1

:: Information technology management ::

_____ is a collective term for all approaches to prepare , support and help individuals, teams, and organizations in making organizational change. The most common change drivers include: technological evolution, process reviews, crisis, and consumer habit changes; pressure from new business entrants, acquisitions, mergers, and organizational restructuring. It includes methods that redirect or redefine the use of resources, business process, budget allocations, or other modes of operation that significantly change a company or organization. Organizational _____ considers the full organization and what needs to change, while _____ may be used solely to refer to how people and teams are affected by such organizational transition. It deals with many different disciplines, from behavioral and social sciences to information technology and business solutions.

Exam Probability: **Low**

45. *Answer choices:*

(see index for correct answer)

- a. ServiceNow
- b. Knowledge balance sheet
- c. IT Project Coordinator
- d. Battle command knowledge system

Guidance: level 1

:: Production and manufacturing ::

_____ consists of organization-wide efforts to "install and make permanent climate where employees continuously improve their ability to provide on demand products and services that customers will find of particular value." "Total" emphasizes that departments in addition to production are obligated to improve their operations; "management" emphasizes that executives are obligated to actively manage quality through funding, training, staffing, and goal setting. While there is no widely agreed-upon approach, TQM efforts typically draw heavily on the previously developed tools and techniques of quality control. TQM enjoyed widespread attention during the late 1980s and early 1990s before being overshadowed by ISO 9000, Lean manufacturing, and Six Sigma.

Exam Probability: **High**

46. *Answer choices:*

(see index for correct answer)

- a. EFQM Excellence Model
- b. Back-story
- c. Variable rate feeder
- d. Total quality management

Guidance: level 1

:: ::

The _____ or just chief executive , is the most senior corporate, executive, or administrative officer in charge of managing an organization especially an independent legal entity such as a company or nonprofit institution. CEOs lead a range of organizations, including public and private corporations, non-profit organizations and even some government organizations . The CEO of a corporation or company typically reports to the board of directors and is charged with maximizing the value of the entity, which may include maximizing the share price, market share, revenues or another element. In the non-profit and government sector, CEOs typically aim at achieving outcomes related to the organization's mission, such as reducing poverty, increasing literacy, etc.

Exam Probability: **High**

47. *Answer choices:*

(see index for correct answer)

- a. Chief executive officer
- b. levels of analysis
- c. empathy
- d. hierarchical perspective

Guidance: level 1

:: Marketing ::

_____ or stock control can be broadly defined as "the activity of checking a shop's stock." However, a more focused definition takes into account the more science-based, methodical practice of not only verifying a business` inventory but also focusing on the many related facets of inventory management "within an organisation to meet the demand placed upon that business economically." Other facets of _____ include supply chain management, production control, financial flexibility, and customer satisfaction. At the root of _____ , however, is the _____ problem, which involves determining when to order, how much to order, and the logistics of those decisions.

Exam Probability: **High**

48. *Answer choices:*

(see index for correct answer)

- a. Channel conflict
- b. Alpha consumer
- c. Promotional mix
- d. Inventory control

Guidance: level 1

:: ::

A _____ is a type of job aid used to reduce failure by compensating for potential limits of human memory and attention. It helps to ensure consistency and completeness in carrying out a task. A basic example is the "to do list". A more advanced _____ would be a schedule, which lays out tasks to be done according to time of day or other factors. A primary task in _____ is documentation of the task and auditing against the documentation.

Exam Probability: **Medium**

49. *Answer choices:*

(see index for correct answer)

- a. information systems assessment
- b. co-culture
- c. Checklist
- d. personal values

Guidance: level 1

:: ::

A _____ is a fund into which a sum of money is added during an employee's employment years, and from which payments are drawn to support the person's retirement from work in the form of periodic payments. A _____ may be a "defined benefit plan" where a fixed sum is paid regularly to a person, or a "defined contribution plan" under which a fixed sum is invested and then becomes available at retirement age. _____ s should not be confused with severance pay; the former is usually paid in regular installments for life after retirement, while the latter is typically paid as a fixed amount after involuntary termination of employment prior to retirement.

Exam Probability: **Medium**

50. *Answer choices:*

(see index for correct answer)

- a. empathy
- b. Character
- c. Pension
- d. process perspective

Guidance: level 1

:: Strategic management ::

_____ is a strategic planning technique used to help a person or organization identify strengths, weaknesses, opportunities, and threats related to business competition or project planning. It is intended to specify the objectives of the business venture or project and identify the internal and external factors that are favorable and unfavorable to achieving those objectives. Users of a _____ often ask and answer questions to generate meaningful information for each category to make the tool useful and identify their competitive advantage. SWOT has been described as the tried-and-true tool of strategic analysis.

Exam Probability: **Low**

51. *Answer choices:*

(see index for correct answer)

- a. Segment architecture
- b. Complementors
- c. The New Age of Innovation
- d. SWOT analysis

Guidance: level 1

:: ::

_____ Corporation was an American energy, commodities, and services company based in Houston, Texas. It was founded in 1985 as a merger between Houston Natural Gas and InterNorth, both relatively small regional companies. Before its bankruptcy on December 3, 2001, _____ employed approximately 29,000 staff and was a major electricity, natural gas, communications and pulp and paper company, with claimed revenues of nearly $101 billion during 2000. Fortune named _____ "America's Most Innovative Company" for six consecutive years.

Exam Probability: **Low**

52. *Answer choices:*

(see index for correct answer)

- a. Sarbanes-Oxley act of 2002
- b. Enron
- c. interpersonal communication
- d. open system

Guidance: level 1

:: ::

A _____ or GM is an executive who has overall responsibility for managing both the revenue and cost elements of a company's income statement, known as profit & loss responsibility. A _____ usually oversees most or all of the firm's marketing and sales functions as well as the day-to-day operations of the business. Frequently, the _____ is responsible for effective planning, delegating, coordinating, staffing, organizing, and decision making to attain desirable profit making results for an organization .

Exam Probability: **High**

53. *Answer choices:*

(see index for correct answer)

- a. process perspective
- b. hierarchical perspective
- c. levels of analysis
- d. deep-level diversity

Guidance: level 1

:: Majority–minority relations ::

_____ , also known as reservation in India and Nepal, positive discrimination / action in the United Kingdom, and employment equity in Canada and South Africa, is the policy of promoting the education and employment of members of groups that are known to have previously suffered from discrimination. Historically and internationally, support for _____ has sought to achieve goals such as bridging inequalities in employment and pay, increasing access to education, promoting diversity, and redressing apparent past wrongs, harms, or hindrances.

Exam Probability: **High**

54. *Answer choices:*

(see index for correct answer)

- a. Affirmative action
- b. cultural dissonance
- c. positive discrimination

Guidance: level 1

:: Manufacturing ::

A _____ is a building for storing goods. _____ s are used by manufacturers, importers, exporters, wholesalers, transport businesses, customs, etc. They are usually large plain buildings in industrial parks on the outskirts of cities, towns or villages.

Exam Probability: **Low**

55. *Answer choices:*

(see index for correct answer)

- a. Useful art
- b. Point cloud
- c. Dimensional metrology
- d. Obeya

Guidance: level 1

:: Evaluation ::

_____ is the practice of being honest and showing a consistent and uncompromising adherence to strong moral and ethical principles and values.In ethics, _____ is regarded as the honesty and truthfulness or accuracy of one's actions. _____ can stand in opposition to hypocrisy, in that judging with the standards of _____ involves regarding internal consistency as a virtue, and suggests that parties holding within themselves apparently conflicting values should account for the discrepancy or alter their beliefs. The word _____ evolved from the Latin adjective integer, meaning whole or complete. In this context, _____ is the inner sense of "wholeness" deriving from qualities such as honesty and consistency of character. As such, one may judge that others "have _____ " to the extent that they act according to the values, beliefs and principles they claim to hold.

Exam Probability: **Low**

56. *Answer choices:*

(see index for correct answer)

- a. American Evaluation Association
- b. Integrity
- c. Server Efficiency Rating Tool
- d. Shifting baseline

Guidance: level 1

:: Teams ::

A _____ usually refers to a group of individuals who work together from different geographic locations and rely on communication technology such as email, FAX, and video or voice conferencing services in order to collaborate. The term can also refer to groups or teams that work together asynchronously or across organizational levels. Powell, Piccoli and Ives define _____ s as "groups of geographically, organizationally and/or time dispersed workers brought together by information and telecommunication technologies to accomplish one or more organizational tasks." According to Ale Ebrahim et. al., _____ s can also be defined as "small temporary groups of geographically, organizationally and/or time dispersed knowledge workers who coordinate their work predominantly with electronic information and communication technologies in order to accomplish one or more organization tasks."

Exam Probability: **Low**

57. *Answer choices:*

(see index for correct answer)

- a. Virtual team
- b. Team-building

:: Business terms ::

A _____ is a short statement of why an organization exists, what its overall goal is, identifying the goal of its operations: what kind of product or service it provides, its primary customers or market, and its geographical region of operation. It may include a short statement of such fundamental matters as the organization's values or philosophies, a business's main competitive advantages, or a desired future state—the "vision".

Exam Probability: **High**

58. *Answer choices:*

(see index for correct answer)

- a. Strategic partner
- b. organic growth
- c. Mission statement
- d. year-to-date

:: ::

In production, research, retail, and accounting, a _____ is the value of money that has been used up to produce something or deliver a service, and hence is not available for use anymore. In business, the _____ may be one of acquisition, in which case the amount of money expended to acquire it is counted as _____ . In this case, money is the input that is gone in order to acquire the thing. This acquisition _____ may be the sum of the _____ of production as incurred by the original producer, and further _____ s of transaction as incurred by the acquirer over and above the price paid to the producer. Usually, the price also includes a mark-up for profit over the _____ of production.

Exam Probability: **Medium**

59. *Answer choices:*

(see index for correct answer)

- a. deep-level diversity
- b. cultural
- c. information systems assessment
- d. imperative

Guidance: level 1

Business law

Corporate law (also known as business law) is the body of law governing the rights, relations, and conduct of persons, companies, organizations and businesses. It refers to the legal practice relating to, or the theory of corporations. Corporate law often describes the law relating to matters which derive directly from the life-cycle of a corporation. It thus encompasses the formation, funding, governance, and death of a corporation.

:: ::

_____ , also referred to as orthostasis, is a human position in which the body is held in an upright position and supported only by the feet.

Exam Probability: **Low**

1. *Answer choices:*

(see index for correct answer)

- a. Character
- b. hierarchical perspective
- c. deep-level diversity
- d. Standing

Guidance: level 1

:: ::

In law, a _____ is a coming together of parties to a dispute, to present information in a tribunal, a formal setting with the authority to adjudicate claims or disputes. One form of tribunal is a court. The tribunal, which may occur before a judge, jury, or other designated trier of fact, aims to achieve a resolution to their dispute.

Exam Probability: **High**

2. *Answer choices:*

(see index for correct answer)

- a. imperative
- b. interpersonal communication
- c. Trial
- d. levels of analysis

Guidance: level 1

:: Fraud ::

The _____ refers to the requirement that certain kinds of contracts be memorialized in writing, signed by the party to be charged, with sufficient content to evidence the contract.

Exam Probability: **High**

3. *Answer choices:*

(see index for correct answer)

- a. Statute of frauds
- b. Money mule
- c. Fraud Squad
- d. Wangiri

Guidance: level 1

:: Business models ::

A _____ is "an autonomous association of persons united voluntarily to meet their common economic, social, and cultural needs and aspirations through a jointly-owned and democratically-controlled enterprise". _____ s may include.

Exam Probability: **Medium**

4. *Answer choices:*

(see index for correct answer)

- a. Gratis
- b. Subsidiary
- c. Volatility, uncertainty, complexity and ambiguity
- d. Cooperative

Guidance: level 1

:: ::

_____ refers to a business or organization attempting to acquire goods or services to accomplish its goals. Although there are several organizations that attempt to set standards in the _____ process, processes can vary greatly between organizations. Typically the word " _____ " is not used interchangeably with the word "procurement", since procurement typically includes expediting, supplier quality, and transportation and logistics in addition to _____ .

Exam Probability: **High**

5. *Answer choices:*

(see index for correct answer)

- a. corporate values
- b. process perspective
- c. interpersonal communication

- d. Purchasing

Guidance: level 1

:: ::

An _____ is a formal or official change made to a law, contract, constitution, or other legal document. It is based on the verb to amend, which means to change for better. _____ s can add, remove, or update parts of these agreements. They are often used when it is better to change the document than to write a new one.

Exam Probability: **Medium**

6. *Answer choices:*

(see index for correct answer)

- a. levels of analysis
- b. Amendment
- c. surface-level diversity
- d. functional perspective

Guidance: level 1

:: Business law ::

A _____ is a legal right granted by a debtor to a creditor over the debtor's property which enables the creditor to have recourse to the property if the debtor defaults in making payment or otherwise performing the secured obligations. One of the most common examples of a _____ is a mortgage: When person, by the action of an expressed conveyance, pledges by a promise to pay a certain sum of money, with certain conditions, on a said date or dates for a said period, that action on the page with wet ink applied on the part of the one wishing the exchange creates the original funds and negotiable Instrument. That action of pledging conveys a promise binding upon the mortgagee which creates a face value upon the Instrument of the amount of currency being asked for in exchange. It is therein in good faith offered to the Bank in exchange for local currency from the Bank to buy a house. The particular country's Bank Acts usually requires the Banks to deliver such fund bearing negotiable instruments to the Countries Main Bank such as is the case in Canada. This creates a _____ in the land the house sits on for the Bank and they file a caveat at land titles on the house as evidence of that _____ . If the mortgagee fails to pay defaulting in his promise to repay the exchange, the bank then applies to the court to for-close on your property to eventually sell the house and apply the proceeds to the outstanding exchange.

Exam Probability: **High**

7. *Answer choices:*

(see index for correct answer)

- a. Time-and-a-half
- b. Security interest
- c. Board of directors
- d. Finance lease

Guidance: level 1

:: Business law ::

An _____ is an agreement in which a producer agrees to sell his or her entire production to the buyer, who in turn agrees to purchase the entire output. Example: an almond grower enters into an _____ with an almond packer: thus the producer has a "home" for output of nuts, and the packer of nuts is happy to try the particular product. The converse of this situation is a requirements contract, under which a seller agrees to supply the buyer with as much of a good or service as the buyer wants, in exchange for the buyer's agreement not to buy that good or service elsewhere.

Exam Probability: **High**

8. *Answer choices:*

(see index for correct answer)

- a. Family and Medical Leave Act of 1993
- b. Advertising regulation
- c. Installment sale
- d. Output contract

Guidance: level 1

:: Criminal law ::

_____ is the body of law that relates to crime. It proscribes conduct perceived as threatening, harmful, or otherwise endangering to the property, health, safety, and moral welfare of people inclusive of one`s self. Most _____ is established by statute, which is to say that the laws are enacted by a legislature. _____ includes the punishment and rehabilitation of people who violate such laws. _____ varies according to jurisdiction, and differs from civil law, where emphasis is more on dispute resolution and victim compensation, rather than on punishment or rehabilitation. Criminal procedure is a formalized official activity that authenticates the fact of commission of a crime and authorizes punitive or rehabilitative treatment of the offender.

Exam Probability: **Medium**

9. *Answer choices:*

(see index for correct answer)

- a. Self-incrimination
- b. mitigating factor
- c. Criminal law
- d. complicit

Guidance: level 1

:: ::

Industrial espionage, _____ , corporate spying or corporate espionage is a form of espionage conducted for commercial purposes instead of purely national security. While _____ is conducted or orchestrated by governments and is international in scope, industrial or corporate espionage is more often national and occurs between companies or corporations.

Exam Probability: **Low**

10. *Answer choices:*

(see index for correct answer)

- a. process perspective
- b. Economic espionage
- c. personal values
- d. hierarchical perspective

Guidance: level 1

:: Euthenics ::

_____ is an ethical framework and suggests that an entity, be it an organization or individual, has an obligation to act for the benefit of society at large. _____ is a duty every individual has to perform so as to maintain a balance between the economy and the ecosystems. A trade-off may exist between economic development, in the material sense, and the welfare of the society and environment, though this has been challenged by many reports over the past decade. _____ means sustaining the equilibrium between the two. It pertains not only to business organizations but also to everyone whose any action impacts the environment. This responsibility can be passive, by avoiding engaging in socially harmful acts, or active, by performing activities that directly advance social goals. _____ must be intergenerational since the actions of one generation have consequences on those following.

Exam Probability: **Medium**

11. *Answer choices:*

(see index for correct answer)

- a. Minnie Cumnock Blodgett
- b. Social responsibility
- c. Euthenics
- d. Family and consumer science

Guidance: level 1

:: Contract law ::

_____ is an equitable remedy in the law of contract, whereby a court issues an order requiring a party to perform a specific act, such as to complete performance of the contract. It is typically available in the sale of land, but otherwise is not generally available if damages are an appropriate alternative. _____ is almost never available for contracts of personal service, although performance may also be ensured through the threat of proceedings for contempt of court.

Exam Probability: **High**

12. *Answer choices:*

(see index for correct answer)

- a. Marriage privatization
- b. History of contract law
- c. Specific performance
- d. Convention on the Law Applicable to Contractual Obligations 1980

Guidance: level 1

:: ::

_____ is the practice of protecting the natural environment by individuals, organizations and governments. Its objectives are to conserve natural resources and the existing natural environment and, where possible, to repair damage and reverse trends.

Exam Probability: **High**

13. *Answer choices:*

(see index for correct answer)

- a. imperative
- b. Environmental Protection
- c. functional perspective
- d. corporate values

Guidance: level 1

:: ::

A contract is a legally-binding agreement which recognises and governs the rights and duties of the parties to the agreement. A contract is legally enforceable because it meets the requirements and approval of the law. An agreement typically involves the exchange of goods, services, money, or promises of any of those. In the event of breach of contract, the law awards the injured party access to legal remedies such as damages and cancellation.

Exam Probability: **Low**

14. *Answer choices:*

(see index for correct answer)

- a. hierarchical
- b. surface-level diversity
- c. Contract law
- d. personal values

:: ::

The Sherman Antitrust Act of 1890 was a United States antitrust law that regulates competition among enterprises, which was passed by Congress under the presidency of Benjamin Harrison.

Exam Probability: **Medium**

15. *Answer choices:*

(see index for correct answer)

- a. process perspective
- b. deep-level diversity
- c. corporate values
- d. functional perspective

:: Asset ::

In financial accounting, an _____ is any resource owned by the business. Anything tangible or intangible that can be owned or controlled to produce value and that is held by a company to produce positive economic value is an _____ . Simply stated, _____ s represent value of ownership that can be converted into cash . The balance sheet of a firm records the monetary value of the _____ s owned by that firm. It covers money and other valuables belonging to an individual or to a business.

Exam Probability: **High**

16. *Answer choices:*

(see index for correct answer)

- a. Fixed asset
- b. Asset

Guidance: level 1

:: ::

_____ is the collection of mechanisms, processes and relations by which corporations are controlled and operated. Governance structures and principles identify the distribution of rights and responsibilities among different participants in the corporation and include the rules and procedures for making decisions in corporate affairs. _____ is necessary because of the possibility of conflicts of interests between stakeholders, primarily between shareholders and upper management or among shareholders.

Exam Probability: **Low**

17. *Answer choices:*

(see index for correct answer)

- a. interpersonal communication
- b. Corporate governance
- c. hierarchical
- d. imperative

Guidance: level 1

:: ::

_____ is an abstract concept of management of complex systems according to a set of rules and trends. In systems theory, these types of rules exist in various fields of biology and society, but the term has slightly different meanings according to context. For example.

Exam Probability: **High**

18. *Answer choices:*

(see index for correct answer)

- a. empathy
- b. interpersonal communication
- c. open system
- d. Sarbanes-Oxley act of 2002

:: Contract law ::

_____ are damages whose amount the parties designate during the formation of a contract for the injured party to collect as compensation upon a specific breach .

Exam Probability: **High**

19. *Answer choices:*

(see index for correct answer)

- a. Last shot
- b. Convention on the Law Applicable to Contractual Obligations 1980
- c. Bonus clause
- d. Break/fix

:: Notes (finance) ::

A _____ , sometimes referred to as a note payable, is a legal instrument , in which one party promises in writing to pay a determinate sum of money to the other , either at a fixed or determinable future time or on demand of the payee, under specific terms.

Exam Probability: **Medium**

20. *Answer choices:*

(see index for correct answer)

- a. note payable
- b. Surplus note
- c. Demand Note
- d. Promissory note

Guidance: level 1

:: Writs ::

In common law, a _____ is a formal _____ ten order issued by a body with administrative or judicial jurisdiction; in modern usage, this body is generally a court. Warrants, prerogative _____ s, and subpoenas are common types of _____ , but many forms exist and have existed.

Exam Probability: **Low**

21. *Answer choices:*

(see index for correct answer)

- a. Writ of execution
- b. Qui tam
- c. Writ

Guidance: level 1

:: ::

In regulatory jurisdictions that provide for it , _____ is a group of laws and organizations designed to ensure the rights of consumers as well as fair trade, competition and accurate information in the marketplace. The laws are designed to prevent the businesses that engage in fraud or specified unfair practices from gaining an advantage over competitors. They may also provides additional protection for those most vulnerable in society. _____ laws are a form of government regulation that aim to protect the rights of consumers. For example, a government may require businesses to disclose detailed information about products—particularly in areas where safety or public health is an issue, such as food.

Exam Probability: **Low**

22. *Answer choices:*

(see index for correct answer)

- a. empathy
- b. deep-level diversity
- c. imperative

- d. Consumer protection

Guidance: level 1

:: Marketing ::

_____ or stock is the goods and materials that a business holds for the ultimate goal of resale .

Exam Probability: **Medium**

23. *Answer choices:*

(see index for correct answer)

- a. Generic trademark
- b. Inventory
- c. Marketing mix
- d. Patronage concentration

Guidance: level 1

:: ::

_____ is the principled guide to action taken by the administrative executive branches of the state with regard to a class of issues, in a manner consistent with law and institutional customs.

Exam Probability: **Low**

24. *Answer choices:*

(see index for correct answer)

- a. hierarchical perspective
- b. imperative
- c. personal values
- d. Public policy

Guidance: level 1

:: Business law ::

A _____ is a contractual arrangement calling for the lessee to pay the lessor for use of an asset. Property, buildings and vehicles are common assets that are _____ d. Industrial or business equipment is also _____ d.

Exam Probability: **Medium**

25. *Answer choices:*

(see index for correct answer)

- a. Legal tender
- b. Teck Corp. Ltd. v. Millar
- c. Certificate of incorporation
- d. Lease

Guidance: level 1

:: Anti-competitive behaviour ::

Restraints of trade is a common law doctrine relating to the enforceability of contractual restrictions on freedom to conduct business. It is a precursor of modern competition law. In an old leading case of Mitchel v Reynolds Lord Smith LC said,

Exam Probability: **High**

26. *Answer choices:*

(see index for correct answer)

- a. Conscious parallelism
- b. SK Hynix
- c. Competition regulator
- d. Ernest Varacalli

Guidance: level 1

:: Personal property law ::

Bailment describes a legal relationship in common law where physical
possession of personal property, or a chattel, is transferred from one person
to another person who subsequently has possession of the property. It arises
when a person gives property to someone else for safekeeping, and is a cause of
action independent of contract or tort.

Exam Probability: **High**

27. *Answer choices:*
(see index for correct answer)

- a. Bailee
- b. bailor

Guidance: level 1

:: ::

Business is the activity of making one`s living or making money by producing
or buying and selling products . Simply put, it is "any activity or enterprise
entered into for profit. It does not mean it is a company, a corporation,
partnership, or have any such formal organization, but it can range from a
street peddler to General Motors."

Exam Probability: **Low**

28. *Answer choices:*

(see index for correct answer)

- a. surface-level diversity
- b. functional perspective
- c. Firm
- d. information systems assessment

Guidance: level 1

:: Contract law ::

An _____ , or simply option, is defined as "a promise which meets the requirements for the formation of a contract and limits the promisor's power to revoke an offer."

Exam Probability: **Medium**

29. *Answer choices:*

(see index for correct answer)

- a. Option contract
- b. Condition precedent
- c. Parametric contract
- d. Listing contract

Guidance: level 1

:: ::

A _____ is an organization, usually a group of people or a company, authorized to act as a single entity and recognized as such in law. Early incorporated entities were established by charter . Most jurisdictions now allow the creation of new _____ s through registration.

Exam Probability: **Low**

30. *Answer choices:*

(see index for correct answer)

- a. corporate values
- b. co-culture
- c. Corporation
- d. cultural

Guidance: level 1

:: ::

_____ , in United States trademark law, is a statutory cause of action that permits a party to petition the Trademark Trial and Appeal Board of the Patent and Trademark Office to cancel a trademark registration that "may disparage or falsely suggest a connection with persons, living or dead, institutions, beliefs, or national symbols, or bring them into contempt or disrepute." Unlike claims regarding the validity of the mark, a _____ claim can be brought "at any time," subject to equitable defenses such as laches.

Exam Probability: **Medium**

31. *Answer choices:*

(see index for correct answer)

- a. Disparagement
- b. personal values
- c. hierarchical perspective
- d. levels of analysis

Guidance: level 1

:: Real estate ::

_____ , real estate, realty, or immovable property In English common law refers to landed properties belonging to some person. It include all structures, crops, buildings, machinery, wells, dams, ponds, mines, canals, and roads, among other things. The term is historic, arising from the now-discontinued form of action, which distinguish between _____ disputes and personal property disputes. Personal property was, and continues to refer to all properties that are not real properties.

Exam Probability: **High**

32. *Answer choices:*
(see index for correct answer)

- a. Exchanging contracts
- b. Gross lease
- c. Real property
- d. Housing estate

Guidance: level 1

:: ::

In general, _____ is a form of dishonesty or criminal activity undertaken by a person or organization entrusted with a position of authority, often to acquire illicit benefit. _____ may include many activities including bribery and embezzlement, though it may also involve practices that are legal in many countries. Political _____ occurs when an office-holder or other governmental employee acts in an official capacity for personal gain. _____ is most commonplace in kleptocracies, oligarchies, narco-states and mafia states.

Exam Probability: **Medium**

33. *Answer choices:*

(see index for correct answer)

- a. Corruption
- b. cultural
- c. levels of analysis
- d. empathy

Guidance: level 1

:: ::

The _____ of 1977 is a United States federal law known primarily for two of its main provisions: one that addresses accounting transparency requirements under the Securities Exchange Act of 1934 and another concerning bribery of foreign officials. The Act was amended in 1988 and in 1998, and has been subject to continued congressional concerns, namely whether its enforcement discourages U.S. companies from investing abroad.

34. *Answer choices:*

(see index for correct answer)

- a. similarity-attraction theory
- b. Sarbanes-Oxley act of 2002
- c. levels of analysis
- d. empathy

Guidance: level 1

:: ::

A _____ is any person who contracts to acquire an asset in return for some form of consideration.

Exam Probability: **Medium**

35. *Answer choices:*

(see index for correct answer)

- a. corporate values
- b. Buyer
- c. hierarchical
- d. information systems assessment

:: Legal doctrines and principles ::

_____ , land acquisition , compulsory purchase , resumption , resumption/compulsory acquisition , or expropriation is the power of a state, provincial, or national government to take private property for public use. However, this power can be legislatively delegated by the state to municipalities, government subdivisions, or even to private persons or corporations, when they are authorized by the legislature to exercise the functions of public character.

Exam Probability: **Low**

36. *Answer choices:*

(see index for correct answer)

- a. Eminent domain
- b. Parol evidence
- c. Abstention doctrine
- d. Act of state

:: ::

At common law, _____ are a remedy in the form of a monetary award to be paid to a claimant as compensation for loss or injury. To warrant the award, the claimant must show that a breach of duty has caused foreseeable loss. To be recognised at law, the loss must involve damage to property, or mental or physical injury; pure economic loss is rarely recognised for the award of _____ .

Exam Probability: **Low**

37. *Answer choices:*

(see index for correct answer)

- a. Damages
- b. co-culture
- c. imperative
- d. hierarchical perspective

Guidance: level 1

:: Contract law ::

In contract law, _____ is an excuse for the nonperformance of duties under a contract, based on a change in circumstances , the nonoccurrence of which was an underlying assumption of the contract, that makes performance of the contract literally impossible.

Exam Probability: **Medium**

38. *Answer choices:*

- a. Franchisor
- b. Impossibility
- c. Cohabitation agreement
- d. Condition precedent

Guidance: level 1

:: Contract law ::

An _____ —or acceleration covenant— in the law of contracts, is a term that fully matures the performance due from a party upon a breach of the contract. Such clauses are most prevalent in mortgages and similar contracts to purchase real estate in installments.

Exam Probability: **Medium**

39. *Answer choices:*

- a. Contract
- b. Revocation
- c. Void contract
- d. Interlineation

Guidance: level 1

:: ::

A _____ , in common law jurisdictions, is a civil wrong that causes a claimant to suffer loss or harm resulting in legal liability for the person who commits the _____ ious act. It can include the intentional infliction of emotional distress, negligence, financial losses, injuries, invasion of privacy, and many other things.

Exam Probability: **Medium**

40. *Answer choices:*

(see index for correct answer)

- a. hierarchical
- b. cultural
- c. Tort
- d. similarity-attraction theory

Guidance: level 1

:: Law ::

_____ is a body of law which defines the role, powers, and structure of different entities within a state, namely, the executive, the parliament or legislature, and the judiciary; as well as the basic rights of citizens and, in federal countries such as the United States and Canada, the relationship between the central government and state, provincial, or territorial governments.

Exam Probability: **High**

41. *Answer choices:*

(see index for correct answer)

- a. Legal case
- b. Comparative law

Guidance: level 1

:: Contract law ::

_____ , in human interactions, is a sincere intention to be fair, open, and honest, regardless of the outcome of the interaction. While some Latin phrases lose their literal meaning over centuries, this is not the case with bona fides; it is still widely used and interchangeable with its generally accepted modern-day English translation of _____ . It is an important concept within law and business. The opposed concepts are bad faith, mala fides and perfidy . In contemporary English, the usage of bona fides is synonymous with credentials and identity. The phrase is sometimes used in job advertisements, and should not be confused with the bona fide occupational qualifications or the employer`s _____ effort, as described below.

42. *Answer choices:*

(see index for correct answer)

- a. Intention to be legally bound
- b. Good faith
- c. Multimarket contact
- d. The Rise and Fall of Freedom of Contract

Guidance: level 1

:: Insolvency ::

_____ is the process in accounting by which a company is brought to an end in the United Kingdom, Republic of Ireland and United States. The assets and property of the company are redistributed. _____ is also sometimes referred to as winding-up or dissolution, although dissolution technically refers to the last stage of _____ . The process of _____ also arises when customs, an authority or agency in a country responsible for collecting and safeguarding customs duties, determines the final computation or ascertainment of the duties or drawback accruing on an entry.

Exam Probability: **High**

43. *Answer choices:*

(see index for correct answer)

- a. Conservatorship
- b. Debt consolidation
- c. Financial distress
- d. George Samuel Ford

Guidance: level 1

:: Legal doctrines and principles ::

The _____ rule is a rule in the Anglo-American common law that governs what kinds of evidence parties to a contract dispute can introduce when trying to determine the specific terms of a contract. The rule also prevents parties who have reduced their agreement to a final written document from later introducing other evidence, such as the content of oral discussions from earlier in the negotiation process, as evidence of a different intent as to the terms of the contract. The rule provides that "extrinsic evidence is inadmissible to vary a written contract". The term "parol" derives from the Anglo-Norman French parol or parole, meaning "word of mouth" or "verbal", and in medieval times referred to oral pleadings in a court case.

Exam Probability: **Medium**

44. *Answer choices:*

(see index for correct answer)

- a. Respondeat superior
- b. compulsory purchase
- c. Nonacquiescence
- d. Parol evidence

:: Insolvency ::

_____ is the state of being unable to pay the money owed, by a person or company, on time; those in a state of _____ are said to be insolvent. There are two forms: cash-flow _____ and balance-sheet _____ .

Exam Probability: **High**

45. *Answer choices:*

(see index for correct answer)

- a. Financial distress
- b. Liquidator
- c. Conservatorship
- d. Insolvency

Guidance: level 1

:: Trade secrets ::

The _____ of 1996 was a 6 title Act of Congress dealing with a wide range of issues, including not only industrial espionage , but the insanity defense, matters regarding the Boys & Girls Clubs of America, requirements for presentence investigation reports, and the United States Sentencing Commission reports regarding encryption or scrambling technology, and other technical and minor amendments.

Exam Probability: **Medium**

46. *Answer choices:*

(see index for correct answer)

- a. Aromat
- b. Rivendell Forest Prods. v. Georgia-Pacific Corp.
- c. Economic Espionage Act
- d. DuPont v. Kolon Industries

Guidance: level 1

:: Contract law ::

A _____ is a contract in which one party agrees to supply as much of a good or service as is required by the other party, and in exchange the other party expressly or implicitly promises that it will obtain its goods or services exclusively from the first party. For example, a grocery store might enter into a contract with the farmer who grows oranges under which the farmer would supply the grocery store with as many oranges as the store could sell. The farmer could sue for breach of contract if the store were thereafter to purchase oranges for this purpose from any other party. The converse of this situation is an output contract, in which one buyer agrees to purchase however much of a good or service the seller is able to produce.

Exam Probability: **High**

47. *Answer choices:*

(see index for correct answer)

- a. Contract price
- b. Offer and acceptance
- c. Domicilium citandi et executandi
- d. Meeting of the minds

Guidance: level 1

:: Contract law ::

_____ is the act of recall or annulment. It is the cancelling of an act, the recalling of a grant or privilege, or the making void of some deed previously existing.

48. *Answer choices:*

(see index for correct answer)

- a. Revocation
- b. Shrink wrap contract
- c. Franchisor
- d. Implied authority

Guidance: level 1

:: Legal terms ::

_____ , a form of alternative dispute resolution , is a way to resolve disputes outside the courts. The dispute will be decided by one or more persons , which renders the " _____ award". An _____ award is legally binding on both sides and enforceable in the courts.

49. *Answer choices:*

(see index for correct answer)

- a. Legal district
- b. Arbitration
- c. Procuration

- d. Plain meaning rule

Guidance: level 1

:: Contract law ::

_____ is a legal cause of action and a type of civil wrong, in which a binding agreement or bargained-for exchange is not honored by one or more of the parties to the contract by non-performance or interference with the other party's performance. Breach occurs when a party to a contract fails to fulfill its obligation as described in the contract, or communicates an intent to fail the obligation or otherwise appears not to be able to perform its obligation under the contract. Where there is _____ , the resulting damages will have to be paid by the party breaching the contract to the aggrieved party.

Exam Probability: **Medium**

50. *Answer choices:*
(see index for correct answer)

- a. Job order contracting
- b. Non est factum
- c. Contract lifecycle management
- d. Breach of contract

Guidance: level 1

:: ::

The _____ is an intergovernmental organization that is concerned with the regulation of international trade between nations. The WTO officially commenced on 1 January 1995 under the Marrakesh Agreement, signed by 124 nations on 15 April 1994, replacing the General Agreement on Tariffs and Trade , which commenced in 1948. It is the largest international economic organization in the world.

Exam Probability: **Low**

51. *Answer choices:*

(see index for correct answer)

- a. information systems assessment
- b. World Trade Organization
- c. process perspective
- d. personal values

Guidance: level 1

:: Real estate valuation ::

_____ or OMV is the price at which an asset would trade in a competitive auction setting. _____ is often used interchangeably with open _____ , fair value or fair _____ , although these terms have distinct definitions in different standards, and may or may not differ in some circumstances.

52. *Answer choices:*

(see index for correct answer)

- a. Real estate benchmarking
- b. International Right of Way Association
- c. E.surv
- d. Market value

Guidance: level 1

:: Psychometrics ::

_____ is a dynamic, structured, interactive process where a neutral third party assists disputing parties in resolving conflict through the use of specialized communication and negotiation techniques. All participants in _____ are encouraged to actively participate in the process. _____ is a "party-centered" process in that it is focused primarily upon the needs, rights, and interests of the parties. The mediator uses a wide variety of techniques to guide the process in a constructive direction and to help the parties find their optimal solution. A mediator is facilitative in that she/he manages the interaction between parties and facilitates open communication. _____ is also evaluative in that the mediator analyzes issues and relevant norms , while refraining from providing prescriptive advice to the parties .

Exam Probability: **High**

53. *Answer choices:*

(see index for correct answer)

- a. Mediation
- b. Criterion-referenced test
- c. Frederic M. Lord
- d. Psychometric software

Guidance: level 1

:: Legal procedure ::

_____ , adjective law, or rules of court comprises the rules by which a court hears and determines what happens in civil, lawsuit, criminal or administrative proceedings. The rules are designed to ensure a fair and consistent application of due process or fundamental justice to all cases that come before a court.

Exam Probability: **Low**

54. *Answer choices:*

(see index for correct answer)

- a. Opening statement
- b. Closing argument
- c. Procedural law
- d. civil procedure

:: Employment discrimination ::

_____ is a form of discrimination based on race, gender, religion, national origin, physical or mental disability, age, sexual orientation, and gender identity by employers. Earnings differentials or occupational differentiation—where differences in pay come from differences in qualifications or responsibilities—should not be confused with _____. Discrimination can be intended and involve disparate treatment of a group or be unintended, yet create disparate impact for a group.

Exam Probability: **Low**

55. *Answer choices:*

(see index for correct answer)

- a. MacBride Principles
- b. Employment discrimination
- c. Marriage bars
- d. Employment discrimination law in the European Union

:: International trade ::

A _____ is a document issued by a carrier to acknowledge receipt of cargo for shipment. Although the term historically related only to carriage by sea, a _____ may today be used for any type of carriage of goods.

Exam Probability: **Low**

56. *Answer choices:*

(see index for correct answer)

- a. Bill of lading
- b. Trade in services
- c. Monopolistic advantage theory
- d. Common external tariff

Guidance: level 1

:: ::

_____ is a marketing communication that employs an openly sponsored, non-personal message to promote or sell a product, service or idea. Sponsors of _____ are typically businesses wishing to promote their products or services. _____ is differentiated from public relations in that an advertiser pays for and has control over the message. It differs from personal selling in that the message is non-personal, i.e., not directed to a particular individual. _____ is communicated through various mass media, including traditional media such as newspapers, magazines, television, radio, outdoor _____ or direct mail; and new media such as search results, blogs, social media, websites or text messages. The actual presentation of the message in a medium is referred to as an advertisement, or "ad" or advert for short.

57. *Answer choices:*

(see index for correct answer)

- a. personal values
- b. deep-level diversity
- c. Advertising
- d. information systems assessment

Guidance: level 1

:: Contract law ::

In contract law, a _____ is a promise which is not a condition of the contract or an innominate term: it is a term "not going to the root of the contract", and which only entitles the innocent party to damages if it is breached: i.e. the _____ is not true or the defaulting party does not perform the contract in accordance with the terms of the _____ . A _____ is not guarantee. It is a mere promise. It may be enforced if it is breached by an award for the legal remedy of damages.

Exam Probability: **Medium**

58. *Answer choices:*

(see index for correct answer)

- a. Perfect tender

- b. Personal contract purchase
- c. Warranty
- d. Void contract

Guidance: level 1

:: ::

The U.S. _____ is an independent agency of the United States federal government. The SEC holds primary responsibility for enforcing the federal securities laws, proposing securities rules, and regulating the securities industry, the nation's stock and options exchanges, and other activities and organizations, including the electronic securities markets in the United States.

Exam Probability: **Low**

59. *Answer choices:*

(see index for correct answer)

- a. empathy
- b. hierarchical perspective
- c. interpersonal communication
- d. imperative

Guidance: level 1

Finance

Finance is a field that is concerned with the allocation (investment) of
assets and liabilities over space and time, often under conditions of risk or
uncertainty. Finance can also be defined as the science of money management.
Participants in the market aim to price assets based on their risk level,
fundamental value, and their expected rate of return. Finance can be split into
three sub-categories: public finance, corporate finance and personal finance.

:: ::

A shareholder is an individual or institution that legally owns one or more shares of stock in a public or private corporation. Shareholders may be referred to as members of a corporation. Legally, a person is not a shareholder in a corporation until their name and other details are entered in the corporation's register of shareholders or members.

Exam Probability: **Medium**

1. *Answer choices:*

(see index for correct answer)

- a. Stockholder
- b. interpersonal communication
- c. open system
- d. personal values

Guidance: level 1

:: Financial risk ::

_____ is the risk that arises for bond owners from fluctuating interest rates. How much _____ a bond has depends on how sensitive its price is to interest rate changes in the market. The sensitivity depends on two things, the bond's time to maturity, and the coupon rate of the bond.

Exam Probability: **Low**

2. *Answer choices:*

(see index for correct answer)

- a. Risk neutral
- b. Foreign exchange risk
- c. Interest rate risk
- d. Investment management

Guidance: level 1

:: ::

In the broadest sense, _____ is any practice which contributes to the sale of products to a retail consumer. At a retail in-store level, _____ refers to the variety of products available for sale and the display of those products in such a way that it stimulates interest and entices customers to make a purchase.

Exam Probability: **Low**

3. *Answer choices:*

(see index for correct answer)

- a. cultural
- b. Character
- c. co-culture
- d. Merchandising

:: Separation of investment and commercial banking ::

A _____ is a type of bank that provides services such as accepting deposits, making business loans, and offering basic investment products that is operated as a business for profit.

Exam Probability: **High**

4. *Answer choices:*

(see index for correct answer)

- a. GLBA
- b. Volcker Rule
- c. Commercial bank
- d. Bank Holding Company Act

:: Free accounting software ::

A _____ is the principal book or computer file for recording and totaling economic transactions measured in terms of a monetary unit of account by account type, with debits and credits in separate columns and a beginning monetary balance and ending monetary balance for each account.

Exam Probability: **High**

5. *Answer choices:*

(see index for correct answer)

- a. JFin
- b. Grisbi
- c. Ledger
- d. JGnash

Guidance: level 1

:: Auditing ::

_____ , as defined by accounting and auditing, is a process for assuring of an organization's objectives in operational effectiveness and efficiency, reliable financial reporting, and compliance with laws, regulations and policies. A broad concept, _____ involves everything that controls risks to an organization.

Exam Probability: **High**

6. *Answer choices:*

(see index for correct answer)

- a. Event data
- b. International Register of Certificated Auditors
- c. Audit Bureau of Circulations
- d. International Association of Airline Internal Auditors

Guidance: level 1

:: Accounting systems ::

In bookkeeping, a _____ statement is a process that explains the difference on a specified date between the bank balance shown in an organization's bank statement, as supplied by the bank and the corresponding amount shown in the organization's own accounting records.

Exam Probability: **Low**

7. *Answer choices:*

(see index for correct answer)

- a. Bank reconciliation
- b. Counting house
- c. Dome Publishing
- d. Entity concept

:: ::

In finance, return is a profit on an investment. It comprises any change in value of the investment, and/or cash flows which the investor receives from the investment, such as interest payments or dividends. It may be measured either in absolute terms or as a percentage of the amount invested. The latter is also called the holding period return.

Exam Probability: **Low**

8. *Answer choices:*

(see index for correct answer)

- a. deep-level diversity
- b. similarity-attraction theory
- c. levels of analysis
- d. Rate of return

:: Generally Accepted Accounting Principles ::

In accounting, _____ is the income that a business have from its normal business activities, usually from the sale of goods and services to customers. _____ is also referred to as sales or turnover. Some companies receive _____ from interest, royalties, or other fees. _____ may refer to business income in general, or it may refer to the amount, in a monetary unit, earned during a period of time, as in "Last year, Company X had _____ of $42 million". Profits or net income generally imply total _____ minus total expenses in a given period. In accounting, in the balance statement it is a subsection of the Equity section and _____ increases equity, it is often referred to as the "top line" due to its position on the income statement at the very top. This is to be contrasted with the "bottom line" which denotes net income .

Exam Probability: **Medium**

9. *Answer choices:*

(see index for correct answer)

- a. Paid in capital
- b. Vendor-specific objective evidence
- c. Cost principle
- d. Consolidation

Guidance: level 1

:: Expense ::

An _____ , operating expenditure, operational expense, operational expenditure or opex is an ongoing cost for running a product, business, or system. Its counterpart, a capital expenditure , is the cost of developing or providing non-consumable parts for the product or system. For example, the purchase of a photocopier involves capex, and the annual paper, toner, power and maintenance costs represents opex. For larger systems like businesses, opex may also include the cost of workers and facility expenses such as rent and utilities.

Exam Probability: **Medium**

10. *Answer choices:*

(see index for correct answer)

- a. Operating expense
- b. Tax expense
- c. Momentem
- d. Interest expense

Guidance: level 1

:: Stock market ::

_____ is freedom from, or resilience against, potential harm caused by others. Beneficiaries of _____ may be of persons and social groups, objects and institutions, ecosystems or any other entity or phenomenon vulnerable to unwanted change by its environment.

11. *Answer choices:*

(see index for correct answer)

- a. Hybrid market
- b. General Standard
- c. Stock certificate
- d. Security

Guidance: level 1

:: Accounting terminology ::

Accounts are typically defined by an identifier and a caption or header and are coded by account type. In computerized accounting systems with computable quantity accounting, the accounts can have a quantity measure definition.

Exam Probability: **High**

12. *Answer choices:*

(see index for correct answer)

- a. Mark-to-market
- b. Chart of accounts
- c. Cash flow management
- d. managerial accounting

:: Mutualism (movement) ::

A _____ is a professionally managed investment fund that pools money from many investors to purchase securities. These investors may be retail or institutional in nature.

Exam Probability: **Medium**

13. *Answer choices:*

(see index for correct answer)

- a. Mutualism
- b. Co-buying
- c. History of the cooperative movement
- d. Winslow Carlton

:: Accounting terminology ::

In management accounting or _____ , managers use the provisions of accounting information in order to better inform themselves before they decide matters within their organizations, which aids their management and performance of control functions.

Exam Probability: **Medium**

14. *Answer choices:*

(see index for correct answer)

- a. Adjusting entries
- b. Fair value accounting
- c. Account
- d. Checkoff

Guidance: level 1

:: Financial markets ::

_____ s are monetary contracts between parties. They can be created, traded, modified and settled. They can be cash , evidence of an ownership interest in an entity , or a contractual right to receive or deliver cash .

Exam Probability: **Medium**

15. *Answer choices:*

(see index for correct answer)

- a. Financial instrument
- b. Market impact
- c. Flight-to-quality
- d. Money market

Guidance: level 1

:: Hazard analysis ::

Broadly speaking, a _____ is the combined effort of 1. identifying and analyzing potential events that may negatively impact individuals, assets, and/or the environment ; and 2. making judgments "on the tolerability of the risk on the basis of a risk analysis" while considering influencing factors . Put in simpler terms, a _____ analyzes what can go wrong, how likely it is to happen, what the potential consequences are, and how tolerable the identified risk is. As part of this process, the resulting determination of risk may be expressed in a quantitative or qualitative fashion. The _____ is an inherent part of an overall risk management strategy, which attempts to, after a _____ , "introduce control measures to eliminate or reduce" any potential risk-related consequences.

Exam Probability: **Medium**

16. *Answer choices:*

(see index for correct answer)

- a. Risk assessment
- b. Hazard identification

- c. Swiss cheese model

Guidance: level 1

:: ::

_____ is a means of protection from financial loss. It is a form of risk management, primarily used to hedge against the risk of a contingent or uncertain loss

Exam Probability: **High**

17. *Answer choices:*

(see index for correct answer)

- a. personal values
- b. hierarchical
- c. open system
- d. cultural

Guidance: level 1

:: Financial economics ::

A _____ is defined to include property of any kind held by an assessee, whether connected with their business or profession or not connected with their business or profession. It includes all kinds of property, movable or immovable, tangible or intangible, fixed or circulating. Thus, land and building, plant and machinery, motorcar, furniture, jewellery, route permits, goodwill, tenancy rights, patents, trademarks, shares, debentures, securities, units, mutual funds, zero-coupon bonds etc. are _____ s.

Exam Probability: **High**

18. *Answer choices:*

(see index for correct answer)

- a. Consumer leverage ratio
- b. Capital asset
- c. Quasilinear utility
- d. Pricing schedule

Guidance: level 1

:: Accounting terminology ::

_____ or capital expense is the money a company spends to buy, maintain, or improve its fixed assets, such as buildings, vehicles, equipment, or land. It is considered a _____ when the asset is newly purchased or when money is used towards extending the useful life of an existing asset, such as repairing the roof.

19. *Answer choices:*

(see index for correct answer)

- a. Accrual
- b. Double-entry accounting
- c. Fund accounting
- d. Cash flow management

Guidance: level 1

:: Business economics ::

In finance, _____ is the risk of losses caused by interest rate changes. The prices of most financial instruments, such as stocks and bonds move inversely with interest rates, so investors are subject to capital loss when rates rise.

Exam Probability: **Low**

20. *Answer choices:*

(see index for correct answer)

- a. Round-tripping
- b. Trade name
- c. Trade working capital

- d. Peer group analysis

Guidance: level 1

:: Business law ::

_____ is where a person's financial liability is limited to a fixed sum, most commonly the value of a person's investment in a company or partnership. If a company with _____ is sued, then the claimants are suing the company, not its owners or investors. A shareholder in a limited company is not personally liable for any of the debts of the company, other than for the amount already invested in the company and for any unpaid amount on the shares in the company, if any. The same is true for the members of a _____ partnership and the limited partners in a limited partnership. By contrast, sole proprietors and partners in general partnerships are each liable for all the debts of the business .

Exam Probability: **High**

21. *Answer choices:*
(see index for correct answer)

- a. Partnership
- b. Participation
- c. Valuation using the Market Penetration Model
- d. Firm offer

Guidance: level 1

MCI, Inc. was an American telecommunication corporation, currently a subsidiary of Verizon Communications, with its main office in Ashburn, Virginia. The corporation was formed originally as a result of the merger of _____ and MCI Communications corporations, and used the name MCI _____ , succeeded by _____ , before changing its name to the present version on April 12, 2003, as part of the corporation's ending of its bankruptcy status. The company traded on NASDAQ as WCOM and MCIP . The corporation was purchased by Verizon Communications with the deal finalizing on January 6, 2006, and is now identified as that company's Verizon Enterprise Solutions division with the local residential divisions being integrated slowly into local Verizon subsidiaries.

Exam Probability: **Low**

22. *Answer choices:*

(see index for correct answer)

- a. imperative
- b. WorldCom
- c. Character
- d. levels of analysis

Guidance: level 1

:: Fixed income market ::

In finance, the _____ is a curve showing several yields or interest rates across different contract lengths for a similar debt contract. The curve shows the relation between the interest rate and the time to maturity, known as the "term", of the debt for a given borrower in a given currency. For example, the U.S. dollar interest rates paid on U.S. Treasury securities for various maturities are closely watched by many traders, and are commonly plotted on a graph such as the one on the right which is informally called "the _____ ". More formal mathematical descriptions of this relation are often called the term structure of interest rates.

Exam Probability: **Medium**

23. *Answer choices:*

(see index for correct answer)

- a. Fixed-income attribution
- b. credit market
- c. Inter-dealer broker
- d. Yield curve

Guidance: level 1

:: Financial economics ::

_____ , Inc. is an independent investment research and financial publishing firm based in New York City, New York, United States, founded in 1931 by Arnold Bernhard. _____ is best known for publishing The _____ Investment Survey, a stock analysis newsletter that is among the most highly regarded and widely used independent investment research resources in global investment and trading markets, tracking approximately 1,700 publicly traded stocks in over 99 industries.

Exam Probability: **Low**

24. *Answer choices:*

(see index for correct answer)

- a. Market correction
- b. Value Line
- c. Pricing schedule
- d. Implementation shortfall

Guidance: level 1

:: Generally Accepted Accounting Principles ::

In accounting, an economic item's _____ is the original nominal monetary value of that item. _____ accounting involves reporting assets and liabilities at their _____ s, which are not updated for changes in the items' values. Consequently, the amounts reported for these balance sheet items often differ from their current economic or market values.

Exam Probability: **High**

25. *Answer choices:*

(see index for correct answer)

- a. Fin 48
- b. Expense
- c. Engagement letter
- d. Historical cost

Guidance: level 1

:: Actuarial science ::

_____ is the addition of interest to the principal sum of a loan or deposit, or in other words, interest on interest. It is the result of reinvesting interest, rather than paying it out, so that interest in the next period is then earned on the principal sum plus previously accumulated interest. _____ is standard in finance and economics.

Exam Probability: **Medium**

26. *Answer choices:*

(see index for correct answer)

- a. Financial modeling
- b. Mortality forecasting

- c. Esscher transform
- d. Value at risk

Guidance: level 1

:: Generally Accepted Accounting Principles ::

A _____ or reacquired stock is stock which is bought back by the issuing company, reducing the amount of outstanding stock on the open market .

Exam Probability: **High**

27. *Answer choices:*

(see index for correct answer)

- a. Depreciation
- b. Shares outstanding
- c. Earnings before interest, taxes, depreciation, and amortization
- d. Long-term liabilities

Guidance: level 1

:: Business ethics ::

In accounting and in most Schools of economic thought, _____ is a rational and unbiased estimate of the potential market price of a good, service, or asset. It takes into account such objectivity factors as.

Exam Probability: **Low**

28. *Answer choices:*

(see index for correct answer)

- a. McJob
- b. Pension spiking
- c. Being Globally Responsible Conference
- d. Contingent work

Guidance: level 1

:: Competition (economics) ::

_____ arises whenever at least two parties strive for a goal which cannot be shared: where one's gain is the other's loss .

Exam Probability: **High**

29. *Answer choices:*

(see index for correct answer)

- a. Currency competition
- b. Competition
- c. Self-competition
- d. Level playing field

Guidance: level 1

:: Generally Accepted Accounting Principles ::

_____ is the accounting classification of an account. It is part of double-entry book-keeping technique.

Exam Probability: **High**

30. *Answer choices:*

(see index for correct answer)

- a. Normal balance
- b. Management accounting principles
- c. Expense
- d. Consolidation

Guidance: level 1

:: Personal finance ::

_____ is income not spent, or deferred consumption. Methods of _____ include putting money aside in, for example, a deposit account, a pension account, an investment fund, or as cash. _____ also involves reducing expenditures, such as recurring costs. In terms of personal finance, _____ generally specifies low-risk preservation of money, as in a deposit account, versus investment, wherein risk is a lot higher; in economics more broadly, it refers to any income not used for immediate consumption.

Exam Probability: **Low**

31. *Answer choices:*

(see index for correct answer)

- a. Saving
- b. Asset location
- c. West One Bridging Index
- d. The Money Tracker

Guidance: level 1

:: Management accounting ::

_____ is the process of recording, classifying, analyzing, summarizing, and allocating costs associated with a process,after that developing various courses of action to control the costs. Its goal is to advise the management on how to optimize business practices and processes based on cost efficiency and capability. _____ provides the detailed cost information that management needs to control current operations and plan for the future.

32. *Answer choices:*

(see index for correct answer)

- a. Customer profitability
- b. Cost accounting
- c. Operating profit margin
- d. Institute of Management Accountants

Guidance: level 1

:: ::

_____ is the field of accounting concerned with the summary, analysis and reporting of financial transactions related to a business. This involves the preparation of financial statements available for public use. Stockholders, suppliers, banks, employees, government agencies, business owners, and other stakeholders are examples of people interested in receiving such information for decision making purposes.

33. *Answer choices:*

(see index for correct answer)

- a. deep-level diversity
- b. open system

- c. levels of analysis
- d. hierarchical

Guidance: level 1

:: ::

A _____ is an individual or institution that legally owns one or more shares of stock in a public or private corporation. _____ s may be referred to as members of a corporation. Legally, a person is not a _____ in a corporation until their name and other details are entered in the corporation's register of _____ s or members.

Exam Probability: **Low**

34. *Answer choices:*

(see index for correct answer)

- a. Shareholder
- b. similarity-attraction theory
- c. Character
- d. open system

Guidance: level 1

:: ::

_____ is a political and social philosophy promoting traditional social institutions in the context of culture and civilization. The central tenets of _____ include tradition, human imperfection, organic society, hierarchy, authority, and property rights. Conservatives seek to preserve a range of institutions such as religion, parliamentary government, and property rights, with the aim of emphasizing social stability and continuity. The more traditional elements—reactionaries—oppose modernism and seek a return to "the way things were".

Exam Probability: **Medium**

35. *Answer choices:*

(see index for correct answer)

- a. functional perspective
- b. Conservatism
- c. corporate values
- d. open system

Guidance: level 1

:: Financial accounting ::

_____ refers to any one of several methods by which a company, for 'financial accounting' or tax purposes, depreciates a fixed asset in such a way that the amount of depreciation taken each year is higher during the earlier years of an asset's life. For financial accounting purposes, _____ is expected to be much more productive during its early years, so that depreciation expense will more accurately represent how much of an asset's usefulness is being used up each year. For tax purposes, _____ provides a way of deferring corporate income taxes by reducing taxable income in current years, in exchange for increased taxable income in future years. This is a valuable tax incentive that encourages businesses to purchase new assets.

Exam Probability: **Medium**

36. *Answer choices:*

(see index for correct answer)

- a. Net worth
- b. Accelerated depreciation
- c. Tax amortization benefit
- d. Accounting identity

Guidance: level 1

:: Accounting journals and ledgers ::

_____ is a daybook or journal which is used to record transactions relating to adjustment entries, opening stock, accounting errors etc. The source documents of this prime entry book are journal voucher, copy of management reports and invoices.

37. *Answer choices:*

(see index for correct answer)

- a. General journal
- b. Subledger
- c. Subsidiary ledger
- d. Journal entry

Guidance: level 1

:: Markets (customer bases) ::

In economics, _____ is the economic price for which a good or service is offered in the marketplace. It is of interest mainly in the study of microeconomics. Market value and _____ are equal only under conditions of market efficiency, equilibrium, and rational expectations.

Exam Probability: **Medium**

38. *Answer choices:*

(see index for correct answer)

- a. Parity product
- b. Vertical market
- c. Market mechanism

- d. Market price

Guidance: level 1

:: Financial ratios ::

_____ is a financial ratio that indicates the percentage of a company's assets that are provided via debt. It is the ratio of total debt and total assets .

Exam Probability: **High**

39. *Answer choices:*
(see index for correct answer)

- a. Debt ratio
- b. Information ratio
- c. Debt service ratio
- d. Import ratio

Guidance: level 1

:: Commerce ::

A _____ , manufacturing plant or a production plant is an industrial site, usually consisting of buildings and machinery, or more commonly a complex having several buildings, where workers manufacture goods or operate machines processing one product into another.

Exam Probability: **Medium**

40. *Answer choices:*

(see index for correct answer)

- a. Fast track
- b. PIN pad
- c. Real prices and ideal prices
- d. Factory

Guidance: level 1

:: Generally Accepted Accounting Principles ::

The _____ principle is a cornerstone of accrual accounting together with the matching principle. They both determine the accounting period in which revenues and expenses are recognized. According to the principle, revenues are recognized when they are realized or realizable, and are earned , no matter when cash is received. In cash accounting – in contrast – revenues are recognized when cash is received no matter when goods or services are sold.

Exam Probability: **Low**

41. *Answer choices:*

(see index for correct answer)

- a. net realisable value
- b. Trial balance
- c. Reserve
- d. Revenue recognition

Guidance: level 1

:: Money market instruments ::

_____ , in the global financial market, is an unsecured promissory note with a fixed maturity of not more than 270 days.

Exam Probability: **Low**

42. *Answer choices:*

(see index for correct answer)

- a. Banker's acceptance
- b. Commercial paper

Guidance: level 1

:: Insolvency ::

_____ is the process in accounting by which a company is brought to an end in the United Kingdom, Republic of Ireland and United States. The assets and property of the company are redistributed. _____ is also sometimes referred to as winding-up or dissolution, although dissolution technically refers to the last stage of _____ . The process of _____ also arises when customs, an authority or agency in a country responsible for collecting and safeguarding customs duties, determines the final computation or ascertainment of the duties or drawback accruing on an entry.

Exam Probability: **Low**

43. *Answer choices:*

(see index for correct answer)

- a. Financial distress
- b. Liquidation
- c. Insolvency law of Russia
- d. Bankruptcy

Guidance: level 1

:: Interest ::

In finance, _____ is the interest on a bond or loan that has accumulated since the principal investment, or since the previous coupon payment if there has been one already.

44. *Answer choices:*

(see index for correct answer)

- a. Penal interest
- b. Fisher hypothesis
- c. Accrued interest
- d. Deposit interest retention tax

Guidance: level 1

:: Pension funds ::

_____ s typically have large amounts of money to invest and are the major investors in listed and private companies. They are especially important to the stock market where large institutional investors dominate. The largest 300 _____ s collectively hold about $6 trillion in assets. In January 2008, The Economist reported that Morgan Stanley estimates that _____ s worldwide hold over US$20 trillion in assets, the largest for any category of investor ahead of mutual funds, insurance companies, currency reserves, sovereign wealth funds, hedge funds, or private equity.

Exam Probability: **High**

45. *Answer choices:*

(see index for correct answer)

- a. Pension led funding
- b. Texas Municipal Retirement System
- c. Pension buyout

Guidance: level 1

:: International Financial Reporting Standards ::

_____ , usually called IFRS, are standards issued by the IFRS Foundation and the International Accounting Standards Board to provide a common global language for business affairs so that company accounts are understandable and comparable across international boundaries. They are a consequence of growing international shareholding and trade and are particularly important for companies that have dealings in several countries. They are progressively replacing the many different national accounting standards. They are the rules to be followed by accountants to maintain books of accounts which are comparable, understandable, reliable and relevant as per the users internal or external. IFRS, with the exception of IAS 29 Financial Reporting in Hyperinflationary Economies and IFRIC 7 Applying the Restatement Approach under IAS 29, are authorized in terms of the historical cost paradigm. IAS 29 and IFRIC 7 are authorized in terms of the units of constant purchasing power paradigm.IAS 2 is related to inventories in this standard we talk about the stock its production process etcIFRS began as an attempt to harmonize accounting across the European Union but the value of harmonization quickly made the concept attractive around the world. However, it has been debated whether or not de facto harmonization has occurred. Standards that were issued by IASC are still within use today and go by the name International Accounting Standards , while standards issued by IASB are called IFRS. IAS were issued between 1973 and 2001 by the Board of the International Accounting Standards Committee . On 1 April 2001, the new International Accounting Standards Board took over from the IASC the responsibility for setting International Accounting Standards. During its first meeting the new Board adopted existing IAS and Standing Interpretations Committee standards . The IASB has continued to develop standards calling the new standards " _____ ".

46. *Answer choices:*

(see index for correct answer)

- a. IAS 2
- b. IAS 7
- c. International Financial Reporting Standards
- d. Convergence of accounting standards

Guidance: level 1

:: Marketing ::

_____ or stock is the goods and materials that a business holds for the ultimate goal of resale .

Exam Probability: **High**

47. *Answer choices:*

(see index for correct answer)

- a. Inventory
- b. Neuromarketing
- c. Mass market
- d. Back to school

:: Generally Accepted Accounting Principles ::

_____ , or non-current liabilities, are liabilities that are due beyond
a year or the normal operation period of the company. The normal operation
period is the amount of time it takes for a company to turn inventory into
cash. On a classified balance sheet, liabilities are separated between current
and _____ to help users assess the company's financial standing in
short-term and long-term periods. _____ give users more information about
the long-term prosperity of the company, while current liabilities inform the
user of debt that the company owes in the current period. On a balance sheet,
accounts are listed in order of liquidity, so _____ come after current
liabilities. In addition, the specific long-term liability accounts are listed
on the balance sheet in order of liquidity. Therefore, an account due within
eighteen months would be listed before an account due within twenty-four
months. Examples of _____ are bonds payable, long-term loans, capital
leases, pension liabilities, post-retirement healthcare liabilities, deferred
compensation, deferred revenues, deferred income taxes, and derivative
liabilities.

Exam Probability: **High**

48. *Answer choices:*

(see index for correct answer)

- a. Fixed investment
- b. Contributed capital
- c. Long-term liabilities
- d. Write-off

:: ::

The U.S. _____ is an independent agency of the United States federal government. The SEC holds primary responsibility for enforcing the federal securities laws, proposing securities rules, and regulating the securities industry, the nation's stock and options exchanges, and other activities and organizations, including the electronic securities markets in the United States.

Exam Probability: **High**

49. *Answer choices:*

(see index for correct answer)

- a. process perspective
- b. functional perspective
- c. imperative
- d. surface-level diversity

:: Margin policy ::

In finance, a _____ is a standardized forward contract, a legal agreement to buy or sell something at a predetermined price at a specified time in the future, between parties not known to each other. The asset transacted is usually a commodity or financial instrument. The predetermined price the parties agree to buy and sell the asset for is known as the forward price. The specified time in the future—which is when delivery and payment occur—is known as the delivery date. Because it is a function of an underlying asset, a _____ is a derivative product.

Exam Probability: **High**

50. *Answer choices:*

(see index for correct answer)

- a. Regulation T
- b. Futures contract

Guidance: level 1

:: ::

_____ is a marketing communication that employs an openly sponsored, non-personal message to promote or sell a product, service or idea. Sponsors of _____ are typically businesses wishing to promote their products or services. _____ is differentiated from public relations in that an advertiser pays for and has control over the message. It differs from personal selling in that the message is non-personal, i.e., not directed to a particular individual. _____ is communicated through various mass media, including traditional media such as newspapers, magazines, television, radio, outdoor _____ or direct mail; and new media such as search results, blogs, social media, websites or text messages. The actual presentation of the message in a medium is referred to as an advertisement, or "ad" or advert for short.

Exam Probability: **Medium**

51. *Answer choices:*

(see index for correct answer)

- a. hierarchical perspective
- b. Sarbanes-Oxley act of 2002
- c. Advertising
- d. Character

Guidance: level 1

:: Accounting terminology ::

_____ is money owed by a business to its suppliers shown as a liability on a company`s balance sheet. It is distinct from notes payable liabilities, which are debts created by formal legal instrument documents.

52. *Answer choices:*

(see index for correct answer)

- a. Record to report
- b. Capital expenditure
- c. Accounts payable
- d. Adjusting entries

Guidance: level 1

:: International trade ::

In finance, an _____ is the rate at which one currency will be exchanged for another. It is also regarded as the value of one country's currency in relation to another currency. For example, an interbank _____ of 114 Japanese yen to the United States dollar means that ¥114 will be exchanged for each US$1 or that US$1 will be exchanged for each ¥114. In this case it is said that the price of a dollar in relation to yen is ¥114, or equivalently that the price of a yen in relation to dollars is $1/114.

Exam Probability: **Medium**

53. *Answer choices:*

(see index for correct answer)

- a. Exchange rate

- b. Gains from trade
- c. Quota share
- d. Ecumenical Advocacy Alliance

Guidance: level 1

:: Income taxes ::

An _____ is a tax imposed on individuals or entities that varies with respective income or profits . _____ generally is computed as the product of a tax rate times taxable income. Taxation rates may vary by type or characteristics of the taxpayer.

Exam Probability: **Medium**

54. *Answer choices:*

(see index for correct answer)

- a. Illinois Fair Tax
- b. Income tax threshold
- c. Lifetime income tax
- d. Income tax

Guidance: level 1

:: Financial markets ::

For an individual, a _____ is the minimum amount of money by which the expected return on a risky asset must exceed the known return on a risk-free asset in order to induce an individual to hold the risky asset rather than the risk-free asset. It is positive if the person is risk averse. Thus it is the minimum willingness to accept compensation for the risk.

Exam Probability: High

55. *Answer choices:*

(see index for correct answer)

- a. Holy grail distribution
- b. Convertible arbitrage
- c. Head fake
- d. Swap spread

Guidance: level 1

:: Expense ::

A company's _____ , or As a result, the computation of the _____ is considerably more complex. Tax law may provide for different treatment of items of income and expenses as a result of tax policy. The differences may be of permanent or temporary nature. Permanent items are in the form of non taxable income and non taxable expenses. Things such as expenses considered not deductible by taxing authorities , the range of tax rates applicable to various levels of income, different tax rates in different jurisdictions, multiple layers of tax on income, and other issues.

56. *Answer choices:*

(see index for correct answer)

- a. Business overhead expense disability insurance
- b. Tax expense
- c. Corporate travel
- d. Interest expense

Guidance: level 1

:: Business economics ::

A _____ is a term used primarily in cost accounting to describe something to which costs are assigned. Common examples of _____ s are: product lines, geographic territories, customers, departments or anything else for which management would like to quantify cost.

Exam Probability: **Medium**

57. *Answer choices:*

(see index for correct answer)

- a. Overnight cost
- b. Cost object
- c. Real net output ratio

- d. Gross operating surplus

Guidance: level 1

:: Bonds (finance) ::

An _____ is a legal contract that reflects or covers a debt or purchase obligation. It specifically refers to two types of practices: in historical usage, an _____ d servant status, and in modern usage, it is an instrument used for commercial debt or real estate transaction.

Exam Probability: **High**

58. *Answer choices:*

(see index for correct answer)

- a. Bid bond
- b. Mortgage bond
- c. Amortizing loan
- d. Indenture

Guidance: level 1

:: Leasing ::

A finance lease is a type of lease in which a finance company is typically the legal owner of the asset for the duration of the lease, while the lessee not only has operating control over the asset, but also has a some share of the economic risks and returns from the change in the valuation of the underlying asset.

Exam Probability: **Medium**

59. *Answer choices:*

(see index for correct answer)

- a. Capital lease
- b. Synthetic lease

Guidance: level 1

Human resource management

    Human resource (HR) management is the strategic approach to the effective management of organization workers so that they help the business gain a competitive advantage. It is designed to maximize employee performance in service of an employer's strategic objectives. HR is primarily concerned with the management of people within organizations, focusing on policies and on systems. HR departments are responsible for overseeing employee-benefits design, employee recruitment, training and development, performance appraisal, and rewarding (e.g., managing pay and benefit systems). HR also concerns itself with organizational change and industrial relations, that is, the balancing of organizational practices with requirements arising from collective bargaining and from governmental laws.

:: Employment ::

_____ is measuring the output of a particular business process or procedure, then modifying the process or procedure to increase the output, increase efficiency, or increase the effectiveness of the process or procedure. _____ can be applied to either individual performance such as an athlete or organizational performance such as a racing team or a commercial business.

Exam Probability: **Medium**

1. *Answer choices:*

(see index for correct answer)

- a. Hourly worker
- b. Ontario Disability Employment Network
- c. Performance improvement
- d. In-basket test

Guidance: level 1

:: United States employment discrimination case law ::

_____ , 557 U.S. 557 , is a US labor law case of the United States Supreme Court on unlawful discrimination through disparate impact under the Civil Rights Act of 1964.

Exam Probability: **High**

2. *Answer choices:*

(see index for correct answer)

- a. Hosanna-Tabor Evangelical Lutheran Church and School v. Equal Employment Opportunity Commission
- b. Price Waterhouse v. Hopkins
- c. Glenn v. Brumby
- d. Ricci v. DeStefano

Guidance: level 1

:: Meetings ::

A _____ is a body of one or more persons that is subordinate to a deliberative assembly. Usually, the assembly sends matters into a _____ as a way to explore them more fully than would be possible if the assembly itself were considering them. _____ s may have different functions and their type of work differ depending on the type of the organization and its needs.

Exam Probability: **High**

3. *Answer choices:*

(see index for correct answer)

- a. Agenda
- b. Audience
- c. Committee
- d. CodeCamp

:: Human resource management ::

Frederick Herzberg, an American psychologist, originally developed the concept of ` _____ ` in 1968, in an article that he published on pioneering studies at A T&T. The concept stemmed from Herzberg's motivator-hygiene theory, which is based on the premise that job attitude is a construct of two independent factors, namely job satisfaction and job dissatisfaction. Job satisfaction encompasses intrinsic factors that arise from the work itself, including achievement and advancement; whilst job dissatisfaction stems from factors external to the actual work, including company policy and the quality of supervision.

Exam Probability: **High**

4. *Answer choices:*

(see index for correct answer)

- a. Co-determination
- b. ROWE
- c. SLT Human Capital Solutions
- d. Job enrichment

:: ::

According to Torrington, a _____ is usually developed by conducting a job analysis, which includes examining the tasks and sequences of tasks necessary to perform the job. The analysis considers the areas of knowledge and skills needed for the job. A job usually includes several roles. According to Hall, the _____ might be broadened to form a person specification or may be known as "terms of reference". The person/job specification can be presented as a stand-alone document, but in practice it is usually included within the _____ . A _____ is often used by employers in the recruitment process.

Exam Probability: **High**

5. *Answer choices:*

(see index for correct answer)

- a. interpersonal communication
- b. Job description
- c. co-culture
- d. process perspective

Guidance: level 1

:: Employment compensation ::

The formula commonly used by compensation professionals to assess the competitiveness of an employee's pay level involves calculating a ""_____ "". _____ is the short form for Comparative ratio.

6. *Answer choices:*

(see index for correct answer)

- a. Dearness allowance
- b. Health Reimbursement Account
- c. Equal pay for equal work
- d. Family meal

Guidance: level 1

:: Business law ::

_____ or employment relations is the multidisciplinary academic field that studies the employment relationship; that is, the complex interrelations between employers and employees, labor/trade unions, employer organizations and the state.

Exam Probability: **Medium**

7. *Answer choices:*

(see index for correct answer)

- a. Secret rebate
- b. License
- c. European Patent Convention

- d. Industrial relations

Guidance: level 1

:: Systems thinking ::

In business management, a _____ is a company that facilitates the learning of its members and continuously transforms itself. The concept was coined through the work and research of Peter Senge and his colleagues.

Exam Probability: **Medium**

8. *Answer choices:*

(see index for correct answer)

- a. Learning organization
- b. Bioterrorism
- c. Involution
- d. Club of Budapest

Guidance: level 1

:: Management ::

A _____ describes the rationale of how an organization creates, delivers, and captures value, in economic, social, cultural or other contexts. The process of _____ construction and modification is also called _____ innovation and forms a part of business strategy.

Exam Probability: **Low**

9. *Answer choices:*

(see index for correct answer)

- a. Submission management
- b. Linear scheduling method
- c. Business model
- d. Stovepipe

Guidance: level 1

:: Workplace ::

_____ is a systematic determination of a subject's merit, worth and significance, using criteria governed by a set of standards. It can assist an organization, program, design, project or any other intervention or initiative to assess any aim, realisable concept/proposal, or any alternative, to help in decision-making; or to ascertain the degree of achievement or value in regard to the aim and objectives and results of any such action that has been completed. The primary purpose of _____ , in addition to gaining insight into prior or existing initiatives, is to enable reflection and assist in the identification of future change.

10. *Answer choices:*

(see index for correct answer)

- a. Evaluation
- b. Feminisation of the workplace
- c. Emotions in the workplace
- d. 360-degree feedback

Guidance: level 1

:: Validity (statistics) ::

_____ is the extent to which a test accurately measures what it is supposed to measure. In the fields of psychological testing and educational testing, "validity refers to the degree to which evidence and theory support the interpretations of test scores entailed by proposed uses of tests". Although classical models divided the concept into various "validities" , the currently dominant view is that validity is a single unitary construct.

11. *Answer choices:*

(see index for correct answer)

- a. Test validity
- b. Internal validity

- c. Construct validity
- d. Statistical conclusion validity

Guidance: level 1

:: ::

An _____ is a process where candidates are examined to determine their suitability for specific types of employment, especially management or military command. The candidates' personality and aptitudes are determined by techniques including interviews, group exercises, presentations, examinations and psychometric testing.

Exam Probability: **High**

12. *Answer choices:*
(see index for correct answer)

- a. personal values
- b. information systems assessment
- c. Assessment center
- d. empathy

Guidance: level 1

:: Employee relations ::

_____ ownership, or employee share ownership, is an ownership interest in a company held by the company's workforce. The ownership interest may be facilitated by the company as part of employees' remuneration or incentive compensation for work performed, or the company itself may be employee owned.

Exam Probability: **Medium**

13. *Answer choices:*

(see index for correct answer)

- a. Employee handbook
- b. employee stock ownership
- c. Employee surveys
- d. Employee engagement

Guidance: level 1

:: Labor terms ::

_____ , often called DI or disability income insurance, or income protection, is a form of insurance that insures the beneficiary`s earned income against the risk that a disability creates a barrier for a worker to complete the core functions of their work. For example, the worker may suffer from an inability to maintain composure in the case of psychological disorders or an injury, illness or condition that causes physical impairment or incapacity to work. It encompasses paid sick leave, short-term disability benefits , and long-term disability benefits . Statistics show that in the US a disabling accident occurs, on average, once every second. In fact, nearly 18.5% of Americans are currently living with a disability, and 1 out of every 4 persons in the US workforce will suffer a disabling injury before retirement.

Exam Probability: **High**

14. *Answer choices:*

(see index for correct answer)

- a. Absence rate
- b. Disability insurance
- c. All other occupational illnesses
- d. Civilian noninstitutional population

Guidance: level 1

:: Parental leave ::

_____ is a type of employment discrimination that occurs when expectant women are fired, not hired, or otherwise discriminated against due to their pregnancy or intention to become pregnant. Common forms of _____ include not being hired due to visible pregnancy or likelihood of becoming pregnant, being fired after informing an employer of one`s pregnancy, being fired after maternity leave, and receiving a pay dock due to pregnancy. Convention on the Elimination of All Forms of Discrimination against Women prohibits dismissal on the grounds of maternity or pregnancy and ensures right to maternity leave or comparable social benefits. The Maternity Protection Convention C 183 proclaims adequate protection for pregnancy as well. Though women have some protection in the United States because of the _____ Act of 1978, it has not completely curbed the incidence of _____. The Equal Rights Amendment could ensure more robust sex equality ensuring that women and men could both work and have children at the same time.

Exam Probability: **Low**

15. *Answer choices:*

(see index for correct answer)

- a. Maternity and Parental Leave, etc Regulations 1999
- b. Geduldig v. Aiello
- c. Parental leave
- d. Pregnancy discrimination

Guidance: level 1

:: Management ::

_____ is a set of activities that ensure goals are met in an effective and efficient manner. _____ can focus on the performance of an organization, a department, an employee, or the processes in place to manage particular tasks. _____ standards are generally organized and disseminated by senior leadership at an organization, and by task owners.

Exam Probability: **Medium**

16. *Answer choices:*

(see index for correct answer)

- a. Performance management
- b. Responsible autonomy
- c. Smiling curve
- d. Enterprise smart grid

Guidance: level 1

:: Business ethics ::

_____ is a pejorative term for a workplace that has very poor, socially unacceptable working conditions. The work may be difficult, dangerous, climatically challenged or underpaid. Workers in _____ s may work long hours with low pay, regardless of laws mandating overtime pay or a minimum wage; child labor laws may also be violated. The Fair Labor Association's "2006 Annual Public Report" inspected factories for FLA compliance in 18 countries including Bangladesh, El Salvador, Colombia, Guatemala, Malaysia, Thailand, Tunisia, Turkey, China, India, Vietnam, Honduras, Indonesia, Brazil, Mexico, and the US. The U.S. Department of Labor's "2015 Findings on the Worst Forms of Child Labor" found that "18 countries did not meet the International Labour Organization's recommendation for an adequate number of inspectors."

Exam Probability: **High**

17. *Answer choices:*

(see index for correct answer)

- a. Ethical consumerism
- b. Cost the limit of price
- c. Resource Conservation and Recovery Act
- d. Sweatshop

Guidance: level 1

:: Unemployment by country ::

Unemployment benefits are payments made by back authorized bodies to unemployed people. In the United States, benefits are funded by a compulsory governmental insurance system, not taxes on individual citizens. Depending on the jurisdiction and the status of the person, those sums may be small, covering only basic needs, or may compensate the lost time proportionally to the previous earned salary.

Exam Probability: **Low**

18. *Answer choices:*

(see index for correct answer)

- a. Unemployment in Brazil
- b. Unemployment in Poland
- c. Unemployment in Spain

Guidance: level 1

:: Business ::

_____ is a trade policy that does not restrict imports or exports; it can also be understood as the free market idea applied to international trade. In government, _____ is predominantly advocated by political parties that hold liberal economic positions while economically left-wing and nationalist political parties generally support protectionism, the opposite of _____ .

Exam Probability: **Low**

19. *Answer choices:*

(see index for correct answer)

- a. Absentee business owner
- b. Attention marketing
- c. Business agility
- d. Free Trade

Guidance: level 1

:: Industrial agreements ::

_____ is a process in labour relations, where a trade union gains a new and superior entitlement from one employer and then uses that agreement as a precedent to demand the same entitlement or a superior one from other employers.

Exam Probability: **Low**

20. *Answer choices:*

(see index for correct answer)

- a. In Place of Strife
- b. Court of Arbitration
- c. Workplace Authority
- d. Mutual gains bargaining

:: Human resource management ::

_____ is the application of information technology for both networking and supporting at least two individual or collective actors in their shared performing of HR activities.

Exam Probability: **Low**

21. *Answer choices:*

(see index for correct answer)

- a. Functional job analysis
- b. E-HRM
- c. Competency-based management
- d. human resource

:: Economic globalization ::

_____ is an agreement in which one company hires another company to be responsible for a planned or existing activity that is or could be done internally,and sometimes involves transferring employees and assets from one firm to another.

Exam Probability: **High**

22. *Answer choices:*

- a. reshoring
- b. global financial

Guidance: level 1

:: Design of experiments ::

In the design of experiments, treatments are applied to experimental units in the treatment group. In comparative experiments, members of the complementary group, the _____ , receive either no treatment or a standard treatment.

Exam Probability: **Medium**

23. *Answer choices:*

- a. Control group

- b. Restricted randomization
- c. Combinatorial design
- d. Exploratory thought

Guidance: level 1

:: Cognitive biases ::

In personality psychology, _____ is the degree to which people believe that they have control over the outcome of events in their lives, as opposed to external forces beyond their control. Understanding of the concept was developed by Julian B. Rotter in 1954, and has since become an aspect of personality studies. A person's "locus" is conceptualized as internal or external .

Exam Probability: **Low**

24. *Answer choices:*

(see index for correct answer)

- a. Hostile media effect
- b. In-group favoritism
- c. Locus of control
- d. Neglect of probability

Guidance: level 1

:: Training ::

_____ is teaching, or developing in oneself or others, any skills and knowledge that relate to specific useful competencies. _____ has specific goals of improving one`s capability, capacity, productivity and performance. It forms the core of apprenticeships and provides the backbone of content at institutes of technology . In addition to the basic _____ required for a trade, occupation or profession, observers of the labor-market recognize as of 2008 the need to continue _____ beyond initial qualifications: to maintain, upgrade and update skills throughout working life. People within many professions and occupations may refer to this sort of _____ as professional development.

Exam Probability: **Low**

25. *Answer choices:*

(see index for correct answer)

- a. Korean Standards Association
- b. Large Group Capacitation
- c. Training
- d. Youth Training Scheme

Guidance: level 1

:: Nepotism ::

_____ is the granting of favour to relatives in various fields, including business, politics, entertainment, sports, religion and other activities. The term originated with the assignment of nephews to important positions by Catholic popes and bishops. Trading parliamentary employment for favors is a modern-day example of _____ . Criticism of _____ , however, can be found in ancient Indian texts such as the Kural literature.

Exam Probability: **Low**

26. *Answer choices:*

(see index for correct answer)

- a. Crachach
- b. Cronyism
- c. Cardinal-nephew
- d. Nepotism

Guidance: level 1

:: United States federal labor legislation ::

The _____ of 1988 is a United States federal law that generally prevents employers from using polygraph tests, either for pre-employment screening or during the course of employment, with certain exemptions.

Exam Probability: **Medium**

27. *Answer choices:*

(see index for correct answer)

- a. Anti-Pinkerton Act
- b. Adamson Act
- c. Reliable Home Heating Act
- d. Pension Protection Act of 2006

Guidance: level 1

:: ::

_____ is a labor union representing almost 1.9 million workers in over 100 occupations in the United States and Canada. SEIU is focused on organizing workers in three sectors: health care , including hospital, home care and nursing home workers; public services ; and property services .

Exam Probability: **High**

28. *Answer choices:*

(see index for correct answer)

- a. Service Employees International Union
- b. hierarchical perspective
- c. personal values
- d. Sarbanes-Oxley act of 2002

:: Job interview ::

A _____ is a job interview in which the applicant is presented with a challenging business scenario that he/she must investigate and propose a solution to. _____ s are designed to test the candidate's analytical skills and "soft" skills within a realistic business context. The case is often a business situation or a business case that the interviewer has worked on in real life.

Exam Probability: **High**

29. *Answer choices:*

(see index for correct answer)

- a. Case interview
- b. Informational interview
- c. Microsoft interview
- d. SOARA

:: Labor rights ::

The _____ is the concept that people have a human _____ , or engage in productive employment, and may not be prevented from doing so. The _____ is enshrined in the Universal Declaration of Human Rights and recognized in international human rights law through its inclusion in the International Covenant on Economic, Social and Cultural Rights, where the _____ emphasizes economic, social and cultural development.

Exam Probability: **Medium**

30. *Answer choices:*

(see index for correct answer)

- a. China Labor Watch
- b. Right to work
- c. Swift raids
- d. The Hyatt 100

Guidance: level 1

:: Business ethics ::

A _____ is a person who exposes any kind of information or activity that is deemed illegal, unethical, or not correct within an organization that is either private or public. The information of alleged wrongdoing can be classified in many ways: violation of company policy/rules, law, regulation, or threat to public interest/national security, as well as fraud, and corruption. Those who become _____ s can choose to bring information or allegations to surface either internally or externally. Internally, a _____ can bring his/her accusations to the attention of other people within the accused organization such as an immediate supervisor. Externally, a _____ can bring allegations to light by contacting a third party outside of an accused organization such as the media, government, law enforcement, or those who are concerned. _____ s, however, take the risk of facing stiff reprisal and retaliation from those who are accused or alleged of wrongdoing.

Exam Probability: **High**

31. *Answer choices:*

(see index for correct answer)

- a. Whistleblower
- b. Ethical corporate social responsibility
- c. Workplace bullying
- d. Institute of Business Ethics

Guidance: level 1

:: Labor ::

_____ s are workers whose main capital is knowledge. Examples include programmers, physicians, pharmacists, architects, engineers, scientists, design thinkers, public accountants, lawyers, and academics, and any other white-collar workers, whose line of work requires the one to "think for a living".

Exam Probability: **Low**

32. *Answer choices:*

(see index for correct answer)

- a. Company store
- b. Knowledge worker
- c. Working Saturday
- d. Labor notes

Guidance: level 1

:: Business ethics ::

_____ is a persistent pattern of mistreatment from others in the workplace that causes either physical or emotional harm. It can include such tactics as verbal, nonverbal, psychological, physical abuse and humiliation. This type of workplace aggression is particularly difficult because, unlike the typical school bully, workplace bullies often operate within the established rules and policies of their organization and their society. In the majority of cases, bullying in the workplace is reported as having been by someone who has authority over their victim. However, bullies can also be peers, and occasionally subordinates. Research has also investigated the impact of the larger organizational context on bullying as well as the group-level processes that impact on the incidence and maintenance of bullying behaviour. Bullying can be covert or overt. It may be missed by superiors; it may be known by many throughout the organization. Negative effects are not limited to the targeted individuals, and may lead to a decline in employee morale and a change in organizational culture. It can also take place as overbearing supervision, constant criticism, and blocking promotions.

Exam Probability: **High**

33. *Answer choices:*

(see index for correct answer)

- a. Being Globally Responsible Conference
- b. Conspiracy of Fools
- c. Corruption of Foreign Public Officials Act
- d. Ethical corporate social responsibility

Guidance: level 1

:: Organizational structure ::

An _____ defines how activities such as task allocation, coordination, and supervision are directed toward the achievement of organizational aims.

Exam Probability: **High**

34. *Answer choices:*

(see index for correct answer)

- a. Organizational structure
- b. Organization of the New York City Police Department
- c. Automated Bureaucracy
- d. Unorganisation

Guidance: level 1

:: Recruitment ::

_____ is a tool companies and organizations use as a way to communicate the good and the bad characteristics of the job during the hiring process of new employees, or as a tool to reestablish job specificity for existing employees. _____ s should provide the individuals with a well-rounded description that details what obligations the individual can expect to perform while working for that specific company. Descriptions may include, but are not limited to, work environment, expectations, and Company policies .

Exam Probability: **Medium**

35. *Answer choices:*

- a. Campus placement
- b. The Select Family of Staffing Companies
- c. Multiple mini interview
- d. Internal labor market

Guidance: level 1

:: Project management ::

Some scenarios associate "this kind of planning" with learning "life skills".
_____ s are necessary, or at least useful, in situations where individuals need to know what time they must be at a specific location to receive a specific service, and where people need to accomplish a set of goals within a set time period.

Exam Probability: **Low**

36. *Answer choices:*

- a. Aggregate project plan
- b. Project manufacturing
- c. Schedule
- d. Cost estimate

:: Industrial agreements ::

_____ is a process of negotiation between employers and a group of employees aimed at agreements to regulate working salaries, working conditions, benefits, and other aspects of workers' compensation and rights for workers. The interests of the employees are commonly presented by representatives of a trade union to which the employees belong. The collective agreements reached by these negotiations usually set out wage scales, working hours, training, health and safety, overtime, grievance mechanisms, and rights to participate in workplace or company affairs.

Exam Probability: **Low**

37. *Answer choices:*

(see index for correct answer)

- a. Workplace Authority
- b. McCrone Agreement
- c. Collective bargaining
- d. Pattern bargaining

:: Training ::

_____ refers to practicing newly acquired skills beyond the point of initial mastery. The term is also often used to refer to the pedagogical theory that this form of practice leads to automaticity or other beneficial consequences.

Exam Probability: **Low**

38. *Answer choices:*

(see index for correct answer)

- a. Hypoventilation training
- b. Arts Party
- c. Overlearning
- d. Person Analysis

Guidance: level 1

:: ::

A _____ is a fund into which a sum of money is added during an employee's employment years, and from which payments are drawn to support the person's retirement from work in the form of periodic payments. A _____ may be a "defined benefit plan" where a fixed sum is paid regularly to a person, or a "defined contribution plan" under which a fixed sum is invested and then becomes available at retirement age. _____ s should not be confused with severance pay; the former is usually paid in regular installments for life after retirement, while the latter is typically paid as a fixed amount after involuntary termination of employment prior to retirement.

39. *Answer choices:*

(see index for correct answer)

- a. similarity-attraction theory
- b. hierarchical
- c. Pension
- d. information systems assessment

Guidance: level 1

:: Survey methodology ::

A _____ is the procedure of systematically acquiring and recording information about the members of a given population. The term is used mostly in connection with national population and housing _____ es; other common _____ es include agriculture, business, and traffic _____ es. The United Nations defines the essential features of population and housing _____ es as "individual enumeration, universality within a defined territory, simultaneity and defined periodicity", and recommends that population _____ es be taken at least every 10 years. United Nations recommendations also cover _____ topics to be collected, official definitions, classifications and other useful information to co-ordinate international practice.

Exam Probability: **Low**

40. *Answer choices:*

(see index for correct answer)

- a. Political forecasting
- b. Census
- c. Sampling
- d. Self-report

Guidance: level 1

:: Asset ::

In financial accounting, an _____ is any resource owned by the business. Anything tangible or intangible that can be owned or controlled to produce value and that is held by a company to produce positive economic value is an _____ . Simply stated, _____ s represent value of ownership that can be converted into cash . The balance sheet of a firm records the monetary value of the _____ s owned by that firm. It covers money and other valuables belonging to an individual or to a business.

Exam Probability: **High**

41. *Answer choices:*
(see index for correct answer)

- a. Current asset
- b. Asset

Guidance: level 1

:: Unemployment ::

In economics, a _____ is a business cycle contraction when there is a general decline in economic activity. Macroeconomic indicators such as GDP , investment spending, capacity utilization, household income, business profits, and inflation fall, while bankruptcies and the unemployment rate rise. In the United Kingdom, it is defined as a negative economic growth for two consecutive quarters.

Exam Probability: **Medium**

42. *Answer choices:*

(see index for correct answer)

- a. Reserve army of labour
- b. JobBridge
- c. Employment Promotion and Protection against Unemployment Convention, 1988
- d. Recession

Guidance: level 1

:: Financial terminology ::

_____ is the cost of maintaining a certain standard of living. Changes in the _____ over time are often operationalized in a cost-of-living index. _____ calculations are also used to compare the cost of maintaining a certain standard of living in different geographic areas. Differences in _____ between locations can also be measured in terms of purchasing power parity rates.

Exam Probability: **High**

43. *Answer choices:*

(see index for correct answer)

- a. Doing a Leeds
- b. Cost of living
- c. Cost price
- d. Custodial participant

Guidance: level 1

:: Validity (statistics) ::

In psychometrics, _____ refers to the extent to which a measure represents all facets of a given construct. For example, a depression scale may lack _____ if it only assesses the affective dimension of depression but fails to take into account the behavioral dimension. An element of subjectivity exists in relation to determining _____, which requires a degree of agreement about what a particular personality trait such as extraversion represents. A disagreement about a personality trait will prevent the gain of a high _____ .

44. *Answer choices:*

(see index for correct answer)

- a. Validation
- b. Predictive validity
- c. Ecological validity
- d. Construct validity

Guidance: level 1

:: ::

_____ is a form of development in which a person called a coach supports a learner or client in achieving a specific personal or professional goal by providing training and guidance. The learner is sometimes called a coachee. Occasionally, _____ may mean an informal relationship between two people, of whom one has more experience and expertise than the other and offers advice and guidance as the latter learns; but _____ differs from mentoring in focusing on specific tasks or objectives, as opposed to more general goals or overall development.

45. *Answer choices:*

(see index for correct answer)

- a. Sarbanes-Oxley act of 2002
- b. empathy
- c. Coaching
- d. personal values

Guidance: level 1

:: Job interview ::

An _____ is a survey conducted with an individual who is separating from an organization or relationship. Most commonly, this occurs between an employee and an organization, a student and an educational institution, or a member and an association. An organization can use the information gained from an _____ to assess what should be improved, changed, or remain intact. More so, an organization can use the results from _____ s to reduce employee, student, or member turnover and increase productivity and engagement, thus reducing the high costs associated with turnover. Some examples of the value of conducting _____ s include shortening the recruiting and hiring process, reducing absenteeism, improving innovation, sustaining performance, and reducing possible litigation if issues mentioned in the _____ are addressed. It is important for each organization to customize its own _____ in order to maintain the highest levels of survey validity and reliability.

Exam Probability: **High**

46. *Answer choices:*

(see index for correct answer)

- a. Situation, Task, Action, Result

- b. Microsoft interview
- c. Exit interview
- d. Programming interview

Guidance: level 1

:: ::

A _____ is monetary compensation paid by an employer to an employee in exchange for work done. Payment may be calculated as a fixed amount for each task completed , or at an hourly or daily rate , or based on an easily measured quantity of work done.

Exam Probability: **Medium**

47. *Answer choices:*

(see index for correct answer)

- a. empathy
- b. surface-level diversity
- c. personal values
- d. Wage

Guidance: level 1

:: Employee relations ::

The _____ can be used to bring together employment and job-related information which employees need to know. It typically has three types of content.

48. *Answer choices:*

(see index for correct answer)

- a. Employee stock
- b. Employee morale
- c. Employee surveys
- d. Employee handbook

Guidance: level 1

:: Majority–minority relations ::

_____ , also known as reservation in India and Nepal, positive discrimination / action in the United Kingdom, and employment equity in Canada and South Africa, is the policy of promoting the education and employment of members of groups that are known to have previously suffered from discrimination. Historically and internationally, support for _____ has sought to achieve goals such as bridging inequalities in employment and pay, increasing access to education, promoting diversity, and redressing apparent past wrongs, harms, or hindrances.

49. *Answer choices:*

(see index for correct answer)

- a. cultural Relativism
- b. Affirmative action
- c. cultural dissonance

Guidance: level 1

:: ::

In business strategy, _____ is establishing a competitive advantage by having the lowest cost of operation in the industry. _____ is often driven by company efficiency, size, scale, scope and cumulative experience .A _____ strategy aims to exploit scale of production, well-defined scope and other economies , producing highly standardized products, using advanced technology.In recent years, more and more companies have chosen a strategic mix to achieve market leadership. These patterns consist of simultaneous _____ , superior customer service and product leadership. Walmart has succeeded across the world due to its _____ strategy. The company has cut down on exesses at every point of production and thus are able to provide the consumers with quality products at low prices.

Exam Probability: **High**

50. *Answer choices:*

(see index for correct answer)

- a. similarity-attraction theory

- b. hierarchical perspective
- c. empathy
- d. Cost leadership

Guidance: level 1

:: Sociological theories ::

A _____ is a systematic process for determining and addressing needs, or "gaps" between current conditions and desired conditions or "wants". The discrepancy between the current condition and wanted condition must be measured to appropriately identify the need. The need can be a desire to improve current performance or to correct a deficiency.

Exam Probability: **High**

51. *Answer choices:*

(see index for correct answer)

- a. comfort zone
- b. Compliance gaining
- c. social construction
- d. resource mobilization

Guidance: level 1

:: Unemployment ::

The _____ is the negative relationship between the levels of unemployment and wages that arises when these variables are expressed in local terms. According to David Blanchflower and Andrew Oswald , the _____ summarizes the fact that "A worker who is employed in an area of high unemployment earns less than an identical individual who works in a region with low joblessness."

Exam Probability: **Medium**

52. *Answer choices:*

(see index for correct answer)

- a. Organization Workshop
- b. Frictional unemployment
- c. Wage curve
- d. Technological unemployment

Guidance: level 1

:: Human resource management ::

_____ is the strategic approach to the effective management of people in an organization so that they help the business to gain a competitive advantage. It is designed to maximize employee performance in service of an employer's strategic objectives. HR is primarily concerned with the management of people within organizations, focusing on policies and on systems. HR departments are responsible for overseeing employee-benefits design, employee recruitment, training and development, performance appraisal, and Reward management . HR also concerns itself with organizational change and industrial relations, that is, the balancing of organizational practices with requirements arising from collective bargaining and from governmental laws.

Exam Probability: **High**

53. *Answer choices:*

(see index for correct answer)

- a. Experticity
- b. Human resource management
- c. Labour is not a commodity
- d. On-ramping

Guidance: level 1

:: Types of marketing ::

In microeconomics and management, _____ is an arrangement in which the supply chain of a company is owned by that company. Usually each member of the supply chain produces a different product or service, and the products combine to satisfy a common need. It is contrasted with horizontal integration, wherein a company produces several items which are related to one another. _____ has also described management styles that bring large portions of the supply chain not only under a common ownership, but also into one corporation .

Exam Probability: **Low**

54. *Answer choices:*

(see index for correct answer)

- a. Proximity marketing
- b. Secret brand
- c. Figure of merit
- d. Direct response

Guidance: level 1

:: ::

The _____ of 1938 29 U.S.C. § 203 is a United States labor law that creates the right to a minimum wage, and "time-and-a-half" overtime pay when people work over forty hours a week. It also prohibits most employment of minors in "oppressive child labor". It applies to employees engaged in interstate commerce or employed by an enterprise engaged in commerce or in the production of goods for commerce, unless the employer can claim an exemption from coverage.

55. *Answer choices:*

(see index for correct answer)

- a. hierarchical perspective
- b. Fair Labor Standards Act
- c. surface-level diversity
- d. functional perspective

Guidance: level 1

:: Free market ::

Piece work is any type of employment in which a worker is paid a fixed _____ for each unit produced or action performed regardless of time.

Exam Probability: **Medium**

56. *Answer choices:*

(see index for correct answer)

- a. Regulated market
- b. Free market

Guidance: level 1

Domestic violence is violence or other abuse by one person against another in a domestic setting, such as in marriage or cohabitation. It may be termed intimate partner violence when committed by a spouse or partner in an intimate relationship against the other spouse or partner, and can take place in heterosexual or same-sex relationships, or between former spouses or partners. Domestic violence can also involve violence against children, parents, or the elderly. It takes a number of forms, including physical, verbal, emotional, economic, religious, reproductive, and sexual abuse, which can range from subtle, coercive forms to marital rape and to violent physical abuse such as choking, beating, female genital mutilation, and acid throwing that results in disfigurement or death. Domestic murders include stoning, bride burning, honor killings, and dowry deaths.

Exam Probability: **Medium**

57. *Answer choices:*

(see index for correct answer)

- a. cultural
- b. interpersonal communication
- c. levels of analysis
- d. process perspective

Guidance: level 1

:: Self ::

_____ is a term that has been used in various psychology theories, often in different ways. The term was originally introduced by the organismic theorist Kurt Goldstein for the motive to realize one`s full potential. In Goldstein`s view, it is the organism`s master motive, the only real motive: "the tendency to actualize itself as fully as possible is the basic drive ... the drive of _____ ." Carl Rogers similarly wrote of "the curative force in psychotherapy  man`s tendency to actualize himself, to become his potentialities ... to express and activate all the capacities of the organism." The concept was brought most fully to prominence in Abraham Maslow`s hierarchy of needs theory as the final level of psychological development that can be achieved when all basic and mental needs are essentially fulfilled and the "actualization" of the full personal potential takes place, although he adapted this viewpoint later on in life to be more flexible.

Exam Probability: **Low**

58. *Answer choices:*

(see index for correct answer)

- a. a person
- b. impression management
- c. Self-actualization
- d. Generalized other

Guidance: level 1

:: Behavior ::

_____ refers to behavior-change procedures that were employed during the 1970s and early 1980s. Based on methodological behaviorism, overt behavior was modified with presumed consequences, including artificial positive and negative reinforcement contingencies to increase desirable behavior, or administering positive and negative punishment and/or extinction to reduce problematic behavior. For the treatment of phobias, habituation and punishment were the basic principles used in flooding, a subcategory of desensitization.

Exam Probability: **High**

59. *Answer choices:*

(see index for correct answer)

- a. theory of planned behavior
- b. Behavior modification

Guidance: level 1

Information systems

Information systems (IS) are formal, sociotechnical, organizational systems designed to collect, process, store, and distribute information. In a sociotechnical perspective Information Systems are composed by four components: technology, process, people and organizational structure.

:: Enterprise architecture ::

Enterprise software, also known as _____ software , is computer software used to satisfy the needs of an organization rather than individual users. Such organizations include businesses, schools, interest-based user groups, clubs, charities, and governments. Enterprise software is an integral part of a information system.

1. *Answer choices:*

(see index for correct answer)

- a. Enterprise life cycle
- b. Enterprise application
- c. Knoa Software
- d. Syclo

Guidance: level 1

:: Information science ::

_____ has been defined as "the branch of ethics that focuses on the relationship between the creation, organization, dissemination, and use of information, and the ethical standards and moral codes governing human conduct in society". It examines the morality that comes from information as a resource, a product, or as a target. It provides a critical framework for considering moral issues concerning informational privacy, moral agency , new environmental issues , problems arising from the life-cycle of information . It is very vital to understand that librarians, archivists, information professionals among others, really understand the importance of knowing how to disseminate proper information as well as being responsible with their actions when addressing information.

Exam Probability: **High**

2. *Answer choices:*

(see index for correct answer)

- a. Semantic Sensor Web
- b. Evolutionary informatics
- c. Biodiversity informatics
- d. Information ethics

Guidance: level 1

:: Data management ::

An _____ is a term used in data warehousing to refer to a system that is used to process the day-to-day transactions of an organization. These systems are designed in a manner that processing of day-to-day transactions is performed efficiently and the integrity of the transactional data is preserved.

Exam Probability: **High**

3. *Answer choices:*

(see index for correct answer)

- a. Parchive
- b. Workflow engine
- c. Junction table
- d. Operational system

Guidance: level 1

:: ::

_____ rate is the ratio of users who click on a specific link to the number of total users who view a page, email, or advertisement. It is commonly used to measure the success of an online advertising campaign for a particular website as well as the effectiveness of email campaigns.

4. *Answer choices:*

(see index for correct answer)

- a. Click-through
- b. similarity-attraction theory
- c. Character
- d. open system

Guidance: level 1

:: Computer memory ::

_____ is a type of non-volatile memory used in computers and other electronic devices. Data stored in ROM can only be modified slowly, with difficulty, or not at all, so it is mainly used to store firmware or application software in plug-in cartridges.

5. *Answer choices:*

(see index for correct answer)

- a. Read-only memory
- b. Word-addressable
- c. Regenerative capacitor memory
- d. Remote direct memory access

Guidance: level 1

:: Information systems ::

A _____ is an information system that supports business or organizational decision-making activities. DSSs serve the management, operations and planning levels of an organization and help people make decisions about problems that may be rapidly changing and not easily specified in advance—i.e. unstructured and semi-structured decision problems. _____ s can be either fully computerized or human-powered, or a combination of both.

Exam Probability: **Medium**

6. *Answer choices:*

(see index for correct answer)

- a. Management information system
- b. FileDirector

- c. Decision support system
- d. NESI

Guidance: level 1

:: Global Positioning System ::

The _____ , originally Navstar GPS, is a satellite-based radionavigation system owned by the United States government and operated by the United States Air Force. It is a global navigation satellite system that provides geolocation and time information to a GPS receiver anywhere on or near the Earth where there is an unobstructed line of sight to four or more GPS satellites. Obstacles such as mountains and buildings block the relatively weak GPS signals.

Exam Probability: **Medium**

7. *Answer choices:*

(see index for correct answer)

- a. Global Positioning System
- b. Precision Lightweight GPS Receiver
- c. Waymarking
- d. MoNav

Guidance: level 1

_____ LLC is an American multinational technology company that specializes in Internet-related services and products, which include online advertising technologies, search engine, cloud computing, software, and hardware. It is considered one of the Big Four technology companies, alongside Amazon, Apple and Facebook.

Exam Probability: **Low**

8. *Answer choices:*

(see index for correct answer)

- a. similarity-attraction theory
- b. Google
- c. functional perspective
- d. process perspective

Guidance: level 1

:: Management ::

A _____ defines or constrains some aspect of business and always resolves to either true or false. _____ s are intended to assert business structure or to control or influence the behavior of the business. _____ s describe the operations, definitions and constraints that apply to an organization. _____ s can apply to people, processes, corporate behavior and computing systems in an organization, and are put in place to help the organization achieve its goals.

Exam Probability: **Low**

9. *Answer choices:*

(see index for correct answer)

- a. Supervisory board
- b. Business rule
- c. Cynefin
- d. Performance management

Guidance: level 1

:: Data management ::

Given organizations' increasing dependency on information technology to run their operations, Business continuity planning covers the entire organization, and Disaster recovery focuses on IT.

Exam Probability: **High**

10. *Answer choices:*

(see index for correct answer)

- a. Consumer relationship system
- b. Data field
- c. H-Store
- d. Small data

Guidance: level 1

:: Industrial design ::

Across the many fields concerned with _____ , including information science, computer science, human-computer interaction, communication, and industrial design, there is little agreement over the meaning of the term " _____ ", although all are related to interaction with computers and other machines with a user interface.

Exam Probability: **Low**

11. *Answer choices:*

(see index for correct answer)

- a. Industrial design right
- b. International Council of Societies of Industrial Design
- c. Preferred number
- d. Interactivity

:: Data management ::

_____ , or IG, is the management of information at an organization. _____ balances the use and security of information. _____ helps with legal compliance, operational transparency, and reducing expenditures associated with legal discovery. An organization can establish a consistent and logical framework for employees to handle data through their _____ policies and procedures. These policies guide proper behavior regarding how organizations and their employees handle electronically stored information .

Exam Probability: **Medium**

12. *Answer choices:*

(see index for correct answer)

- a. Junction table
- b. Data verification
- c. Log trigger
- d. Nonlinear medium

:: Fraud ::

_____ is the deliberate use of someone else's identity, usually as a method to gain a financial advantage or obtain credit and other benefits in the other person's name, and perhaps to the other person's disadvantage or loss. The person whose identity has been assumed may suffer adverse consequences, especially if they are held responsible for the perpetrator's actions.

_____ occurs when someone uses another's personally identifying information, like their name, identifying number, or credit card number, without their permission, to commit fraud or other crimes. The term _____ was coined in 1964. Since that time, the definition of _____ has been statutorily prescribed throughout both the U.K. and the United States as the theft of personally identifying information, generally including a person's name, date of birth, social security number, driver's license number, bank account or credit card numbers, PIN numbers, electronic signatures, fingerprints, passwords, or any other information that can be used to access a person's financial resources.

Exam Probability: **Medium**

13. *Answer choices:*

(see index for correct answer)

- a. Regummed stamp
- b. Lottery scam
- c. Identity theft
- d. Check washing

Guidance: level 1

:: Policy ::

A _____ is a statement or a legal document that discloses some or all of the ways a party gathers, uses, discloses, and manages a customer or client's data. It fulfills a legal requirement to protect a customer or client's privacy. Personal information can be anything that can be used to identify an individual, not limited to the person's name, address, date of birth, marital status, contact information, ID issue, and expiry date, financial records, credit information, medical history, where one travels, and intentions to acquire goods and services. In the case of a business it is often a statement that declares a party's policy on how it collects, stores, and releases personal information it collects. It informs the client what specific information is collected, and whether it is kept confidential, shared with partners, or sold to other firms or enterprises. Privacy policies typically represent a broader, more generalized treatment, as opposed to data use statements, which tend to be more detailed and specific.

Exam Probability: **Low**

14. *Answer choices:*

(see index for correct answer)

- a. Privacy policy
- b. Policy Monitoring
- c. Haldane principle
- d. Security policy

Guidance: level 1

:: Payment systems ::

A _____ is any system used to settle financial transactions through the transfer of monetary value. This includes the institutions, instruments, people, rules, procedures, standards, and technologies that make it exchange possible. A common type of _____ is called an operational network that links bank accounts and provides for monetary exchange using bank deposits. Some _____ s also include credit mechanisms, which are essentially a different aspect of payment.

Exam Probability: **Medium**

15. *Answer choices:*

(see index for correct answer)

- a. Net Element
- b. Cruise ship ID card
- c. Payment system
- d. Zimswitch

Guidance: level 1

:: Computer networking ::

A backbone is a part of computer network that interconnects various pieces of network, providing a path for the exchange of information between different LANs or subnetworks. A backbone can tie together diverse networks in the same building, in different buildings in a campus environment, or over wide areas. Normally, the backbone's capacity is greater than the networks connected to it.

Exam Probability: **Medium**

16. *Answer choices:*

(see index for correct answer)

- a. Multicast router discovery
- b. Cloud-based networking
- c. Vyatta
- d. Backbone network

Guidance: level 1

:: Data quality ::

_____ or data cleaning is the process of detecting and correcting corrupt or inaccurate records from a record set, table, or database and refers to identifying incomplete, incorrect, inaccurate or irrelevant parts of the data and then replacing, modifying, or deleting the dirty or coarse data. _____ may be performed interactively with data wrangling tools, or as batch processing through scripting.

Exam Probability: **Medium**

17. *Answer choices:*

(see index for correct answer)

- a. Data Quality Campaign
- b. Data Quality Firewall

- c. Data integrity
- d. Data cleansing

Guidance: level 1

:: Internet advertising ::

_____ is software that aims to gather information about a person or organization, sometimes without their knowledge, that may send such information to another entity without the consumer's consent, that asserts control over a device without the consumer's knowledge, or it may send such information to another entity with the consumer's consent, through cookies.

Exam Probability: **Low**

18. *Answer choices:*

(see index for correct answer)

- a. Spyware
- b. Memolink
- c. LiftDNA
- d. Ivi.ru

Guidance: level 1

:: Information technology management ::

An _____ , acceptable usage policy or fair use policy, is a set of rules applied by the owner, creator or administrator of a network, website, or service, that restrict the ways in which the network, website or system may be used and sets guidelines as to how it should be used. AUP documents are written for corporations, businesses, universities, schools, internet service providers , and website owners, often to reduce the potential for legal action that may be taken by a user, and often with little prospect of enforcement.

Exam Probability: **Low**

19. *Answer choices:*

(see index for correct answer)

- a. Quality Engineering
- b. Acceptable use policy
- c. Socitm
- d. Change management

Guidance: level 1

:: Information technology management ::

In information technology to _____ means to move from one place to another, information to detailed data by focusing in on something. In a GUI-environment, "drilling-down" may involve clicking on some representation in order to reveal more detail.

Exam Probability: **Medium**

20. *Answer choices:*

(see index for correct answer)

- a. Drill down
- b. Corporate taxonomy
- c. Downtime
- d. Information model

Guidance: level 1

:: Digital rights management ::

_____ tools or technological protection measures are a set of access control technologies for restricting the use of proprietary hardware and copyrighted works. DRM technologies try to control the use, modification, and distribution of copyrighted works , as well as systems within devices that enforce these policies.

Exam Probability: **Medium**

21. *Answer choices:*

(see index for correct answer)

- a. DIVX
- b. Trace vector decoder
- c. Compliance and Robustness
- d. Digital rights management

:: Information technology management ::

The term _____ is used to refer to periods when a system is unavailable. _____ or outage duration refers to a period of time that a system fails to provide or perform its primary function. Reliability, availability, recovery, and unavailability are related concepts. The unavailability is the proportion of a time-span that a system is unavailable or offline. This is usually a result of the system failing to function because of an unplanned event, or because of routine maintenance .

Exam Probability: **Medium**

22. *Answer choices:*

(see index for correct answer)

- a. Information technology operations
- b. Information repository
- c. Document management system
- d. Problem management

:: Supply chain management terms ::

In business and finance, _____ is a system of organizations, people, activities, information, and resources involved in moving a product or service from supplier to customer. _____ activities involve the transformation of natural resources, raw materials, and components into a finished product that is delivered to the end customer. In sophisticated _____ systems, used products may re-enter the _____ at any point where residual value is recyclable. _____ s link value chains.

Exam Probability: **High**

23. *Answer choices:*

(see index for correct answer)

- a. Work in process
- b. Last mile
- c. Direct shipment
- d. inventory management

Guidance: level 1

:: Data interchange standards ::

_____ is the concept of businesses electronically communicating information that was traditionally communicated on paper, such as purchase orders and invoices. Technical standards for EDI exist to facilitate parties transacting such instruments without having to make special arrangements.

Exam Probability: **High**

24. *Answer choices:*

(see index for correct answer)

- a. Uniform Communication Standard
- b. ASC X12
- c. Electronic data interchange
- d. Domain Application Protocol

Guidance: level 1

:: ::

A _____ is a research instrument consisting of a series of questions for the purpose of gathering information from respondents. The _____ was invented by the Statistical Society of London in 1838.

Exam Probability: **Low**

25. *Answer choices:*

(see index for correct answer)

- a. Questionnaire
- b. imperative
- c. Sarbanes-Oxley act of 2002
- d. empathy

Guidance: level 1

:: Virtual economies ::

_____ is an online virtual world, developed and owned by the San Francisco-based firm Linden Lab and launched on June 23, 2003. By 2013, _____ had approximately one million regular users; at the end of 2017 active user count totals "between 800,000 and 900,000". In many ways, _____ is similar to massively multiplayer online role-playing games; however, Linden Lab is emphatic that their creation is not a game: "There is no manufactured conflict, no set objective".

Exam Probability: **Medium**

26. *Answer choices:*

(see index for correct answer)

- a. Empire Avenue
- b. Second Life
- c. Alter Aeon
- d. Zynga

Guidance: level 1

:: Fault tolerance ::

_____ is the property that enables a system to continue operating properly in the event of the failure of some of its components. If its operating quality decreases at all, the decrease is proportional to the severity of the failure, as compared to a naively designed system, in which even a small failure can cause total breakdown. _____ is particularly sought after in high-availability or life-critical systems. The ability of maintaining functionality when portions of a system break down is referred to as graceful degradation.

Exam Probability: **Medium**

27. *Answer choices:*

(see index for correct answer)

- a. Systematic fault
- b. Triple modular redundancy
- c. Fault tolerance
- d. Emergency power system

Guidance: level 1

:: ::

A _____ , sometimes called a passcode, is a memorized secret used to confirm the identity of a user. Using the terminology of the NIST Digital Identity Guidelines, the secret is memorized by a party called the claimant while the party verifying the identity of the claimant is called the verifier. When the claimant successfully demonstrates knowledge of the _____ to the verifier through an established authentication protocol, the verifier is able to infer the claimant's identity.

Exam Probability: **High**

28. *Answer choices:*

(see index for correct answer)

- a. cultural
- b. Password
- c. levels of analysis
- d. co-culture

Guidance: level 1

:: Information technology organisations ::

The Internet Corporation for Assigned Names and Numbers is a nonprofit organization responsible for coordinating the maintenance and procedures of several databases related to the namespaces and numerical spaces of the Internet, ensuring the network's stable and secure operation. _____ performs the actual technical maintenance work of the Central Internet Address pools and DNS root zone registries pursuant to the Internet Assigned Numbers Authority function contract. The contract regarding the IANA stewardship functions between _____ and the National Telecommunications and Information Administration of the United States Department of Commerce ended on October 1, 2016, formally transitioning the functions to the global multistakeholder community.

Exam Probability: **Medium**

29. *Answer choices:*

(see index for correct answer)

- a. Information and Communications Technology Council
- b. ICANN
- c. Information Technology Association of Canada
- d. Parliamentary Information Technology Committee

Guidance: level 1

:: Computer security standards ::

The _____ for Information Technology Security Evaluation is an international standard for computer security certification. It is currently in version 3.1 revision 5.

Exam Probability: **High**

30. *Answer choices:*

(see index for correct answer)

- a. CVSS
- b. Common Criteria
- c. AFSSI-5020
- d. S/MIME

Guidance: level 1

:: ::

A _____ is an organized collection of data, generally stored and accessed electronically from a computer system. Where _____ s are more complex they are often developed using formal design and modeling techniques.

Exam Probability: **High**

31. *Answer choices:*

(see index for correct answer)

- a. functional perspective
- b. Database
- c. Character
- d. surface-level diversity

:: ::

A _____ is a control panel usually located directly ahead of a vehicle's driver, displaying instrumentation and controls for the vehicle's operation.

Exam Probability: **Low**

32. *Answer choices:*

(see index for correct answer)

- a. similarity-attraction theory
- b. personal values
- c. information systems assessment
- d. surface-level diversity

:: Information systems ::

_____ is the process of creating, sharing, using and managing the knowledge and information of an organisation. It refers to a multidisciplinary approach to achieving organisational objectives by making the best use of knowledge.

Exam Probability: **High**

33. *Answer choices:*

(see index for correct answer)

- a. Information processor
- b. Enhanced publication
- c. German Emigrants Database
- d. DIKW Pyramid

Guidance: level 1

:: ::

_____ consists of tailoring a service or a product to accommodate specific individuals, sometimes tied to groups or segments of individuals. A wide variety of organizations use _____ to improve customer satisfaction, digital sales conversion, marketing results, branding, and improved website metrics as well as for advertising. _____ is a key element in social media and recommender systems.

Exam Probability: **Medium**

34. *Answer choices:*

(see index for correct answer)

- a. Character
- b. surface-level diversity
- c. interpersonal communication
- d. Personalization

Guidance: level 1

:: Systems theory ::

A _____ is a group of interacting or interrelated entities that form a unified whole. A _____ is delineated by its spatial and temporal boundaries, surrounded and influenced by its environment, described by its structure and purpose and expressed in its functioning.

Exam Probability: **Medium**

35. *Answer choices:*

(see index for correct answer)

- a. transient state
- b. Viable System Model
- c. steady state
- d. process system

:: Management ::

In organizational studies, _____ is the efficient and effective development of an organization's resources when they are needed. Such resources may include financial resources, inventory, human skills, production resources, or information technology and natural resources.

Exam Probability: **Medium**

36. *Answer choices:*

(see index for correct answer)

- a. Core competency
- b. Sensemaking
- c. Resource management
- d. Local management board

:: Commerce websites ::

_____ is an American classified advertisements website with sections devoted to jobs, housing, for sale, items wanted, services, community service, gigs, résumés, and discussion forums.

Exam Probability: **Medium**

37. *Answer choices:*

(see index for correct answer)

- a. Cityblis
- b. Craigslist
- c. CozyCot
- d. CitizenShipper

Guidance: level 1

:: ::

The _____ is a unit of digital information that most commonly consists of eight bits, representing a binary number. Historically, the _____ was the number of bits used to encode a single character of text in a computer and for this reason it is the smallest addressable unit of memory in many computer architectures.

Exam Probability: **Medium**

38. *Answer choices:*

(see index for correct answer)

- a. Sarbanes-Oxley act of 2002
- b. open system
- c. Byte
- d. levels of analysis

Guidance: level 1

:: Information technology ::

_____ is the reorientation of product and service designs to focus on the end user as an individual consumer, in contrast with an earlier era of only organization-oriented offerings . Technologies whose first commercialization was at the inter-organization level thus have potential for later _____ . The emergence of the individual consumer as the primary driver of product and service design is most commonly associated with the IT industry, as large business and government organizations dominated the early decades of computer usage and development. Thus the microcomputer revolution, in which electronic computing moved from exclusively enterprise and government use to include personal computing, is a cardinal example of _____ . But many technology-based products, such as calculators and mobile phones, have also had their origins in business markets, and only over time did they become dominated by high-volume consumer usage, as these products commoditized and prices fell. An example of enterprise software that became consumer software is optical character recognition software, which originated with banks and postal systems but eventually became personal productivity software.

Exam Probability: **Low**

39. *Answer choices:*

(see index for correct answer)

- a. Information and communications technology
- b. Consumerization
- c. CineGrid
- d. Software-defined data center

Guidance: level 1

:: Supply chain management ::

ERP is usually referred to as a category of business management software — typically a suite of integrated applications—that an organization can use to collect, store, manage, and interpret data from these many business activities.

Exam Probability: **High**

40. *Answer choices:*
(see index for correct answer)

- a. Supply chain surplus
- b. Supply network operations
- c. Interorganizational system
- d. Application service provider

Guidance: level 1

:: Cryptography ::

In cryptography, _____ is the process of encoding a message or information in such a way that only authorized parties can access it and those who are not authorized cannot. _____ does not itself prevent interference, but denies the intelligible content to a would-be interceptor. In an _____ scheme, the intended information or message, referred to as plaintext, is encrypted using an _____ algorithm – a cipher – generating ciphertext that can be read only if decrypted. For technical reasons, an _____ scheme usually uses a pseudo-random _____ key generated by an algorithm. It is in principle possible to decrypt the message without possessing the key, but, for a well-designed _____ scheme, considerable computational resources and skills are required. An authorized recipient can easily decrypt the message with the key provided by the originator to recipients but not to unauthorized users.

Exam Probability: **Low**

41. *Answer choices:*

(see index for correct answer)

- a. Anonymous matching
- b. plaintext
- c. Encryption
- d. cryptosystem

Guidance: level 1

:: Computer data ::

In computer science, _____ is the ability to access an arbitrary element of a sequence in equal time or any datum from a population of addressable elements roughly as easily and efficiently as any other, no matter how many elements may be in the set. It is typically contrasted to sequential access.

Exam Probability: **Medium**

42. *Answer choices:*

(see index for correct answer)

- a. Random access
- b. AS3
- c. Fuzzy backup
- d. Data efficiency

Guidance: level 1

:: Data management ::

Data aggregation is the compiling of information from databases with intent to prepare combined datasets for data processing.

Exam Probability: **High**

43. *Answer choices:*

(see index for correct answer)

- a. Data aggregator
- b. Scriptella
- c. Learning object metadata
- d. Data archive

:: Data analysis ::

_____ is a process of inspecting, cleansing, transforming, and modeling data with the goal of discovering useful information, informing conclusions, and supporting decision-making. _____ has multiple facets and approaches, encompassing diverse techniques under a variety of names, and is used in different business, science, and social science domains. In today's business world, _____ plays a role in making decisions more scientific and helping businesses operate more effectively.

Exam Probability: **High**

44. *Answer choices:*

(see index for correct answer)

- a. Data analysis
- b. Univariate analysis
- c. Natural Language Toolkit
- d. Random mapping

:: Google services ::

_____ is a discontinued image organizer and image viewer for organizing and editing digital photos, plus an integrated photo-sharing website, originally created by a company named Lifescape in 2002. In July 2004, Google acquired _____ from Lifescape and began offering it as freeware. " _____ " is a blend of the name of Spanish painter Pablo Picasso, the phrase mi casa and "pic" for pictures.

Exam Probability: **Low**

45. *Answer choices:*

(see index for correct answer)

- a. Picasa
- b. Google APIs
- c. App Inventor for Android
- d. Google Blog Search

:: Information technology audit ::

_____ is the act of using a computer to take or alter electronic data, or to gain unlawful use of a computer or system. In the United States, _____ is specifically proscribed by the _____ and Abuse Act, which criminalizes computer-related acts under federal jurisdiction. Types of _____ include.

Exam Probability: **Low**

46. *Answer choices:*

(see index for correct answer)

- a. Computer fraud
- b. SekChek Local
- c. Computer forensics
- d. ACL

Guidance: level 1

:: Data management ::

A _____ , or metadata repository, as defined in the IBM Dictionary of Computing, is a "centralized repository of information about data such as meaning, relationships to other data, origin, usage, and format". Oracle defines it as a collection of tables with metadata. The term can have one of several closely related meanings pertaining to databases and database management systems .

Exam Probability: **High**

47. *Answer choices:*

(see index for correct answer)

- a. Distributed concurrency control
- b. Technical data management system
- c. Chunked transfer encoding
- d. Database-centric architecture

Guidance: level 1

:: E-commerce ::

Electronic governance or e-governance is the application of information and communication technology for delivering government services, exchange of information, communication transactions, integration of various stand-alone systems and services between government-to-citizen , _____ , government-to-government , government-to-employees as well as back-office processes and interactions within the entire government framework. Through e-governance, government services are made available to citizens in a convenient, efficient, and transparent manner. The three main target groups that can be distinguished in governance concepts are government, citizens, andbusinesses/interest groups. In e-governance, there are no distinct boundaries.

Exam Probability: **High**

48. *Answer choices:*

(see index for correct answer)

- a. Allbiz
- b. USAePay
- c. Government-to-business
- d. TXT402

Guidance: level 1

:: ::

Collaborative software or _____ is application software designed to help people involved in a common task to achieve their goals. One of the earliest definitions of collaborative software is "intentional group processes plus software to support them".

Exam Probability: **Medium**

49. *Answer choices:*

(see index for correct answer)

- a. levels of analysis
- b. empathy
- c. process perspective
- d. hierarchical perspective

Guidance: level 1

In linguistics, a _____ is the smallest element that can be uttered in isolation with objective or practical meaning.

Exam Probability: **Medium**

50. *Answer choices:*

(see index for correct answer)

- a. Word
- b. empathy
- c. hierarchical
- d. corporate values

Guidance: level 1

:: E-commerce ::

_____ is a type of fraud that occurs on the Internet in pay-per-click online advertising. In this type of advertising, the owners of websites that post the ads are paid an amount of money determined by how many visitors to the sites click on the ads. Fraud occurs when a person, automated script or computer program imitates a legitimate user of a web browser, clicking on such an ad without having an actual interest in the target of the ad's link.
_____ is the subject of some controversy and increasing litigation due to the advertising networks being a key beneficiary of the fraud.

51. *Answer choices:*

(see index for correct answer)

- a. Internet Marketing Conference
- b. Electronic sell-through
- c. Location-based commerce
- d. Click fraud

Guidance: level 1

:: Data management ::

In computing, a _____ , also known as an enterprise _____ , is a system used for reporting and data analysis, and is considered a core component of business intelligence. DWs are central repositories of integrated data from one or more disparate sources. They store current and historical data in one single place that are used for creating analytical reports for workers throughout the enterprise.

Exam Probability: **High**

52. *Answer choices:*

(see index for correct answer)

- a. Commit
- b. Data warehouse

- c. Scriptella
- d. Locks with ordered sharing

Guidance: level 1

:: ::

_____ is the fundamental facilities and systems serving a country, city, or other area, including the services and facilities necessary for its economy to function. _____ is composed of public and private physical improvements such as roads, bridges, tunnels, water supply, sewers, electrical grids, and telecommunications . In general, it has also been defined as "the physical components of interrelated systems providing commodities and services essential to enable, sustain, or enhance societal living conditions".

Exam Probability: **Medium**

53. *Answer choices:*

(see index for correct answer)

- a. cultural
- b. Infrastructure
- c. hierarchical
- d. Sarbanes-Oxley act of 2002

Guidance: level 1

:: Data privacy ::

The _____ is an information security standard for organizations that handle branded credit cards from the major card schemes.

Exam Probability: **Low**

54. *Answer choices:*

(see index for correct answer)

- a. Payment Card Industry Data Security Standard
- b. Information privacy law
- c. Opt-out
- d. Habeas data

Guidance: level 1

:: Data management ::

_____ is a form of intellectual property that grants the creator of an original creative work an exclusive legal right to determine whether and under what conditions this original work may be copied and used by others, usually for a limited term of years. The exclusive rights are not absolute but limited by limitations and exceptions to _____ law, including fair use. A major limitation on _____ on ideas is that _____ protects only the original expression of ideas, and not the underlying ideas themselves.

55. *Answer choices:*

(see index for correct answer)

- a. Hierarchical classifier
- b. Secure electronic delivery service
- c. Copyright
- d. Log trigger

Guidance: level 1

:: E-commerce ::

Electronic governance or e-governance is the application of information and communication technology for delivering government services, exchange of information, communication transactions, integration of various stand-alone systems and services between _____ , government-to-business , government-to-government , government-to-employees as well as back-office processes and interactions within the entire government framework. Through e-governance, government services are made available to citizens in a convenient, efficient, and transparent manner. The three main target groups that can be distinguished in governance concepts are government, citizens, andbusinesses/interest groups. In e-governance, there are no distinct boundaries.

Exam Probability: **High**

56. *Answer choices:*

(see index for correct answer)

- a. Lyoness
- b. Government-to-citizen
- c. The Cluetrain Manifesto
- d. Dark store

Guidance: level 1

:: Satellite navigation systems ::

_____ Galilei was an Italian astronomer, physicist and engineer, sometimes described as a polymath. _____ has been called the "father of observational astronomy", the "father of modern physics", the "father of the scientific method", and the "father of modern science".

Exam Probability: **Low**

57. *Answer choices:*

(see index for correct answer)

- a. Advanced driver assistance systems
- b. Galileo
- c. United States v. Pineda-Moreno
- d. European Satellite Navigation Competition

Guidance: level 1

:: Outsourcing ::

A service-level agreement is a commitment between a service provider and a client. Particular aspects of the service – quality, availability, responsibilities – are agreed between the service provider and the service user. The most common component of SLA is that the services should be provided to the customer as agreed upon in the contract. As an example, Internet service providers and telcos will commonly include _____ s within the terms of their contracts with customers to define the level of service being sold in plain language terms. In this case the SLA will typically have a technical definition in mean time between failures , mean time to repair or mean time to recovery ; identifying which party is responsible for reporting faults or paying fees; responsibility for various data rates; throughput; jitter; or similar measurable details.

Exam Probability: **Low**

58. *Answer choices:*

(see index for correct answer)

- a. Cloud storage
- b. Farmshoring
- c. Service level agreement
- d. Selfsourcing

Guidance: level 1

:: Industrial automation ::

_____ is the technology by which a process or procedure is performed with minimal human assistance. _____ or automatic control is the use of various control systems for operating equipment such as machinery, processes in factories, boilers and heat treating ovens, switching on telephone networks, steering and stabilization of ships, aircraft and other applications and vehicles with minimal or reduced human intervention.

Exam Probability: **High**

59. *Answer choices:*

(see index for correct answer)

- a. Critical Manufacturing
- b. CANopen
- c. Process automation system
- d. IODD

Guidance: level 1

Marketing

Marketing is the study and management of exchange relationships. Marketing is the business process of creating relationships with and satisfying customers. With its focus on the customer, marketing is one of the premier components of business management.

Marketing is defined by the American Marketing Association as "the activity, set of institutions, and processes for creating, communicating, delivering, and exchanging offerings that have value for customers, clients, partners, and society at large."

:: Direct marketing ::

_____ is a form of advertising where organizations communicate directly to customers through a variety of media including cell phone text messaging, email, websites, online adverts, database marketing, fliers, catalog distribution, promotional letters, targeted television, newspapers, magazine advertisements, and outdoor advertising. Among practitioners, it is also known as direct response marketing.

Exam Probability: **Low**

1. *Answer choices:*

(see index for correct answer)

- a. Direct marketing
- b. World Perfume
- c. Colony Brands
- d. Boardroom, Inc.

Guidance: level 1

:: Marketing analytics ::

_____ is a long-term, forward-looking approach to planning with the fundamental goal of achieving a sustainable competitive advantage. Strategic planning involves an analysis of the company's strategic initial situation prior to the formulation, evaluation and selection of market-oriented competitive position that contributes to the company's goals and marketing objectives.

2. *Answer choices:*

(see index for correct answer)

- a. Marketing strategy
- b. Marketing performance measurement and management
- c. Marketing mix modeling
- d. Advertising adstock

Guidance: level 1

:: Retailing ::

_____ is the process of selling consumer goods or services to customers through multiple channels of distribution to earn a profit. _____ ers satisfy demand identified through a supply chain. The term " _____ er" is typically applied where a service provider fills the small orders of a large number of individuals, who are end-users, rather than large orders of a small number of wholesale, corporate or government clientele. Shopping generally refers to the act of buying products. Sometimes this is done to obtain final goods, including necessities such as food and clothing; sometimes it takes place as a recreational activity. Recreational shopping often involves window shopping and browsing: it does not always result in a purchase.

Exam Probability: **Medium**

3. *Answer choices:*

(see index for correct answer)

- a. Shopping list
- b. Garage sale
- c. Retail
- d. Endcap

Guidance: level 1

:: Packaging ::

In work place, _____ or job _____ means good ranking with the hypothesized conception of requirements of a role. There are two types of job _____ s: contextual and task. Task _____ is related to cognitive ability while contextual _____ is dependent upon personality. Task _____ are behavioral roles that are recognized in job descriptions and by remuneration systems, they are directly related to organizational _____, whereas, contextual _____ are value based and additional behavioral roles that are not recognized in job descriptions and covered by compensation; they are extra roles that are indirectly related to organizational _____.
Citizenship _____ like contextual _____ means a set of individual activity/contribution that supports the organizational culture.

Exam Probability: **Low**

4. *Answer choices:*

(see index for correct answer)

- a. Performance
- b. Package tracking
- c. Flexographic ink

- d. Video game packaging

Guidance: level 1

:: Evaluation methods ::

_____ is a scientific method of observation to gather non-numerical data. This type of research "refers to the meanings, concepts definitions, characteristics, metaphors, symbols, and description of things" and not to their "counts or measures." This research answers why and how a certain phenomenon may occur rather than how often. _____ approaches are employed across many academic disciplines, focusing particularly on the human elements of the social and natural sciences; in less academic contexts, areas of application include qualitative market research, business, service demonstrations by non-profits, and journalism.

Exam Probability: **Medium**

5. *Answer choices:*

(see index for correct answer)

- a. Reference class forecasting
- b. Business excellence
- c. Program process monitoring
- d. Qualitative research

Guidance: level 1

:: Decision theory ::

Within economics the concept of _____ is used to model worth or value, but its usage has evolved significantly over time. The term was introduced initially as a measure of pleasure or satisfaction within the theory of utilitarianism by moral philosophers such as Jeremy Bentham and John Stuart Mill. But the term has been adapted and reapplied within neoclassical economics, which dominates modern economic theory, as a _____ function that represents a consumer's preference ordering over a choice set. As such, it is devoid of its original interpretation as a measurement of the pleasure or satisfaction obtained by the consumer from that choice.

Exam Probability: **Low**

6. *Answer choices:*

(see index for correct answer)

- a. Utility
- b. Superiority and inferiority ranking method
- c. Strategic assumptions
- d. Health management system

Guidance: level 1

:: Cognitive dissonance ::

In the field of psychology, _____ is the mental discomfort experienced by a person who holds two or more contradictory beliefs, ideas, or values. This discomfort is triggered by a situation in which a person's belief clashes with new evidence perceived by the person. When confronted with facts that contradict beliefs, ideals, and values, people will try to find a way to resolve the contradiction to reduce their discomfort.

Exam Probability: **Medium**

7. *Answer choices:*

(see index for correct answer)

- a. Hypocrisy
- b. Doublespeak
- c. Cognitive dissonance
- d. Emotional conflict

Guidance: level 1

:: Management ::

A _____ is a comprehensive document or blueprint that outlines the advertising and marketing efforts for the coming year. It describes business activities involved in accomplishing specific marketing objectives within a set time frame. A _____ also includes a description of the current marketing position of a business, a discussion of the target market and a description of the marketing mix that a business will use to achieve their marketing goals. A _____ has a formal structure, but can be used as a formal or informal document which makes it very flexible. It contains some historical data, future predictions, and methods or strategies to achieve the marketing objectives. _____ s start with the identification of customer needs through a market research and how the business can satisfy these needs while generating an acceptable return. This includes processes such as market situation analysis, action programs, budgets, sales forecasts, strategies and projected financial statements. A _____ can also be described as a technique that helps a business to decide on the best use of its resources to achieve corporate objectives. It can also contain a full analysis of the strengths and weaknesses of a company, its organization and its products.

Exam Probability: **Medium**

8. *Answer choices:*

(see index for correct answer)

- a. Process-based management
- b. Marketing plan
- c. One in, one out policy
- d. Scenario planning

Guidance: level 1

:: ::

Retail is the process of selling consumer goods or services to customers through multiple channels of distribution to earn a profit. Retailers satisfy demand identified through a supply chain. The term "retailer" is typically applied where a service provider fills the small orders of a large number of individuals, who are end-users, rather than large orders of a small number of wholesale, corporate or government clientele. Shopping generally refers to the act of buying products. Sometimes this is done to obtain final goods, including necessities such as food and clothing; sometimes it takes place as a recreational activity. Recreational shopping often involves window shopping and browsing: it does not always result in a purchase.

Exam Probability: **Low**

9. *Answer choices:*

(see index for correct answer)

- a. Retailing
- b. empathy
- c. Sarbanes-Oxley act of 2002
- d. open system

Guidance: level 1

:: ::

_____ is the means to see, hear, or become aware of something or someone through our fundamental senses. The term _____ derives from the Latin word perceptio, and is the organization, identification, and interpretation of sensory information in order to represent and understand the presented information, or the environment.

Exam Probability: **Medium**

10. *Answer choices:*

(see index for correct answer)

- a. Sarbanes-Oxley act of 2002
- b. hierarchical perspective
- c. Perception
- d. process perspective

Guidance: level 1

:: Marketing ::

_____ is based on a marketing concept which can be adopted by an organization as a strategy for business expansion. Where implemented, a franchisor licenses its know-how, procedures, intellectual property, use of its business model, brand, and rights to sell its branded products and services to a franchisee. In return the franchisee pays certain fees and agrees to comply with certain obligations, typically set out in a Franchise Agreement.

Exam Probability: **Medium**

11. *Answer choices:*

(see index for correct answer)

- a. Cause-related loyalty marketing
- b. Franchising
- c. Price
- d. Digital strategy

Guidance: level 1

:: Brokered programming ::

An _____ is a form of television commercial, which generally includes a toll-free telephone number or website. Most often used as a form of direct response television , long-form _____ s are typically 28:30 or 58:30 minutes in length. _____ s are also known as paid programming . This phenomenon started in the United States, where _____ s were typically shown overnight , outside peak prime time hours for commercial broadcasters. Some television stations chose to air _____ s as an alternative to the former practice of signing off. Some channels air _____ s 24 hours. Some stations also choose to air _____ s during the daytime hours mostly on weekends to fill in for unscheduled network or syndicated programming. By 2009, most _____ spending in the U.S. occurred during the early morning, daytime and evening hours, or in the afternoon. Stations in most countries around the world have instituted similar media structures. The _____ industry is worth over $200 billion.

Exam Probability: **Medium**

12. *Answer choices:*

(see index for correct answer)

- a. One Magnificent Morning
- b. Leased access
- c. Toonzai
- d. Brokered programming

Guidance: level 1

:: Business law ::

A _____ is an arrangement where parties, known as partners, agree to cooperate to advance their mutual interests. The partners in a _____ may be individuals, businesses, interest-based organizations, schools, governments or combinations. Organizations may partner to increase the likelihood of each achieving their mission and to amplify their reach. A _____ may result in issuing and holding equity or may be only governed by a contract.

Exam Probability: **Low**

13. *Answer choices:*
(see index for correct answer)

- a. Law of agency
- b. Oppression remedy
- c. Unfair business practices
- d. Starting a Business Index

:: Industry ::

_____ describes various measures of the efficiency of production. Often , a _____ measure is expressed as the ratio of an aggregate output to a single input or an aggregate input used in a production process, i.e. output per unit of input. Most common example is the labour _____ measure, e.g., such as GDP per worker. There are many different definitions of _____ and the choice among them depends on the purpose of the _____ measurement and/or data availability. The key source of difference between various _____ measures is also usually related to how the outputs and the inputs are aggregated into scalars to obtain such a ratio-type measure of _____ .

Exam Probability: **High**

14. *Answer choices:*

(see index for correct answer)

- a. Precision Machined Products Association
- b. Productivity
- c. Industrial control system
- d. Private sector

:: Management ::

In business, a _____ is the attribute that allows an organization to outperform its competitors. A _____ may include access to natural resources, such as high-grade ores or a low-cost power source, highly skilled labor, geographic location, high entry barriers, and access to new technology.

Exam Probability: **Medium**

15. *Answer choices:*

(see index for correct answer)

- a. Quality control
- b. Supply chain network
- c. Competitive advantage
- d. Peer pressure

Guidance: level 1

:: Data analysis ::

_____ is a process of inspecting, cleansing, transforming, and modeling data with the goal of discovering useful information, informing conclusions, and supporting decision-making. _____ has multiple facets and approaches, encompassing diverse techniques under a variety of names, and is used in different business, science, and social science domains. In today's business world, _____ plays a role in making decisions more scientific and helping businesses operate more effectively.

Exam Probability: **Low**

16. *Answer choices:*

(see index for correct answer)

- a. Imputation
- b. Lulu smoothing
- c. Data Discovery and Query Builder
- d. Anscombe transform

Guidance: level 1

:: Reputation management ::

A _____ is an astronomical object consisting of a luminous spheroid of plasma held together by its own gravity. The nearest _____ to Earth is the Sun. Many other _____ s are visible to the naked eye from Earth during the night, appearing as a multitude of fixed luminous points in the sky due to their immense distance from Earth. Historically, the most prominent _____ s were grouped into constellations and asterisms, the brightest of which gained proper names. Astronomers have assembled _____ catalogues that identify the known _____ s and provide standardized stellar designations. However, most of the estimated 300 sextillion _____ s in the Universe are invisible to the naked eye from Earth, including all _____ s outside our galaxy, the Milky Way.

Exam Probability: **Medium**

17. *Answer choices:*

(see index for correct answer)

- a. ClaimID
- b. personal brand
- c. Conversocial
- d. Star

:: Investment ::

In finance, the benefit from an _____ is called a return. The return may consist of a gain realised from the sale of property or an _____ , unrealised capital appreciation , or _____ income such as dividends, interest, rental income etc., or a combination of capital gain and income. The return may also include currency gains or losses due to changes in foreign currency exchange rates.

Exam Probability: **High**

18. *Answer choices:*

(see index for correct answer)

- a. Do-it-yourself investing
- b. Investment certificate
- c. Investment
- d. Asian option

:: Summary statistics ::

_____ is the number of occurrences of a repeating event per unit of time. It is also referred to as temporal _____ , which emphasizes the contrast to spatial _____ and angular _____ . The period is the duration of time of one cycle in a repeating event, so the period is the reciprocal of the _____ . For example: if a newborn baby's heart beats at a _____ of 120 times a minute, its period—the time interval between beats—is half a second . _____ is an important parameter used in science and engineering to specify the rate of oscillatory and vibratory phenomena, such as mechanical vibrations, audio signals , radio waves, and light.

Exam Probability: **High**

19. *Answer choices:*

(see index for correct answer)

- a. Higher-order statistics
- b. Nonparametric skew
- c. Robin Hood index
- d. Multiple of the median

Guidance: level 1

:: Brand management ::

_____ refers to the extent to which customers are able to recall or recognise a brand. _____ is a key consideration in consumer behavior, advertising management, brand management and strategy development. The consumer's ability to recognise or recall a brand is central to purchasing decision-making. Purchasing cannot proceed unless a consumer is first aware of a product category and a brand within that category. Awareness does not necessarily mean that the consumer must be able to recall a specific brand name, but he or she must be able to recall sufficient distinguishing features for purchasing to proceed. For instance, if a consumer asks her friend to buy her some gum in a "blue pack", the friend would be expected to know which gum to buy, even though neither friend can recall the precise brand name at the time.

Exam Probability: **Medium**

20. *Answer choices:*

(see index for correct answer)

- a. Umbrella brand
- b. Branded entertainment
- c. Brand awareness
- d. Barloworld Limited

Guidance: level 1

:: ::

_____ Company, commonly referred to as _____ , is an American multinational corporation headquartered in Detroit that designs, manufactures, markets, and distributes vehicles and vehicle parts, and sells financial services, with global headquarters in Detroit's Renaissance Center. It was originally founded by William C. Durant on September 16, 1908 as a holding company. The company is the largest American automobile manufacturer, and one of the world's largest. As of 2018, _____ is ranked #10 on the Fortune 500 rankings of the largest United States corporations by total revenue.

Exam Probability: **Medium**

21. *Answer choices:*

(see index for correct answer)

- a. co-culture
- b. General Motors
- c. personal values
- d. deep-level diversity

Guidance: level 1

:: Evaluation methods ::

In natural and social sciences, and sometimes in other fields, _____ is the systematic empirical investigation of observable phenomena via statistical, mathematical, or computational techniques. The objective of _____ is to develop and employ mathematical models, theories, and hypotheses pertaining to phenomena. The process of measurement is central to _____ because it provides the fundamental connection between empirical observation and mathematical expression of quantitative relationships.

Exam Probability: **Medium**

22. *Answer choices:*

(see index for correct answer)

- a. Advanced Concept Technology Demonstration
- b. Quantitative research
- c. Case series
- d. Reference class forecasting

Guidance: level 1

:: Data interchange standards ::

_____ is the concept of businesses electronically communicating information that was traditionally communicated on paper, such as purchase orders and invoices. Technical standards for EDI exist to facilitate parties transacting such instruments without having to make special arrangements.

Exam Probability: **Low**

23. *Answer choices:*

(see index for correct answer)

- a. ASC X12
- b. Common Alerting Protocol
- c. Interaction protocol
- d. Uniform Communication Standard

Guidance: level 1

:: Product management ::

_____ or brand stretching is a marketing strategy in which a firm marketing a product with a well-developed image uses the same brand name in a different product category. The new product is called a spin-off. Organizations use this strategy to increase and leverage brand equity . An example of a _____ is Jello-gelatin creating Jello pudding pops. It increases awareness of the brand name and increases profitability from offerings in more than one product category.

Exam Probability: **High**

24. *Answer choices:*

(see index for correct answer)

- a. Diffusion of innovations
- b. Product cost management
- c. Product management

- d. Brand extension

Guidance: level 1

:: ::

An _____ , often referred to as a creative agency or an ad agency, is a business dedicated to creating, planning, and handling advertising and sometimes other forms of promotion and marketing for its clients. An ad agency is generally independent from the client; it may be an internal department or agency that provides an outside point of view to the effort of selling the client's products or services, or an outside firm. An agency can also handle overall marketing and branding strategies promotions for its clients, which may include sales as well.

Exam Probability: **High**

25. *Answer choices:*

(see index for correct answer)

- a. Advertising agency
- b. Character
- c. open system
- d. cultural

Guidance: level 1

:: Behaviorism ::

In behavioral psychology, _____ is a consequence applied that will strengthen an organism's future behavior whenever that behavior is preceded by a specific antecedent stimulus. This strengthening effect may be measured as a higher frequency of behavior , longer duration , greater magnitude , or shorter latency . There are two types of _____ , known as positive _____ and negative _____ ; positive is where by a reward is offered on expression of the wanted behaviour and negative is taking away an undesirable element in the persons environment whenever the desired behaviour is achieved.

Exam Probability: **Medium**

26. *Answer choices:*

(see index for correct answer)

- a. chaining
- b. Reinforcement
- c. social facilitation
- d. Systematic desensitization

Guidance: level 1

:: Television commercials ::

_____ is a phenomenon whereby something new and somehow valuable is formed. The created item may be intangible or a physical object .

Exam Probability: **High**

27. *Answer choices:*

(see index for correct answer)

- a. Original Chicken Sandwich
- b. Cheer Up!
- c. Creativity
- d. Fridge

Guidance: level 1

:: ::

_____ , or auditory perception, is the ability to perceive sounds by detecting vibrations, changes in the pressure of the surrounding medium through time, through an organ such as the ear. The academic field concerned with _____ is auditory science.

Exam Probability: **High**

28. *Answer choices:*

(see index for correct answer)

- a. co-culture
- b. corporate values
- c. process perspective

- d. open system

Guidance: level 1

:: ::

_____ s are formal, sociotechnical, organizational systems designed to collect, process, store, and distribute information. In a sociotechnical perspective, _____ s are composed by four components: task, people, structure , and technology.

Exam Probability: **High**

29. *Answer choices:*

(see index for correct answer)

- a. similarity-attraction theory
- b. Information system
- c. imperative
- d. co-culture

Guidance: level 1

:: ::

In legal terminology, a _____ is any formal legal document that sets out the facts and legal reasons that the filing party or parties believes are sufficient to support a claim against the party or parties against whom the claim is brought that entitles the plaintiff to a remedy. For example, the Federal Rules of Civil Procedure that govern civil litigation in United States courts provide that a civil action is commenced with the filing or service of a pleading called a _____. Civil court rules in states that have incorporated the Federal Rules of Civil Procedure use the same term for the same pleading.

Exam Probability: **Medium**

30. *Answer choices:*
(see index for correct answer)

- a. hierarchical
- b. co-culture
- c. corporate values
- d. functional perspective

Guidance: level 1

:: Product management ::

`_____` is a phrase used in the marketing industry which describes the value of having a well-known brand name, based on the idea that the owner of a well-known brand name can generate more revenue simply from brand recognition; that is from products with that brand name than from products with a less well known name, as consumers believe that a product with a well-known name is better than products with less well-known names.

Exam Probability: **High**

31. *Answer choices:*

(see index for correct answer)

- a. Consumer adoption of technological innovations
- b. Brand equity
- c. Diffusion of innovations
- d. Discontinuation

Guidance: level 1

:: Management ::

The term _____ refers to measures designed to increase the degree of autonomy and self-determination in people and in communities in order to enable them to represent their interests in a responsible and self-determined way, acting on their own authority. It is the process of becoming stronger and more confident, especially in controlling one's life and claiming one's rights. _____ as action refers both to the process of self-_____ and to professional support of people, which enables them to overcome their sense of powerlessness and lack of influence, and to recognize and use their resources. To do work with power.

Exam Probability: **Low**

32. *Answer choices:*

(see index for correct answer)

- a. Earned schedule
- b. Marketing management
- c. Empowerment
- d. Downstream

Guidance: level 1

:: Production economics ::

In microeconomics, _____ are the cost advantages that enterprises obtain due to their scale of operation , with cost per unit of output decreasing with increasing scale.

33. *Answer choices:*

(see index for correct answer)

- a. Economies of scale
- b. Peer production
- c. Diminishing returns
- d. Marginal product of labor

Guidance: level 1

:: Generally Accepted Accounting Principles ::

Expenditure is an outflow of money to another person or group to pay for an item or service, or for a category of costs. For a tenant, rent is an _____ . For students or parents, tuition is an _____ . Buying food, clothing, furniture or an automobile is often referred to as an _____ . An _____ is a cost that is "paid" or "remitted", usually in exchange for something of value. Something that seems to cost a great deal is "expensive". Something that seems to cost little is "inexpensive". " _____ s of the table" are _____ s of dining, refreshments, a feast, etc.

34. *Answer choices:*

(see index for correct answer)

- a. Gross profit
- b. net realisable value
- c. Expense
- d. Earnings before interest, taxes and depreciation

Guidance: level 1

:: Pricing ::

_____ is a pricing strategy in which the selling price is determined by adding a specific amount markup to a product's unit cost. An alternative pricing method is value-based pricing.

Exam Probability: **Low**

35. *Answer choices:*

(see index for correct answer)

- a. Electricity pricing
- b. Cost-plus pricing
- c. Rational pricing
- d. indifference pricing

Guidance: level 1

:: Marketing ::

_____ is research conducted for a problem that has not been studied more clearly, intended to establish priorities, develop operational definitions and improve the final research design. _____ helps determine the best research design, data-collection method and selection of subjects. It should draw definitive conclusions only with extreme caution. Given its fundamental nature, _____ often relies on techniques such as.

Exam Probability: **Medium**

36. *Answer choices:*

(see index for correct answer)

- a. Accreditation in Public Relations
- b. Adobe Social
- c. Penetration pricing
- d. Adobe Analytics

Guidance: level 1

:: Stock market ::

The _____ of a corporation is all of the shares into which ownership of the corporation is divided. In American English, the shares are commonly known as " _____ s". A single share of the _____ represents fractional ownership of the corporation in proportion to the total number of shares. This typically entitles the _____ holder to that fraction of the company's earnings, proceeds from liquidation of assets , or voting power, often dividing these up in proportion to the amount of money each _____ holder has invested. Not all _____ is necessarily equal, as certain classes of _____ may be issued for example without voting rights, with enhanced voting rights, or with a certain priority to receive profits or liquidation proceeds before or after other classes of shareholders.

Exam Probability: **Medium**

37. *Answer choices:*

(see index for correct answer)

- a. Stock split
- b. Stock
- c. American Depositary Share
- d. CEE Stock Exchange Group

Guidance: level 1

:: Business models ::

A _____, _____ company or daughter company is a company that is owned or controlled by another company, which is called the parent company, parent, or holding company. The _____ can be a company, corporation, or limited liability company. In some cases it is a government or state-owned enterprise. In some cases, particularly in the music and book publishing industries, subsidiaries are referred to as imprints.

Exam Probability: **Medium**

38. *Answer choices:*

(see index for correct answer)

- a. Premium business model
- b. Meta learning
- c. IASME
- d. Subsidiary

Guidance: level 1

:: Monopoly (economics) ::

A _____ exists when a specific person or enterprise is the only supplier of a particular commodity. This contrasts with a monopsony which relates to a single entity's control of a market to purchase a good or service, and with oligopoly which consists of a few sellers dominating a market. Monopolies are thus characterized by a lack of economic competition to produce the good or service, a lack of viable substitute goods, and the possibility of a high _____ price well above the seller's marginal cost that leads to a high _____ profit. The verb monopolise or monopolize refers to the process by which a company gains the ability to raise prices or exclude competitors. In economics, a _____ is a single seller. In law, a _____ is a business entity that has significant market power, that is, the power to charge overly high prices. Although monopolies may be big businesses, size is not a characteristic of a _____ . A small business may still have the power to raise prices in a small industry .

Exam Probability: **Low**

39. *Answer choices:*

(see index for correct answer)

- a. Monopoly
- b. Network effect
- c. Competition Commission
- d. Dominance

Guidance: level 1

:: ::

_____ are interactive computer-mediated technologies that facilitate the creation and sharing of information, ideas, career interests and other forms of expression via virtual communities and networks. The variety of stand-alone and built-in _____ services currently available introduces challenges of definition; however, there are some common features.

Exam Probability: **Medium**

40. *Answer choices:*

(see index for correct answer)

- a. corporate values
- b. Social media
- c. levels of analysis
- d. personal values

Guidance: level 1

:: ::

_____ is the act of conveying meanings from one entity or group to another through the use of mutually understood signs, symbols, and semiotic rules.

Exam Probability: **Medium**

41. *Answer choices:*

(see index for correct answer)

- a. empathy
- b. interpersonal communication
- c. information systems assessment
- d. Communication

Guidance: level 1

:: Advertising techniques ::

In promotion and of advertising, a _____ or show consists of a person's written or spoken statement extolling the virtue of a product. The term " _____ " most commonly applies to the sales-pitches attributed to ordinary citizens, whereas the word "endorsement" usually applies to pitches by celebrities. _____ s can be part of communal marketing. Sometimes, the cartoon character can be a _____ in a commercial.

Exam Probability: **Low**

42. *Answer choices:*

(see index for correct answer)

- a. Unipole sign
- b. Inconsistent comparison
- c. Testimonial
- d. Below the line

:: Direct marketing ::

_____ is a method of direct marketing in which a salesperson solicits prospective customers to buy products or services, either over the phone or through a subsequent face to face or Web conferencing appointment scheduled during the call. _____ can also include recorded sales pitches programmed to be played over the phone via automatic dialing.

Exam Probability: **High**

43. *Answer choices:*

(see index for correct answer)

- a. Direct mail fundraising
- b. Telemarketing
- c. American Family Publishers
- d. International Masters Publishers

Guidance: level 1

:: Advertising ::

A _____ is a document used by creative professionals and agencies to develop creative deliverables: visual design, copy, advertising, web sites, etc. The document is usually developed by the requestor and approved by the creative team of designers, writers, and project managers. In some cases, the project's _____ may need creative director approval before work will commence.

Exam Probability: **Medium**

44. *Answer choices:*

(see index for correct answer)

- a. Cost per acquisition
- b. Flurry
- c. Media planning
- d. Visual pollution

Guidance: level 1

:: Contract law ::

In contract law, a _____ is a promise which is not a condition of the contract or an innominate term: it is a term "not going to the root of the contract", and which only entitles the innocent party to damages if it is breached: i.e. the _____ is not true or the defaulting party does not perform the contract in accordance with the terms of the _____ . A _____ is not guarantee. It is a mere promise. It may be enforced if it is breached by an award for the legal remedy of damages.

45. *Answer choices:*

(see index for correct answer)

- a. Franchisor
- b. Broad Agency Announcement
- c. Bonus clause
- d. Performance Based Contracting

Guidance: level 1

:: ::

A _____ is any person who contracts to acquire an asset in return for some form of consideration.

46. *Answer choices:*

(see index for correct answer)

- a. process perspective
- b. similarity-attraction theory
- c. Sarbanes-Oxley act of 2002
- d. corporate values

:: Survey methodology ::

An _____ is a conversation where questions are asked and answers are given. In common parlance, the word " _____ " refers to a one-on-one conversation between an _____ er and an _____ ee. The _____ er asks questions to which the _____ ee responds, usually so information may be transferred from _____ ee to _____ er . Sometimes, information can be transferred in both directions. It is a communication, unlike a speech, which produces a one-way flow of information.

Exam Probability: **Low**

47. *Answer choices:*

(see index for correct answer)

- a. Swiss Centre of Expertise in the Social Sciences
- b. Interview
- c. Scale analysis
- d. Survey sampling

:: Marketing ::

_____ is the percentage of a market accounted for by a specific entity. In a survey of nearly 200 senior marketing managers, 67% responded that they found the revenue- "dollar _____" metric very useful, while 61% found "unit _____" very useful.

Exam Probability: **High**

48. *Answer choices:*

(see index for correct answer)

- a. Promo
- b. National brand
- c. Market share
- d. Lead management

Guidance: level 1

:: ::

A _____ is a research instrument consisting of a series of questions for the purpose of gathering information from respondents. The _____ was invented by the Statistical Society of London in 1838.

Exam Probability: **Medium**

49. *Answer choices:*

(see index for correct answer)

- a. hierarchical perspective
- b. deep-level diversity
- c. surface-level diversity
- d. information systems assessment

Guidance: level 1

:: Financial economics ::

In management, business value is an informal term that includes all forms of value that determine the health and well-being of the firm in the long run. Business value expands concept of value of the firm beyond economic value to include other forms of value such as employee value, _____ , supplier value, channel partner value, alliance partner value, managerial value, and societal value. Many of these forms of value are not directly measured in monetary terms.

Exam Probability: **Medium**

50. *Answer choices:*

(see index for correct answer)

- a. Customer value
- b. Journal of Financial and Quantitative Analysis
- c. Financial innovation
- d. Investment protection

:: Marketing ::

_____ is a marketing practice of individuals or organizations . It allows them to sell products or services to other companies or organizations that resell them, use them in their products or services or use them to support their works.

Exam Probability: **Medium**

51. *Answer choices:*
(see index for correct answer)

- a. Business marketing
- b. Matomy Media
- c. Distributed presence
- d. Marketing intelligence

:: ::

_____ is the production of products for use or sale using labour and machines, tools, chemical and biological processing, or formulation. The term may refer to a range of human activity, from handicraft to high tech, but is most commonly applied to industrial design, in which raw materials are transformed into finished goods on a large scale. Such finished goods may be sold to other manufacturers for the production of other, more complex products, such as aircraft, household appliances, furniture, sports equipment or automobiles, or sold to wholesalers, who in turn sell them to retailers, who then sell them to end users and consumers.

Exam Probability: **High**

52. *Answer choices:*

(see index for correct answer)

- a. hierarchical
- b. Manufacturing
- c. corporate values
- d. interpersonal communication

Guidance: level 1

:: Marketing ::

_____ , in marketing, manufacturing, call centres and management, is the use of flexible computer-aided manufacturing systems to produce custom output. Such systems combine the low unit costs of mass production processes with the flexibility of individual customization.

53. *Answer choices:*

(see index for correct answer)

- a. Mass customization
- b. Movie packaging
- c. elaboration likelihood model
- d. One Town One Product

Guidance: level 1

:: ::

Bloomberg Businessweek is an American weekly business magazine published since 2009 by Bloomberg L.P. Businessweek, founded in 1929, aimed to provide information and interpretation about events in the business world. The magazine is headquartered in New York City. Megan Murphy served as editor from November 2016; she stepped down from the role in January 2018 and Joel Weber was appointed in her place. The magazine is published 47 times a year.

Exam Probability: **Medium**

54. *Answer choices:*

(see index for correct answer)

- a. hierarchical perspective
- b. levels of analysis

- c. functional perspective
- d. co-culture

Guidance: level 1

:: Marketing ::

A _____ is a group of customers within a business's serviceable available market at which a business aims its marketing efforts and resources. A _____ is a subset of the total market for a product or service. The _____ typically consists of consumers who exhibit similar characteristics and are considered most likely to buy a business's market offerings or are likely to be the most profitable segments for the business to service.

Exam Probability: **High**

55. *Answer choices:*

(see index for correct answer)

- a. Target market
- b. Macromarketing
- c. Mass customization
- d. Discounts and allowances

Guidance: level 1

:: Debt ::

_____ is the trust which allows one party to provide money or resources to another party wherein the second party does not reimburse the first party immediately , but promises either to repay or return those resources at a later date. In other words, _____ is a method of making reciprocity formal, legally enforceable, and extensible to a large group of unrelated people.

Exam Probability: **Low**

56. *Answer choices:*

(see index for correct answer)

- a. Debt-lag
- b. Floating charge
- c. Terminal debt
- d. Internal debt

Guidance: level 1

:: ::

_____ LLC is an American multinational technology company that specializes in Internet-related services and products, which include online advertising technologies, search engine, cloud computing, software, and hardware. It is considered one of the Big Four technology companies, alongside Amazon, Apple and Facebook.

Exam Probability: **High**

57. *Answer choices:*

(see index for correct answer)

- a. open system
- b. process perspective
- c. Google
- d. levels of analysis

Guidance: level 1

:: ::

_____ , in general use, is a devotion and faithfulness to a nation, cause, philosophy, country, group, or person. Philosophers disagree on what can be an object of _____ , as some argue that _____ is strictly interpersonal and only another human being can be the object of _____ . The definition of _____ in law and political science is the fidelity of an individual to a nation, either one`s nation of birth, or one`s declared home nation by oath .

Exam Probability: **Low**

58. *Answer choices:*

(see index for correct answer)

- a. levels of analysis
- b. information systems assessment
- c. similarity-attraction theory

- d. Character

Guidance: level 1

:: Health promotion ::

_____ , as defined by the World _____ Organization , is "a state of complete physical, mental and social well-being and not merely the absence of disease or infirmity." This definition has been subject to controversy, as it may have limited value for implementation. _____ may be defined as the ability to adapt and manage physical, mental and social challenges throughout life.

Exam Probability: **High**

59. *Answer choices:*
(see index for correct answer)

- a. High-deductible health plan
- b. Breastfeeding promotion
- c. ParticipACTION
- d. Unwarranted variation

Guidance: level 1

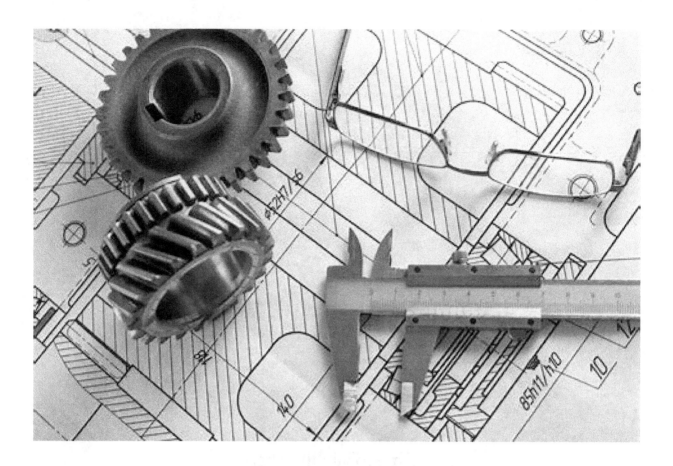

Manufacturing

Manufacturing is the production of merchandise for use or sale using labor and machines, tools, chemical and biological processing, or formulation. The term may refer to a range of human activity, from handicraft to high tech, but is most commonly applied to industrial design , in which raw materials are transformed into finished goods on a large scale. Such finished goods may be sold to other manufacturers for the production of other, more complex products, such as aircraft, household appliances, furniture, sports equipment or automobiles, or sold to wholesalers, who in turn sell them to retailers, who then sell them to end users and consumers.

:: Product management ::

_____ is the state of being which occurs when an object, service, or practice is no longer wanted even though it may still be in good working order; however, the international standard EN62402 _____ Management - Application Guide defines _____ as being the "transition from availability of products by the original manufacturer or supplier to unavailability". _____ frequently occurs because a replacement has become available that has, in sum, more advantages compared to the disadvantages incurred by maintaining or repairing the original. Obsolete also refers to something that is already disused or discarded, or antiquated. Typically, _____ is preceded by a gradual decline in popularity.

Exam Probability: **Medium**

1. *Answer choices:*

(see index for correct answer)

- a. Consumer adoption of technological innovations
- b. Product cost management
- c. Obsolescence
- d. Product management

Guidance: level 1

:: Product development ::

In business and engineering, _____ covers the complete process of bringing a new product to market. A central aspect of NPD is product design, along with various business considerations. _____ is described broadly as the transformation of a market opportunity into a product available for sale. The product can be tangible or intangible , though sometimes services and other processes are distinguished from "products." NPD requires an understanding of customer needs and wants, the competitive environment, and the nature of the market.Cost, time and quality are the main variables that drive customer needs. Aiming at these three variables, innovative companies develop continuous practices and strategies to better satisfy customer requirements and to increase their own market share by a regular development of new products. There are many uncertainties and challenges which companies must face throughout the process. The use of best practices and the elimination of barriers to communication are the main concerns for the management of the NPD .

Exam Probability: **Low**

2. *Answer choices:*

(see index for correct answer)

- a. WhiteBoard Product Solutions
- b. DFMA
- c. Product design specification
- d. New product development

Guidance: level 1

:: Packaging materials ::

_____ is a non-crystalline, amorphous solid that is often transparent and has widespread practical, technological, and decorative uses in, for example, window panes, tableware, and optoelectronics. The most familiar, and historically the oldest, types of manufactured _____ are "silicate _____ es" based on the chemical compound silica , the primary constituent of sand. The term _____ , in popular usage, is often used to refer only to this type of material, which is familiar from use as window _____ and in _____ bottles. Of the many silica-based _____ es that exist, ordinary glazing and container _____ is formed from a specific type called soda-lime _____ , composed of approximately 75% silicon dioxide , sodium oxide from sodium carbonate , calcium oxide , also called lime, and several minor additives.

Exam Probability: **Low**

3. *Answer choices:*

(see index for correct answer)

- a. Polymethylpentene
- b. Glass
- c. Paper
- d. Bubble wrap

Guidance: level 1

:: Debt ::

_____ is the trust which allows one party to provide money or resources to another party wherein the second party does not reimburse the first party immediately , but promises either to repay or return those resources at a later date. In other words, _____ is a method of making reciprocity formal, legally enforceable, and extensible to a large group of unrelated people.

Exam Probability: **Low**

4. *Answer choices:*

(see index for correct answer)

- a. Credit
- b. Debtors Anonymous
- c. Perpetual subordinated debt
- d. Bad debt

Guidance: level 1

:: Materials science ::

An _____ is a polymer with viscoelasticity and very weak intermolecular forces, and generally low Young's modulus and high failure strain compared with other materials. The term, a portmanteau of elastic polymer, is often used interchangeably with rubber, although the latter is preferred when referring to vulcanisates. Each of the monomers which link to form the polymer is usually a compound of several elements among carbon, hydrogen, oxygen and silicon. _____ s are amorphous polymers maintained above their glass transition temperature, so that considerable molecular reconformation, without breaking of covalent bonds, is feasible. At ambient temperatures, such rubbers are thus relatively soft and deformable. Their primary uses are for seals, adhesives and molded flexible parts. Application areas for different types of rubber are manifold and cover segments as diverse as tires, soles for shoes, and damping and insulating elements. The importance of these rubbers can be judged from the fact that global revenues are forecast to rise to US$56 billion in 2020.

Exam Probability: **Medium**

5. *Answer choices:*

(see index for correct answer)

- a. Maxwell material
- b. Sticking probability
- c. Surface modification
- d. Solvus

Guidance: level 1

:: Metalworking ::

A _____ is a round object with various uses. It is used in _____ games, where the play of the game follows the state of the _____ as it is hit, kicked or thrown by players. _____ s can also be used for simpler activities, such as catch or juggling. _____ s made from hard-wearing materials are used in engineering applications to provide very low friction bearings, known as _____ bearings. Black-powder weapons use stone and metal _____ s as projectiles.

Exam Probability: **High**

6. *Answer choices:*

(see index for correct answer)

- a. Autofrettage
- b. Faggoting
- c. Forming
- d. Ball

Guidance: level 1

:: Inventory ::

The _____ is the level of inventory which triggers an action to replenish that particular inventory stock. It is a minimum amount of an item which a firm holds in stock, such that, when stock falls to this amount, the item must be reordered. It is normally calculated as the forecast usage during the replenishment lead time plus safety stock. In the EOQ model, it was assumed that there is no time lag between ordering and procuring of materials. Therefore the _____ for replenishing the stocks occurs at that level when the inventory level drops to zero and because instant delivery by suppliers, the stock level bounce back.

Exam Probability: **Medium**

7. *Answer choices:*

(see index for correct answer)

- a. Stock control
- b. Reorder point
- c. LIFO
- d. Cost of goods sold

Guidance: level 1

:: Unit operations ::

_____ is a discipline of thermal engineering that concerns the generation, use, conversion, and exchange of thermal energy between physical systems. _____ is classified into various mechanisms, such as thermal conduction, thermal convection, thermal radiation, and transfer of energy by phase changes. Engineers also consider the transfer of mass of differing chemical species, either cold or hot, to achieve _____ . While these mechanisms have distinct characteristics, they often occur simultaneously in the same system.

Exam Probability: **Low**

8. *Answer choices:*

(see index for correct answer)

- a. Distillation
- b. Separation process
- c. Sedimentation coefficient
- d. Heat transfer

Guidance: level 1

:: Management accounting ::

" _____ s are the structural determinants of the cost of an activity, reflecting any linkages or interrelationships that affect it". Therefore we could assume that the _____ s determine the cost behavior within the activities, reflecting the links that these have with other activities and relationships that affect them.

9. *Answer choices:*

(see index for correct answer)

- a. Dual overhead rate
- b. Entity-level controls
- c. Cost driver
- d. Factory overhead

Guidance: level 1

:: Quality ::

A _____ is an initiating cause of either a condition or a causal chain that leads to an outcome or effect of interest. The term denotes the earliest, most basic, 'deepest', cause for a given behavior; most often a fault. The idea is that you can only see an error by its manifest signs. Those signs can be widespread, multitudinous, and convoluted, whereas the _____ leading to them often is a lot simpler.

Exam Probability: **High**

10. *Answer choices:*

(see index for correct answer)

- a. Diamond clarity
- b. Process architecture

- c. Robustification
- d. Root cause

Guidance: level 1

:: ::

A _____ or till is a mechanical or electronic device for registering and calculating transactions at a point of sale. It is usually attached to a drawer for storing cash and other valuables. A modern _____ is usually attached to a printer that can print out receipts for record-keeping purposes.

Exam Probability: **Medium**

11. *Answer choices:*

(see index for correct answer)

- a. Cash register
- b. hierarchical perspective
- c. open system
- d. deep-level diversity

Guidance: level 1

:: Management ::

_____ is a method of quality control which employs statistical methods to monitor and control a process. This helps to ensure that the process operates efficiently, producing more specification-conforming products with less waste . SPC can be applied to any process where the "conforming product" output can be measured. Key tools used in SPC include run charts, control charts, a focus on continuous improvement, and the design of experiments. An example of a process where SPC is applied is manufacturing lines.

Exam Probability: **High**

12. *Answer choices:*

(see index for correct answer)

- a. Mission critical
- b. Statistical process control
- c. Resource management
- d. Fredmund Malik

Guidance: level 1

:: Quality assurance ::

The _____ is a United States-based nonprofit tax-exempt 501 organization that accredits more than 21,000 US health care organizations and programs. The international branch accredits medical services from around the world. A majority of US state governments recognize _____ accreditation as a condition of licensure for the receipt of Medicaid and Medicare reimbursements.

13. *Answer choices:*

(see index for correct answer)

- a. Quality Assurance Agency for Higher Education
- b. Federation of Swiss Private Schools
- c. Static testing
- d. The Compliance Team

Guidance: level 1

:: ::

A _____ consists of an orchestrated and repeatable pattern of business activity enabled by the systematic organization of resources into processes that transform materials, provide services, or process information. It can be depicted as a sequence of operations, the work of a person or group, the work of an organization of staff, or one or more simple or complex mechanisms.

Exam Probability: **High**

14. *Answer choices:*

(see index for correct answer)

- a. personal values
- b. Sarbanes-Oxley act of 2002

- c. cultural
- d. Workflow

Guidance: level 1

:: Project management ::

A _____ is a professional in the field of project management. _____ s have the responsibility of the planning, procurement and execution of a project, in any undertaking that has a defined scope, defined start and a defined finish; regardless of industry. _____ s are first point of contact for any issues or discrepancies arising from within the heads of various departments in an organization before the problem escalates to higher authorities. Project management is the responsibility of a _____ . This individual seldom participates directly in the activities that produce the end result, but rather strives to maintain the progress, mutual interaction and tasks of various parties in such a way that reduces the risk of overall failure, maximizes benefits, and minimizes costs.

Exam Probability: **High**

15. *Answer choices:*
(see index for correct answer)

- a. Small-scale project management
- b. Project manager
- c. Theory Z of Ouchi
- d. Rapid Results

:: Sensitivity analysis ::

_____ is the study of how the uncertainty in the output of a mathematical model or system can be divided and allocated to different sources of uncertainty in its inputs. A related practice is uncertainty analysis, which has a greater focus on uncertainty quantification and propagation of uncertainty; ideally, uncertainty and _____ should be run in tandem.

Exam Probability: **Medium**

16. *Answer choices:*

(see index for correct answer)

- a. Sensitivity analysis
- b. Elementary effects method
- c. Variance-based sensitivity analysis
- d. Fourier amplitude sensitivity testing

:: Goods ::

In most contexts, the concept of _____ denotes the conduct that should be preferred when posed with a choice between possible actions. _____ is generally considered to be the opposite of evil, and is of interest in the study of morality, ethics, religion and philosophy. The specific meaning and etymology of the term and its associated translations among ancient and contemporary languages show substantial variation in its inflection and meaning depending on circumstances of place, history, religious, or philosophical context.

Exam Probability: **Low**

17. *Answer choices:*

(see index for correct answer)

- a. Refined goods
- b. Good
- c. Composite good
- d. Durable good

Guidance: level 1

:: Project management ::

A _____ is a source or supply from which a benefit is produced and it has some utility. _____ s can broadly be classified upon their availability—they are classified into renewable and non-renewable _____ s.Examples of non renewable _____ s are coal ,crude oil natural gas nuclear energy etc. Examples of renewable _____ s are air,water,wind,solar energy etc. They can also be classified as actual and potential on the basis of level of development and use, on the basis of origin they can be classified as biotic and abiotic, and on the basis of their distribution, as ubiquitous and localized . An item becomes a _____ with time and developing technology. Typically, _____ s are materials, energy, services, staff, knowledge, or other assets that are transformed to produce benefit and in the process may be consumed or made unavailable. Benefits of _____ utilization may include increased wealth, proper functioning of a system, or enhanced well-being. From a human perspective a natural _____ is anything obtained from the environment to satisfy human needs and wants. From a broader biological or ecological perspective a _____ satisfies the needs of a living organism .

Exam Probability: **High**

18. *Answer choices:*

(see index for correct answer)

- a. Starmad
- b. Assumption-based planning
- c. Resource
- d. Value of work done

Guidance: level 1

:: Building materials ::

_____ is an alloy of iron and carbon, and sometimes other elements. Because of its high tensile strength and low cost, it is a major component used in buildings, infrastructure, tools, ships, automobiles, machines, appliances, and weapons.

Exam Probability: **Medium**

19. *Answer choices:*

(see index for correct answer)

- a. Steel
- b. Orangeburg pipe
- c. Shelf angle
- d. Martensitic stainless steel

Guidance: level 1

:: Information technology management ::

_____ is the discipline of engineering concerned with the principles and practice of product and service quality assurance and control. In the software development, it is the management, development, operation and maintenance of IT systems and enterprise architectures with a high quality standard.

Exam Probability: **Medium**

20. *Answer choices:*

(see index for correct answer)

- a. EFx Factory
- b. DocSTAR
- c. Distributed development
- d. Telematics

Guidance: level 1

:: Project management ::

Contemporary business and science treat as a _____ any undertaking, carried out individually or collaboratively and possibly involving research or design, that is carefully planned to achieve a particular aim.

Exam Probability: **Low**

21. *Answer choices:*

(see index for correct answer)

- a. Effective Development Group
- b. Project
- c. Rapid Results
- d. Market requirements document

Guidance: level 1

:: Metal heat treatments ::

_____ is a group of industrial and metalworking processes used to alter the physical, and sometimes chemical, properties of a material. The most common application is metallurgical. Heat treatments are also used in the manufacture of many other materials, such as glass. Heat treatment involves the use of heating or chilling, normally to extreme temperatures, to achieve a desired result such as hardening or softening of a material. Heat treatment techniques include annealing, case hardening, precipitation strengthening, tempering, carburizing, normalizing and quenching. It is noteworthy that while the term heat treatment applies only to processes where the heating and cooling are done for the specific purpose of altering properties intentionally, heating and cooling often occur incidentally during other manufacturing processes such as hot forming or welding.

Exam Probability: **Medium**

22. *Answer choices:*

(see index for correct answer)

- a. Heat treating
- b. Martempering
- c. Case hardening
- d. Hardening

Guidance: level 1

:: Manufacturing ::

A _____ is an object used to extend the ability of an individual to modify features of the surrounding environment. Although many animals use simple _____ s, only human beings, whose use of stone _____ s dates back hundreds of millennia, use _____ s to make other _____ s. The set of _____ s needed to perform different tasks that are part of the same activity is called gear or equipment.

Exam Probability: **High**

23. *Answer choices:*

(see index for correct answer)

- a. Clean Driving Zone
- b. Notions
- c. Acheson process
- d. Tool

Guidance: level 1

:: Supply chain management ::

_____ is the process of finding and agreeing to terms, and acquiring goods, services, or works from an external source, often via a tendering or competitive bidding process. _____ is used to ensure the buyer receives goods, services, or works at the best possible price when aspects such as quality, quantity, time, and location are compared. Corporations and public bodies often define processes intended to promote fair and open competition for their business while minimizing risks such as exposure to fraud and collusion.

Exam Probability: **High**

24. *Answer choices:*

(see index for correct answer)

- a. Procurement
- b. CTSI-Global
- c. Suppliers and Parts database
- d. Application service provider

Guidance: level 1

:: Management ::

_____ is a category of business activity made possible by software tools that aim to provide customers with both independence from vendors and better means for engaging with vendors. These same tools can also apply to individuals' relations with other institutions and organizations.

Exam Probability: **Low**

25. *Answer choices:*

(see index for correct answer)

- a. Director
- b. Gemba
- c. Vendor relationship management

- d. Maryland StateStat

:: Elementary mathematics ::

In mathematics, a _____ is an enumerated collection of objects in which repetitions are allowed. Like a set, it contains members . The number of elements is called the length of the _____ . Unlike a set, the same elements can appear multiple times at different positions in a _____ , and order matters. Formally, a _____ can be defined as a function whose domain is either the set of the natural numbers or the set of the first n natural numbers . The position of an element in a _____ is its rank or index; it is the natural number from which the element is the image. It depends on the context or a specific convention, if the first element has index 0 or 1.
 When a symbol has been chosen for denoting a _____ , the nth element of the _____ is denoted by this symbol with n as subscript; for example, the nth element of the Fibonacci _____ is generally denoted Fn.

Exam Probability: **Medium**

26. *Answer choices:*
(see index for correct answer)

- a. Argument of a function
- b. Identity function
- c. Radix
- d. Magnitude

:: Industrial engineering ::

_____ , in its contemporary conceptualisation, is a comparison of perceived expectations of a service with perceived performance , giving rise to the equation SQ=P-E. This conceptualistion of _____ has its origins in the expectancy-disconfirmation paradigm.

Exam Probability: **Medium**

27. *Answer choices:*

(see index for correct answer)

- a. Systematic layout planning
- b. Worker-machine activity chart
- c. Service quality
- d. Therblig

Guidance: level 1

:: ::

Some scenarios associate "this kind of planning" with learning "life skills".Schedules are necessary, or at least useful, in situations where individuals need to know what time they must be at a specific location to receive a specific service, and where people need to accomplish a set of goals within a set time period.

Exam Probability: **High**

28. *Answer choices:*

(see index for correct answer)

- a. cultural
- b. Scheduling
- c. similarity-attraction theory
- d. Character

Guidance: level 1

:: Production economics ::

In economics and related disciplines, a _____ is a cost in making any economic trade when participating in a market.

Exam Probability: **Medium**

29. *Answer choices:*

(see index for correct answer)

- a. Producer's risk
- b. Multifactor productivity
- c. Fragmentation
- d. Transaction cost

Guidance: level 1

:: Production and manufacturing ::

_____ is a concept in purchasing and project management for securing the quality and timely delivery of goods and components.

Exam Probability: **High**

30. *Answer choices:*

(see index for correct answer)

- a. Verband der Automobilindustrie
- b. Rolled throughput yield
- c. Order to cash
- d. PCR food testing

Guidance: level 1

:: Project management ::

Rolling-wave planning is the process of project planning in waves as the project proceeds and later details become clearer; similar to the techniques used in agile software development approaches like Scrum..

Exam Probability: **Medium**

31. *Answer choices:*
(see index for correct answer)

- a. Rolling Wave planning
- b. Punch list
- c. Gantt chart
- d. Participatory impact pathways analysis

Guidance: level 1

:: Industries ::

The _____ comprises the companies that produce industrial chemicals. Central to the modern world economy, it converts raw materials into more than 70,000 different products. The plastics industry contains some overlap, as most chemical companies produce plastic as well as other chemicals.

Exam Probability: **High**

32. *Answer choices:*

(see index for correct answer)

- a. Professional sports
- b. Sustainable industries
- c. Energy industry
- d. Housing industry

Guidance: level 1

:: Chemical reactions ::

A _____ is a process that leads to the chemical transformation of one set of chemical substances to another. Classically, _____ s encompass changes that only involve the positions of electrons in the forming and breaking of chemical bonds between atoms, with no change to the nuclei , and can often be described by a chemical equation. Nuclear chemistry is a sub-discipline of chemistry that involves the _____ s of unstable and radioactive elements where both electronic and nuclear changes can occur.

Exam Probability: **Medium**

33. *Answer choices:*

(see index for correct answer)

- a. Harpoon reaction
- b. Adduct purification
- c. Isomerization

- d. Hydrolysis

Guidance: level 1

:: Business planning ::

_____ is an organization's process of defining its strategy, or direction, and making decisions on allocating its resources to pursue this strategy. It may also extend to control mechanisms for guiding the implementation of the strategy. _____ became prominent in corporations during the 1960s and remains an important aspect of strategic management. It is executed by strategic planners or strategists, who involve many parties and research sources in their analysis of the organization and its relationship to the environment in which it competes.

Exam Probability: **Low**

34. *Answer choices:*
(see index for correct answer)

- a. operational planning
- b. Community Futures
- c. Strategic planning
- d. Open Options Corporation

Guidance: level 1

:: Quality management ::

_____ is a not-for-profit membership foundation in Brussels, established in 1989 to increase the competitiveness of the European economy. The initial impetus for forming _____ was a response to the work of W. Edwards Deming and the development of the concepts of Total Quality Management.

Exam Probability: **Low**

35. *Answer choices:*

(see index for correct answer)

- a. European Quality in Social Services
- b. EFQM
- c. External quality assessment
- d. QC Reporting

Guidance: level 1

:: Supply chain management ::

A _____ is a type of auction in which the traditional roles of buyer and seller are reversed. Thus, there is one buyer and many potential sellers. In an ordinary auction , buyers compete to obtain goods or services by offering increasingly higher prices. In contrast, in a _____ , the sellers compete to obtain business from the buyer and prices will typically decrease as the sellers underbid each other.

36. *Answer choices:*

(see index for correct answer)

- a. Universal Product Code
- b. Transactional IT
- c. Global supply-chain finance
- d. Materials management

Guidance: level 1

:: Production and manufacturing ::

_____ is a systematic method to improve the "value" of goods or products and services by using an examination of function. Value, as defined, is the ratio of function to cost. Value can therefore be manipulated by either improving the function or reducing the cost. It is a primary tenet of _____ that basic functions be preserved and not be reduced as a consequence of pursuing value improvements.

Exam Probability: **High**

37. *Answer choices:*

(see index for correct answer)

- a. Product lifecycle management
- b. Value engineering

- c. STEP-NC
- d. ISO/TS 16949

Guidance: level 1

:: Production economics ::

_____ is the joint use of a resource or space. It is also the process of dividing and distributing. In its narrow sense, it refers to joint or alternating use of inherently finite goods, such as a common pasture or a shared residence. Still more loosely, "_____" can actually mean giving something as an outright gift: for example, to "share" one's food really means to give some of it as a gift. _____ is a basic component of human interaction, and is responsible for strengthening social ties and ensuring a person's well-being.

Exam Probability: **High**

38. *Answer choices:*

(see index for correct answer)

- a. Sharing
- b. HMI quality
- c. Industrial production index
- d. Socially optimal firm size

Guidance: level 1

:: Quality assurance ::

Organizations that issue credentials or certify third parties against
official standards are themselves formally accredited by _____ bodies ;
hence they are sometimes known as "accredited certification bodies". The
_____ process ensures that their certification practices are acceptable,
typically meaning that they are competent to test and certify third parties,
behave ethically and employ suitable quality assurance.

Exam Probability: **Medium**

39. *Answer choices:*

(see index for correct answer)

- a. Healthcare Quality Association on Accreditation
- b. SUBSAFE
- c. Accreditation
- d. Healthcare Facilities Accreditation Program

Guidance: level 1

:: Costs ::

In process improvement efforts, _____ or cost of quality is a means to
quantify the total cost of quality-related efforts and deficiencies. It was
first described by Armand V. Feigenbaum in a 1956 Harvard Business Review
article.

40. *Answer choices:*

(see index for correct answer)

- a. Quality costs
- b. Average cost
- c. Opportunity cost
- d. Cost per paper

Guidance: level 1

:: ::

_____ is the quantity of three-dimensional space enclosed by a closed surface, for example, the space that a substance or shape occupies or contains. _____ is often quantified numerically using the SI derived unit, the cubic metre. The _____ of a container is generally understood to be the capacity of the container; i. e., the amount of fluid that the container could hold, rather than the amount of space the container itself displaces. Three dimensional mathematical shapes are also assigned _____ s. _____ s of some simple shapes, such as regular, straight-edged, and circular shapes can be easily calculated using arithmetic formulas. _____ s of complicated shapes can be calculated with integral calculus if a formula exists for the shape's boundary. One-dimensional figures and two-dimensional shapes are assigned zero _____ in the three-dimensional space.

Exam Probability: **High**

41. *Answer choices:*

(see index for correct answer)

- a. interpersonal communication
- b. deep-level diversity
- c. Volume
- d. surface-level diversity

Guidance: level 1

:: ::

In sales, commerce and economics, a _____ is the recipient of a good, service, product or an idea - obtained from a seller, vendor, or supplier via a financial transaction or exchange for money or some other valuable consideration.

Exam Probability: **Low**

42. *Answer choices:*

(see index for correct answer)

- a. Customer
- b. deep-level diversity
- c. similarity-attraction theory
- d. functional perspective

:: Business process ::

_____ is the value to an enterprise which is derived from the techniques, procedures, and programs that implement and enhance the delivery of goods and services. _____ is one of the three components of structural capital, itself a component of intellectual capital. _____ can be seen as the value of processes to any entity, whether for profit or not-for profit, but is most commonly used in reference to for-profit entities.

Exam Probability: **Medium**

43. *Answer choices:*

(see index for correct answer)

- a. Change order
- b. Process capital
- c. Bonita BPM
- d. IDS Scheer

:: Metrics ::

_____ is a computer model developed by the University of Idaho, that uses Landsat satellite data to compute and map evapotranspiration . _____ calculates ET as a residual of the surface energy balance, where ET is estimated by keeping account of total net short wave and long wave radiation at the vegetation or soil surface, the amount of heat conducted into soil, and the amount of heat convected into the air above the surface. The difference in these three terms represents the amount of energy absorbed during the conversion of liquid water to vapor, which is ET. _____ expresses near-surface temperature gradients used in heat convection as indexed functions of radio _____ surface temperature, thereby eliminating the need for absolutely accurate surface temperature and the need for air-temperature measurements.

Exam Probability: **Medium**

44. *Answer choices:*

(see index for correct answer)

- a. Accommodation index
- b. Software metric
- c. Full-time equivalent
- d. Guide number

Guidance: level 1

:: Business planning ::

_____ is a critical component to the successful delivery of any project, programme or activity. A stakeholder is any individual, group or organization that can affect, be affected by, or perceive itself to be affected by a programme.

Exam Probability: **Medium**

45. *Answer choices:*

(see index for correct answer)

- a. Strategic planning
- b. Stakeholder management
- c. Customer Demand Planning
- d. Gap analysis

Guidance: level 1

:: Industrial organization ::

In economics, specifically general equilibrium theory, a perfect market is defined by several idealizing conditions, collectively called _____ . In theoretical models where conditions of _____ hold, it has been theoretically demonstrated that a market will reach an equilibrium in which the quantity supplied for every product or service, including labor, equals the quantity demanded at the current price. This equilibrium would be a Pareto optimum.

Exam Probability: **High**

46. *Answer choices:*

(see index for correct answer)

- a. American system of manufacturing
- b. Perfect competition
- c. domestic system
- d. Switching barriers

Guidance: level 1

:: Project management ::

A _____ is a type of bar chart that illustrates a project schedule, named after its inventor, Henry Gantt , who designed such a chart around the years 1910–1915. Modern _____ s also show the dependency relationships between activities and current schedule status.

Exam Probability: **Medium**

47. *Answer choices:*

(see index for correct answer)

- a. TargetProcess
- b. Gantt chart
- c. 10,000ft
- d. Lean project management

:: Management ::

_____ is the practice of initiating, planning, executing, controlling, and closing the work of a team to achieve specific goals and meet specific success criteria at the specified time.

Exam Probability: **Medium**

48. *Answer choices:*

(see index for correct answer)

- a. Design management
- b. Business process mapping
- c. Fall guy
- d. Project management

:: Business ::

The seller, or the provider of the goods or services, completes a sale in response to an acquisition, appropriation, requisition or a direct interaction with the buyer at the point of sale. There is a passing of title of the item, and the settlement of a price, in which agreement is reached on a price for which transfer of ownership of the item will occur. The seller, not the purchaser typically executes the sale and it may be completed prior to the obligation of payment. In the case of indirect interaction, a person who sells goods or service on behalf of the owner is known as a _____ man or _____ woman or _____ person, but this often refers to someone selling goods in a store/shop, in which case other terms are also common, including _____ clerk, shop assistant, and retail clerk.

Exam Probability: **Medium**

49. *Answer choices:*

(see index for correct answer)

- a. Qualifying event
- b. Sales
- c. Ian McLeod
- d. Business partnering

Guidance: level 1

:: Management accounting ::

_____ are costs that are not directly accountable to a cost object .
_____ may be either fixed or variable. _____ include administration,
personnel and security costs. These are those costs which are not directly
related to production. Some _____ may be overhead. But some overhead
costs can be directly attributed to a project and are direct costs.

Exam Probability: **Low**

50. *Answer choices:*

(see index for correct answer)

- a. RCA open-source application
- b. Indirect costs
- c. Notional profit
- d. Net present value

Guidance: level 1

:: Management ::

A process is a unique combination of tools, materials, methods, and people
engaged in producing a measurable output; for example a manufacturing line for
machine parts. All processes have inherent statistical variability which can
be evaluated by statistical methods.

Exam Probability: **Medium**

51. *Answer choices:*

(see index for correct answer)

- a. Business-oriented architecture
- b. Executive compensation
- c. Sensemaking
- d. Process capability

Guidance: level 1

:: Quality management ::

_____ ensures that an organization, product or service is consistent. It has four main components: quality planning, quality assurance, quality control and quality improvement. _____ is focused not only on product and service quality, but also on the means to achieve it. _____ , therefore, uses quality assurance and control of processes as well as products to achieve more consistent quality. What a customer wants and is willing to pay for it determines quality. It is written or unwritten commitment to a known or unknown consumer in the market . Thus, quality can be defined as fitness for intended use or, in other words, how well the product performs its intended function

Exam Probability: **Medium**

52. *Answer choices:*

(see index for correct answer)

- a. Quality Management Maturity Grid
- b. TL 9000

- c. Quality management
- d. Flemish Quality Management Center

Guidance: level 1

:: Data management ::

_____ is an object-oriented program and library developed by CERN. It was originally designed for particle physics data analysis and contains several features specific to this field, but it is also used in other applications such as astronomy and data mining. The latest release is 6.16.00, as of 2018-11-14.

Exam Probability: **Medium**

53. *Answer choices:*
(see index for correct answer)

- a. ROOT
- b. Microsoft Office PerformancePoint Server
- c. Disaster recovery plan
- d. Versomatic

Guidance: level 1

:: Asset ::

In financial accounting, an _____ is any resource owned by the business. Anything tangible or intangible that can be owned or controlled to produce value and that is held by a company to produce positive economic value is an _____ . Simply stated, _____ s represent value of ownership that can be converted into cash . The balance sheet of a firm records the monetary value of the _____ s owned by that firm. It covers money and other valuables belonging to an individual or to a business.

Exam Probability: **Medium**

54. *Answer choices:*

(see index for correct answer)

- a. Fixed asset
- b. Current asset

Guidance: level 1

:: Management ::

A supply-chain network is an evolution of the basic supply chain. Due to rapid technological advancement, organisations with a basic supply chain can develop this chain into a more complex structure involving a higher level of interdependence and connectivity between more organisations, this constitutes a supply-chain network.

Exam Probability: **High**

55. *Answer choices:*

(see index for correct answer)

- a. Supply chain network
- b. Marketing plan
- c. Managerial hubris
- d. Certified management consultant

Guidance: level 1

:: Information technology management ::

The term _____ is used to refer to periods when a system is unavailable. _____ or outage duration refers to a period of time that a system fails to provide or perform its primary function. Reliability, availability, recovery, and unavailability are related concepts. The unavailability is the proportion of a time-span that a system is unavailable or offline. This is usually a result of the system failing to function because of an unplanned event, or because of routine maintenance .

Exam Probability: **Medium**

56. *Answer choices:*

(see index for correct answer)

- a. ITIL security management
- b. Storage virtualization
- c. Downtime

- d. Enterprise content management

Guidance: level 1

:: Information technology management ::

_____ is a collective term for all approaches to prepare , support and help individuals, teams, and organizations in making organizational change. The most common change drivers include: technological evolution, process reviews, crisis, and consumer habit changes; pressure from new business entrants, acquisitions, mergers, and organizational restructuring. It includes methods that redirect or redefine the use of resources, business process, budget allocations, or other modes of operation that significantly change a company or organization. Organizational _____ considers the full organization and what needs to change, while _____ may be used solely to refer to how people and teams are affected by such organizational transition. It deals with many different disciplines, from behavioral and social sciences to information technology and business solutions.

Exam Probability: **Medium**

57. *Answer choices:*

(see index for correct answer)

- a. Change management
- b. Customer communications management
- c. HP FutureSmart firmware
- d. IT Interaction Model

Guidance: level 1

:: Lean manufacturing ::

_____ is a scheduling system for lean manufacturing and just-in-time manufacturing . Taiichi Ohno, an industrial engineer at Toyota, developed _____ to improve manufacturing efficiency. _____ is one method to achieve JIT. The system takes its name from the cards that track production within a factory. For many in the automotive sector, _____ is known as the "Toyota nameplate system" and as such the term is not used by some other automakers.

Exam Probability: **High**

58. *Answer choices:*

(see index for correct answer)

- a. The Machine That Changed the World
- b. Lean software development
- c. Kanban
- d. JobShopLean

Guidance: level 1

:: Management ::

_____ is the discipline of strategically planning for, and managing, all interactions with third party organizations that supply goods and/or services to an organization in order to maximize the value of those interactions. In practice, SRM entails creating closer, more collaborative relationships with key suppliers in order to uncover and realize new value and reduce risk of failure.

Exam Probability: **Low**

59. *Answer choices:*

(see index for correct answer)

- a. Business process improvement
- b. Supplier relationship management
- c. Interim management
- d. PDCA

Guidance: level 1

Commerce

Commerce relates to "the exchange of goods and services, especially on a large scale." It includes legal, economic, political, social, cultural and technological systems that operate in any country or internationally.

:: ::

The _____ or just chief executive , is the most senior corporate, executive, or administrative officer in charge of managing an organization especially an independent legal entity such as a company or nonprofit institution. CEOs lead a range of organizations, including public and private corporations, non-profit organizations and even some government organizations . The CEO of a corporation or company typically reports to the board of directors and is charged with maximizing the value of the entity, which may include maximizing the share price, market share, revenues or another element. In the non-profit and government sector, CEOs typically aim at achieving outcomes related to the organization`s mission, such as reducing poverty, increasing literacy, etc.

Exam Probability: **Low**

1. *Answer choices:*

(see index for correct answer)

- a. Chief executive officer
- b. hierarchical
- c. functional perspective
- d. surface-level diversity

Guidance: level 1

:: Marketing ::

_____ or stock control can be broadly defined as "the activity of checking a shop's stock." However, a more focused definition takes into account the more science-based, methodical practice of not only verifying a business' inventory but also focusing on the many related facets of inventory management "within an organisation to meet the demand placed upon that business economically." Other facets of _____ include supply chain management, production control, financial flexibility, and customer satisfaction. At the root of _____ , however, is the _____ problem, which involves determining when to order, how much to order, and the logistics of those decisions.

Exam Probability: **Medium**

2. *Answer choices:*

(see index for correct answer)

- a. Inventory control
- b. Lingerie party
- c. Customer newsletter service
- d. Market sector

Guidance: level 1

:: Project management ::

In political science, an _____ is a means by which a petition signed by a certain minimum number of registered voters can force a government to choose to either enact a law or hold a public vote in parliament in what is called indirect _____ , or under direct _____ , the proposition is immediately put to a plebiscite or referendum, in what is called a Popular initiated Referendum or citizen-initiated referendum).

3. *Answer choices:*

(see index for correct answer)

- a. Mandated lead arranger
- b. Initiative
- c. Dependency
- d. Bid manager

Guidance: level 1

:: Goods ::

In most contexts, the concept of _____ denotes the conduct that should be preferred when posed with a choice between possible actions. _____ is generally considered to be the opposite of evil, and is of interest in the study of morality, ethics, religion and philosophy. The specific meaning and etymology of the term and its associated translations among ancient and contemporary languages show substantial variation in its inflection and meaning depending on circumstances of place, history, religious, or philosophical context.

4. *Answer choices:*

(see index for correct answer)

- a. Complementary good
- b. Experience good
- c. Neutral good
- d. Global public good

Guidance: level 1

:: Computer access control ::

_____ is the act of confirming the truth of an attribute of a single piece of data claimed true by an entity. In contrast with identification, which refers to the act of stating or otherwise indicating a claim purportedly attesting to a person's thing's identity, _____ is the process of actually confirming that identity. It might involve confirming the identity of a person by validating their identity documents, verifying the authenticity of a website with a digital certificate, determining the age of an artifact by carbon dating, or ensuring that a product is what its packaging and labeling claim to be. In other words, _____ often involves verifying the validity of at least one form of identification.

Exam Probability: **Low**

5. *Answer choices:*

(see index for correct answer)

- a. Credential lag
- b. Authentication
- c. Wilmagate
- d. Identity driven networking

Guidance: level 1

:: Business law ::

A _____ is a group of people who jointly supervise the activities of an organization, which can be either a for-profit business, nonprofit organization, or a government agency. Such a board's powers, duties, and responsibilities are determined by government regulations and the organization's own constitution and bylaws. These authorities may specify the number of members of the board, how they are to be chosen, and how often they are to meet.

Exam Probability: **Medium**

6. *Answer choices:*

(see index for correct answer)

- a. Limited liability
- b. Board of directors
- c. Security interest
- d. Sole proprietorship

Guidance: level 1

:: ::

The _____ is a U.S. business-focused, English-language international daily newspaper based in New York City. The Journal, along with its Asian and European editions, is published six days a week by Dow Jones & Company, a division of News Corp. The newspaper is published in the broadsheet format and online. The Journal has been printed continuously since its inception on July 8, 1889, by Charles Dow, Edward Jones, and Charles Bergstresser.

Exam Probability: **Medium**

7. *Answer choices:*

(see index for correct answer)

- a. deep-level diversity
- b. Wall Street Journal
- c. hierarchical perspective
- d. process perspective

Guidance: level 1

:: ::

Competition law is a law that promotes or seeks to maintain market competition by regulating anti-competitive conduct by companies. Competition law is implemented through public and private enforcement. Competition law is known as " _____ law" in the United States for historical reasons, and as "anti-monopoly law" in China and Russia. In previous years it has been known as trade practices law in the United Kingdom and Australia. In the European Union, it is referred to as both _____ and competition law.

Exam Probability: **Low**

8. *Answer choices:*

(see index for correct answer)

- a. cultural
- b. Antitrust
- c. Character
- d. levels of analysis

Guidance: level 1

:: Banking ::

A _____ is a financial institution that accepts deposits from the public and creates credit. Lending activities can be performed either directly or indirectly through capital markets. Due to their importance in the financial stability of a country, _____ s are highly regulated in most countries. Most nations have institutionalized a system known as fractional reserve _____ ing under which _____ s hold liquid assets equal to only a portion of their current liabilities. In addition to other regulations intended to ensure liquidity, _____ s are generally subject to minimum capital requirements based on an international set of capital standards, known as the Basel Accords.

Exam Probability: **High**

9. *Answer choices:*

(see index for correct answer)

- a. Prescreen
- b. Bank
- c. Direct debit
- d. Master transaction agreement

Guidance: level 1

:: Insolvency ::

_____ is the process in accounting by which a company is brought to an end in the United Kingdom, Republic of Ireland and United States. The assets and property of the company are redistributed. _____ is also sometimes referred to as winding-up or dissolution, although dissolution technically refers to the last stage of _____ . The process of _____ also arises when customs, an authority or agency in a country responsible for collecting and safeguarding customs duties, determines the final computation or ascertainment of the duties or drawback accruing on an entry.

Exam Probability: **High**

10. *Answer choices:*

(see index for correct answer)

- a. Liquidation
- b. Personal Insolvency Arrangement
- c. George Samuel Ford
- d. Insolvency law of Russia

Guidance: level 1

:: E-commerce ::

_____ is the activity of buying or selling of products on online services or over the Internet. Electronic commerce draws on technologies such as mobile commerce, electronic funds transfer, supply chain management, Internet marketing, online transaction processing, electronic data interchange , inventory management systems, and automated data collection systems.

11. *Answer choices:*

(see index for correct answer)

- a. Electronic Commerce Regulations 2002
- b. Mobilpenge
- c. Camgirl
- d. Steam

Guidance: level 1

:: ::

Business Model Canvas is a strategic management and lean startup template for developing new or documenting existing business models. It is a visual chart with elements describing a firm's or product's value proposition, infrastructure, customers, and finances. It assists firms in aligning their activities by illustrating potential trade-offs.

Exam Probability: **Low**

12. *Answer choices:*

(see index for correct answer)

- a. functional perspective
- b. personal values

- c. surface-level diversity
- d. hierarchical

Guidance: level 1

:: ::

An _____ is an area of the production, distribution, or trade, and consumption of goods and services by different agents. Understood in its broadest sense, `The _____ is defined as a social domain that emphasize the practices, discourses, and material expressions associated with the production, use, and management of resources`. Economic agents can be individuals, businesses, organizations, or governments. Economic transactions occur when two parties agree to the value or price of the transacted good or service, commonly expressed in a certain currency. However, monetary transactions only account for a small part of the economic domain.

Exam Probability: **Medium**

13. *Answer choices:*

(see index for correct answer)

- a. Economy
- b. hierarchical
- c. empathy
- d. surface-level diversity

Guidance: level 1

:: ::

In law, a _____ is a coming together of parties to a dispute, to present information in a tribunal, a formal setting with the authority to adjudicate claims or disputes. One form of tribunal is a court. The tribunal, which may occur before a judge, jury, or other designated trier of fact, aims to achieve a resolution to their dispute.

Exam Probability: **Low**

14. *Answer choices:*

(see index for correct answer)

- a. Trial
- b. deep-level diversity
- c. levels of analysis
- d. similarity-attraction theory

Guidance: level 1

:: ::

_____ is a means of protection from financial loss. It is a form of risk management, primarily used to hedge against the risk of a contingent or uncertain loss

15. *Answer choices:*

(see index for correct answer)

- a. co-culture
- b. levels of analysis
- c. Insurance
- d. personal values

Guidance: level 1

:: Scientific method ::

In the social sciences and life sciences, a _____ is a research method involving an up-close, in-depth, and detailed examination of a subject of study , as well as its related contextual conditions.

Exam Probability: **High**

16. *Answer choices:*

(see index for correct answer)

- a. pilot project
- b. Preference test
- c. explanatory research
- d. Case study

:: Land value taxation ::

_____ , sometimes referred to as dry _____ , is the solid surface of Earth that is not permanently covered by water. The vast majority of human activity throughout history has occurred in _____ areas that support agriculture, habitat, and various natural resources. Some life forms have developed from predecessor species that lived in bodies of water.

Exam Probability: **Medium**

17. *Answer choices:*

(see index for correct answer)

- a. Harry Gunnison Brown
- b. Land
- c. Henry George
- d. Georgism

:: ::

An _____ is the production of goods or related services within an economy. The major source of revenue of a group or company is the indicator of its relevant _____ . When a large group has multiple sources of revenue generation, it is considered to be working in different industries.
Manufacturing _____ became a key sector of production and labour in European and North American countries during the Industrial Revolution, upsetting previous mercantile and feudal economies. This came through many successive rapid advances in technology, such as the production of steel and coal.

Exam Probability: **Low**

18. *Answer choices:*

(see index for correct answer)

- a. similarity-attraction theory
- b. open system
- c. personal values
- d. deep-level diversity

Guidance: level 1

:: ::

In law, an _____ is the process in which cases are reviewed, where parties request a formal change to an official decision. _____ s function both as a process for error correction as well as a process of clarifying and interpreting law. Although appellate courts have existed for thousands of years, common law countries did not incorporate an affirmative right to _____ into their jurisprudence until the 19th century.

Exam Probability: **Low**

19. *Answer choices:*

(see index for correct answer)

- a. corporate values
- b. open system
- c. functional perspective
- d. cultural

Guidance: level 1

:: Supply chain management ::

_____ is the process of finding and agreeing to terms, and acquiring goods, services, or works from an external source, often via a tendering or competitive bidding process. _____ is used to ensure the buyer receives goods, services, or works at the best possible price when aspects such as quality, quantity, time, and location are compared. Corporations and public bodies often define processes intended to promote fair and open competition for their business while minimizing risks such as exposure to fraud and collusion.

20. *Answer choices:*

(see index for correct answer)

- a. Distribution software
- b. Wave picking
- c. Journal of Supply Chain Management
- d. Retalix

Guidance: level 1

:: ::

In marketing jargon, product lining is offering several related products for sale individually. Unlike product bundling, where several products are combined into one group, which is then offered for sale as a units, product lining involves offering the products for sale separately. A line can comprise related products of various sizes, types, colors, qualities, or prices. Line depth refers to the number of subcategories a category has. Line consistency refers to how closely related the products that make up the line are. Line vulnerability refers to the percentage of sales or profits that are derived from only a few products in the line.

Exam Probability: **Medium**

21. *Answer choices:*

(see index for correct answer)

- a. imperative
- b. Sarbanes-Oxley act of 2002
- c. open system
- d. co-culture

Guidance: level 1

:: ::

In economics _____ is a theoretical concept where all markets are in equilibrium, and all prices and quantities have fully adjusted and are in equilibrium. The _____ contrasts with the short run where there are some constraints and markets are not fully in equilibrium.

Exam Probability: **Medium**

22. *Answer choices:*

(see index for correct answer)

- a. interpersonal communication
- b. corporate values
- c. Long run
- d. process perspective

Guidance: level 1

:: E-commerce ::

_____ is a method of e-commerce where shoppers` friends become involved in the shopping experience. _____ attempts to use technology to mimic the social interactions found in physical malls and stores. With the rise of mobile devices, _____ is now extending beyond the online world and into the offline world of shopping.

Exam Probability: **High**

23. *Answer choices:*

(see index for correct answer)

- a. Wildcard certificate
- b. Social shopping
- c. Yemeksepeti
- d. MonkeySports

Guidance: level 1

:: ::

_____ s are formal, sociotechnical, organizational systems designed to collect, process, store, and distribute information. In a sociotechnical perspective, _____ s are composed by four components: task, people, structure , and technology.

24. *Answer choices:*

(see index for correct answer)

- a. Information system
- b. information systems assessment
- c. corporate values
- d. deep-level diversity

Guidance: level 1

:: Commerce ::

_____ relates to "the exchange of goods and services, especially on a large scale". It includes legal, economic, political, social, cultural and technological systems that operate in a country or in international trade.

Exam Probability: **High**

25. *Answer choices:*

(see index for correct answer)

- a. Commerce
- b. International Marketmakers Combination
- c. Bargaining power
- d. Staple right

:: Service industries ::

_____ are the economic services provided by the finance industry, which encompasses a broad range of businesses that manage money, including credit unions, banks, credit-card companies, insurance companies, accountancy companies, consumer-finance companies, stock brokerages, investment funds, individual managers and some government-sponsored enterprises. _____ companies are present in all economically developed geographic locations and tend to cluster in local, national, regional and international financial centers such as London, New York City, and Tokyo.

Exam Probability: **Low**

26. *Answer choices:*

(see index for correct answer)

- a. Financial services in Singapore
- b. Financial services in Japan
- c. Graham Company
- d. Financial services

:: Industrial automation ::

_____ is the technology by which a process or procedure is performed with minimal human assistance. _____ or automatic control is the use of various control systems for operating equipment such as machinery, processes in factories, boilers and heat treating ovens, switching on telephone networks, steering and stabilization of ships, aircraft and other applications and vehicles with minimal or reduced human intervention.

Exam Probability: **Low**

27. *Answer choices:*

(see index for correct answer)

- a. Stack light
- b. TANGO
- c. Automation
- d. DirectLOGIC

Guidance: level 1

:: Management ::

Logistics is generally the detailed organization and implementation of a complex operation. In a general business sense, logistics is the management of the flow of things between the point of origin and the point of consumption in order to meet requirements of customers or corporations. The resources managed in logistics may include tangible goods such as materials, equipment, and supplies, as well as food and other consumable items. The logistics of physical items usually involves the integration of information flow, materials handling, production, packaging, inventory, transportation, warehousing, and often security.

Exam Probability: **Low**

28. *Answer choices:*

(see index for correct answer)

- a. Logistics Management
- b. Capability management
- c. Investment control
- d. Balanced scorecard

Guidance: level 1

:: ::

_____ is the administration of an organization, whether it is a business, a not-for-profit organization, or government body. _____ includes the activities of setting the strategy of an organization and coordinating the efforts of its employees to accomplish its objectives through the application of available resources, such as financial, natural, technological, and human resources. The term " _____ " may also refer to those people who manage an organization.

Exam Probability: **High**

29. *Answer choices:*

(see index for correct answer)

- a. Management
- b. co-culture
- c. Character
- d. hierarchical perspective

Guidance: level 1

:: Management accounting ::

_____ , or dollar contribution per unit, is the selling price per unit minus the variable cost per unit. "Contribution" represents the portion of sales revenue that is not consumed by variable costs and so contributes to the coverage of fixed costs. This concept is one of the key building blocks of break-even analysis.

30. *Answer choices:*

(see index for correct answer)

- a. Contribution margin
- b. Indirect costs
- c. Grenzplankostenrechnung
- d. Bridge life-cycle cost analysis

Guidance: level 1

:: ::

A _____ is a fund into which a sum of money is added during an employee's employment years, and from which payments are drawn to support the person's retirement from work in the form of periodic payments. A _____ may be a "defined benefit plan" where a fixed sum is paid regularly to a person, or a "defined contribution plan" under which a fixed sum is invested and then becomes available at retirement age. _____ s should not be confused with severance pay; the former is usually paid in regular installments for life after retirement, while the latter is typically paid as a fixed amount after involuntary termination of employment prior to retirement.

Exam Probability: **Low**

31. *Answer choices:*

(see index for correct answer)

- a. Character
- b. hierarchical
- c. Sarbanes-Oxley act of 2002
- d. deep-level diversity

Guidance: level 1

:: Human resource management ::

_____ are the people who make up the workforce of an organization, business sector, or economy. "Human capital" is sometimes used synonymously with " _____ ", although human capital typically refers to a narrower effect . Likewise, other terms sometimes used include manpower, talent, labor, personnel, or simply people.

Exam Probability: **High**

32. *Answer choices:*

(see index for correct answer)

- a. Leadership development
- b. Expense management
- c. T-shaped skills
- d. Vendor on premises

Guidance: level 1

:: Export and import control ::

" _____ " means the Government Service which is responsible for the administration of _____ law and the collection of duties and taxes and which also has the responsibility for the application of other laws and regulations relating to the importation, exportation, movement or storage of goods.

Exam Probability: **Low**

33. *Answer choices:*

(see index for correct answer)

- a. Import parity price
- b. Plant Protection and Quarantine
- c. Wassenaar Arrangement
- d. Customs

Guidance: level 1

:: ::

In business, overhead or overhead expense refers to an ongoing expense of operating a business. Overheads are the expenditure which cannot be conveniently traced to or identified with any particular cost unit, unlike operating expenses such as raw material and labor. Therefore, overheads cannot be immediately associated with the products or services being offered, thus do not directly generate profits. However, overheads are still vital to business operations as they provide critical support for the business to carry out profit making activities. For example, _____ s such as the rent for a factory allows workers to manufacture products which can then be sold for a profit. Such expenses are incurred for output generally and not for particular work order; e.g., wages paid to watch and ward staff, heating and lighting expenses of factory, etc. Overheads are also very important cost element along with direct materials and direct labor.

Exam Probability: **High**

34. *Answer choices:*

(see index for correct answer)

- a. personal values
- b. co-culture
- c. hierarchical
- d. Sarbanes-Oxley act of 2002

Guidance: level 1

:: ::

_____ is getting a diploma or academic degree or the ceremony that is sometimes associated with it, in which students become graduates. The date of _____ is often called _____ day. The _____ ceremony itself is also called commencement, convocation or invocation.

Exam Probability: **High**

35. *Answer choices:*

(see index for correct answer)

- a. similarity-attraction theory
- b. process perspective
- c. co-culture
- d. levels of analysis

Guidance: level 1

:: Dot-com bubble ::

_____ is an internet portal launched in 1995 that provides a variety of content including news and weather, a metasearch engine, a web-based email, instant messaging, stock quotes, and a customizable user homepage. It is currently operated by IAC Applications of IAC, and _____ Networks. In the U.S., the main _____ site has long been a personal start page called My _____ . _____ also operates an e-mail service, although it is no longer open for new customers.

Exam Probability: **High**

36. *Answer choices:*

(see index for correct answer)

- a. E-Dreams
- b. Excite
- c. The Industry Standard
- d. Internet time

Guidance: level 1

:: ::

_____ is a term frequently used in marketing. It is a measure of how products and services supplied by a company meet or surpass customer expectation. _____ is defined as "the number of customers, or percentage of total customers, whose reported experience with a firm, its products, or its services exceeds specified satisfaction goals."

Exam Probability: **Medium**

37. *Answer choices:*

(see index for correct answer)

- a. similarity-attraction theory
- b. levels of analysis
- c. Customer satisfaction
- d. deep-level diversity

:: Payment systems ::

_____ s are part of a payment system issued by financial institutions, such as a bank, to a customer that enables its owner to access the funds in the customer's designated bank accounts, or through a credit account and make payments by electronic funds transfer and access automated teller machines . Such cards are known by a variety of names including bank cards, ATM cards, MAC , client cards, key cards or cash cards.

Exam Probability: **Medium**

38. *Answer choices:*

(see index for correct answer)

- a. BASE24
- b. VocaLink
- c. PA-DSS
- d. Boleto

:: Contract law ::

A _____ is a legally-binding agreement which recognises and governs the rights and duties of the parties to the agreement. A _____ is legally enforceable because it meets the requirements and approval of the law. An agreement typically involves the exchange of goods, services, money, or promises of any of those. In the event of breach of _____ , the law awards the injured party access to legal remedies such as damages and cancellation.

Exam Probability: **Low**

39. *Answer choices:*

(see index for correct answer)

- a. Frustration of purpose
- b. Contract
- c. Fair Food Program
- d. Collateral assurance

Guidance: level 1

:: ::

_____ Corporation is an American multinational technology company with headquarters in Redmond, Washington. It develops, manufactures, licenses, supports and sells computer software, consumer electronics, personal computers, and related services. Its best known software products are the _____ Windows line of operating systems, the _____ Office suite, and the Internet Explorer and Edge Web browsers. Its flagship hardware products are the Xbox video game consoles and the _____ Surface lineup of touchscreen personal computers. As of 2016, it is the world's largest software maker by revenue, and one of the world's most valuable companies. The word " _____ " is a portmanteau of "microcomputer" and "software". _____ is ranked No. 30 in the 2018 Fortune 500 rankings of the largest United States corporations by total revenue.

Exam Probability: **Low**

40. *Answer choices:*

(see index for correct answer)

- a. open system
- b. Microsoft
- c. hierarchical
- d. functional perspective

Guidance: level 1

:: Meetings ::

A _____ is a body of one or more persons that is subordinate to a deliberative assembly. Usually, the assembly sends matters into a _____ as a way to explore them more fully than would be possible if the assembly itself were considering them. _____ s may have different functions and their type of work differ depending on the type of the organization and its needs.

Exam Probability: **Low**

41. *Answer choices:*

(see index for correct answer)

- a. Program book
- b. CodeCamp
- c. Committee
- d. Evoma

Guidance: level 1

:: Stock market ::

_____ is freedom from, or resilience against, potential harm caused by others. Beneficiaries of _____ may be of persons and social groups, objects and institutions, ecosystems or any other entity or phenomenon vulnerable to unwanted change by its environment.

Exam Probability: **Medium**

42. *Answer choices:*

(see index for correct answer)

- a. Underweight
- b. Abnormal return
- c. Security
- d. The Congressional Effect

Guidance: level 1

:: Business models ::

A _____ is "an autonomous association of persons united voluntarily to meet their common economic, social, and cultural needs and aspirations through a jointly-owned and democratically-controlled enterprise". _____ s may include.

Exam Probability: **Medium**

43. *Answer choices:*

(see index for correct answer)

- a. Very small business
- b. Cooperative
- c. Pay to play
- d. Collective business system

:: ::

A _____ is a person who trades in commodities produced by other people. Historically, a _____ is anyone who is involved in business or trade. _____ s have operated for as long as industry, commerce, and trade have existed. During the 16th-century, in Europe, two different terms for _____ s emerged: One term, meerseniers, described local traders such as bakers, grocers, etc.; while a new term, koopman (Dutch: koopman, described _____ s who operated on a global stage, importing and exporting goods over vast distances, and offering added-value services such as credit and finance.

Exam Probability: **Medium**

44. *Answer choices:*

(see index for correct answer)

- a. empathy
- b. Merchant
- c. imperative
- d. corporate values

:: Real estate ::

_____ s serve several societal needs – primarily as shelter from weather, security, living space, privacy, to store belongings, and to comfortably live and work. A _____ as a shelter represents a physical division of the human habitat and the outside .

Exam Probability: **High**

45. *Answer choices:*

(see index for correct answer)

- a. Conditional sale
- b. Chambre de bonne
- c. Real estate transaction
- d. Latifundium

Guidance: level 1

:: Business law ::

A _____ is a contractual arrangement calling for the lessee to pay the lessor for use of an asset. Property, buildings and vehicles are common assets that are _____ d. Industrial or business equipment is also _____ d.

Exam Probability: **Medium**

46. *Answer choices:*

(see index for correct answer)

- a. Uniform Commercial Code
- b. Board of directors
- c. Partnership
- d. Lease

Guidance: level 1

:: ::

In mathematics, computer science and operations research, mathematical optimization or mathematical programming is the selection of a best element from some set of available alternatives.

Exam Probability: **Low**

47. *Answer choices:*

(see index for correct answer)

- a. Optimum
- b. empathy
- c. imperative
- d. surface-level diversity

Guidance: level 1

:: Commercial item transport and distribution ::

Wholesaling or distributing is the sale of goods or merchandise to retailers; to industrial, commercial, institutional, or other professional business users; or to other _____ rs and related subordinated services. In general, it is the sale of goods to anyone other than a standard consumer.

Exam Probability: **Medium**

48. *Answer choices:*

(see index for correct answer)

- a. Affreightment
- b. Wholesale
- c. Pallet
- d. Containerization

Guidance: level 1

:: Cryptography ::

In cryptography, _____ is the process of encoding a message or information in such a way that only authorized parties can access it and those who are not authorized cannot. _____ does not itself prevent interference, but denies the intelligible content to a would-be interceptor. In an _____ scheme, the intended information or message, referred to as plaintext, is encrypted using an _____ algorithm – a cipher – generating ciphertext that can be read only if decrypted. For technical reasons, an _____ scheme usually uses a pseudo-random _____ key generated by an algorithm. It is in principle possible to decrypt the message without possessing the key, but, for a well-designed _____ scheme, considerable computational resources and skills are required. An authorized recipient can easily decrypt the message with the key provided by the originator to recipients but not to unauthorized users.

Exam Probability: **Low**

49. *Answer choices:*

(see index for correct answer)

- a. plaintext
- b. Encryption
- c. cryptosystem
- d. ciphertext

Guidance: level 1

:: Stock market ::

The _____ of a corporation is all of the shares into which ownership of the corporation is divided. In American English, the shares are commonly known as "_____ s". A single share of the _____ represents fractional ownership of the corporation in proportion to the total number of shares. This typically entitles the _____ holder to that fraction of the company's earnings, proceeds from liquidation of assets , or voting power, often dividing these up in proportion to the amount of money each _____ holder has invested. Not all _____ is necessarily equal, as certain classes of _____ may be issued for example without voting rights, with enhanced voting rights, or with a certain priority to receive profits or liquidation proceeds before or after other classes of shareholders.

Exam Probability: **High**

50. *Answer choices:*

(see index for correct answer)

- a. Mr. Market
- b. Pattern day trader
- c. Stock
- d. Uptick rule

Guidance: level 1

:: ::

In legal terminology, a _____ is any formal legal document that sets out the facts and legal reasons that the filing party or parties believes are sufficient to support a claim against the party or parties against whom the claim is brought that entitles the plaintiff to a remedy . For example, the Federal Rules of Civil Procedure that govern civil litigation in United States courts provide that a civil action is commenced with the filing or service of a pleading called a _____ . Civil court rules in states that have incorporated the Federal Rules of Civil Procedure use the same term for the same pleading.

Exam Probability: **Low**

51. *Answer choices:*

(see index for correct answer)

- a. personal values
- b. similarity-attraction theory
- c. hierarchical perspective
- d. co-culture

Guidance: level 1

:: Organizational structure ::

An _____ defines how activities such as task allocation, coordination, and supervision are directed toward the achievement of organizational aims.

Exam Probability: **High**

52. *Answer choices:*

- a. Automated Bureaucracy
- b. Followership
- c. Blessed Unrest
- d. Unorganisation

Guidance: level 1

:: ::

_____ , also referred to as orthostasis, is a human position in which the body is held in an upright position and supported only by the feet.

Exam Probability: **High**

53. *Answer choices:*

- a. hierarchical perspective
- b. cultural
- c. surface-level diversity
- d. Standing

Guidance: level 1

:: Human resource management ::

An organizational chart is a diagram that shows the structure of an organization and the relationships and relative ranks of its parts and positions/jobs. The term is also used for similar diagrams, for example ones showing the different elements of a field of knowledge or a group of languages.

Exam Probability: **Low**

54. *Answer choices:*

(see index for correct answer)

- a. Management development
- b. Organization chart
- c. Vendor on premises
- d. Kelly Services

Guidance: level 1

:: ::

Regulatory economics is the economics of regulation. It is the application of law by government or independent administrative agencies for various purposes, including remedying market failure, protecting the environment, centrally-planning an economy, enriching well-connected firms, or benefiting politicians.

55. *Answer choices:*

(see index for correct answer)

- a. hierarchical
- b. Sarbanes-Oxley act of 2002
- c. Character
- d. Economic regulation

Guidance: level 1

:: Income ::

In business and accounting, net income is an entity's income minus cost of goods sold, expenses and taxes for an accounting period. It is computed as the residual of all revenues and gains over all expenses and losses for the period, and has also been defined as the net increase in shareholders' equity that results from a company's operations. In the context of the presentation of financial statements, the IFRS Foundation defines net income as synonymous with profit and loss. The difference between revenue and the cost of making a product or providing a service, before deducting overheads, payroll, taxation, and interest payments. This is different from operating income .

Exam Probability: **High**

56. *Answer choices:*

(see index for correct answer)

- a. Implied level of government service
- b. Trinity study
- c. Pay grade
- d. Income Per User

Guidance: level 1

:: ::

_____ or standardisation is the process of implementing and developing technical standards based on the consensus of different parties that include firms, users, interest groups, standards organizations and governments. _____ can help maximize compatibility, interoperability, safety, repeatability, or quality. It can also facilitate commoditization of formerly custom processes. In social sciences, including economics, the idea of _____ is close to the solution for a coordination problem, a situation in which all parties can realize mutual gains, but only by making mutually consistent decisions. This view includes the case of "spontaneous _____ processes", to produce de facto standards.

Exam Probability: **High**

57. *Answer choices:*

(see index for correct answer)

- a. Standardization
- b. functional perspective
- c. information systems assessment
- d. surface-level diversity

:: ::

_____ is the practice of deliberately managing the spread of information between an individual or an organization and the public. _____ may include an organization or individual gaining exposure to their audiences using topics of public interest and news items that do not require direct payment. This differentiates it from advertising as a form of marketing communications. _____ is the idea of creating coverage for clients for free, rather than marketing or advertising. But now, advertising is also a part of greater PR Activities.An example of good _____ would be generating an article featuring a client, rather than paying for the client to be advertised next to the article. The aim of _____ is to inform the public, prospective customers, investors, partners, employees, and other stakeholders and ultimately persuade them to maintain a positive or favorable view about the organization, its leadership, products, or political decisions. _____ professionals typically work for PR and marketing firms, businesses and companies, government, and public officials as PIOs and nongovernmental organizations, and nonprofit organizations. Jobs central to _____ include account coordinator, account executive, account supervisor, and media relations manager.

Exam Probability: **Low**

58. *Answer choices:*

(see index for correct answer)

- a. hierarchical perspective
- b. imperative
- c. co-culture

- d. Public relations

Guidance: level 1

:: Economics terminology ::

_____ is the total receipts a seller can obtain from selling goods or services to buyers. It can be written as P × Q, which is the price of the goods multiplied by the quantity of the sold goods.

Exam Probability: **High**

59. *Answer choices:*

(see index for correct answer)

- a. Total revenue
- b. Capital stock
- c. Capital cost
- d. payee

Guidance: level 1

Business ethics

Business ethics (also known as corporate ethics) is a form of applied ethics or professional ethics, that examines ethical principles and moral or ethical problems that can arise in a business environment. It applies to all aspects of business conduct and is relevant to the conduct of individuals and entire organizations. These ethics originate from individuals, organizational statements or from the legal system. These norms, values, ethical, and unethical practices are what is used to guide business. They help those businesses maintain a better connection with their stakeholders.

:: Water law ::

The _____ is the primary federal law in the United States governing water pollution. Its objective is to restore and maintain the chemical, physical, and biological integrity of the nation's waters; recognizing the responsibilities of the states in addressing pollution and providing assistance to states to do so, including funding for publicly owned treatment works for the improvement of wastewater treatment; and maintaining the integrity of wetlands. It is one of the United States' first and most influential modern environmental laws. As with many other major U.S. federal environmental statutes, it is administered by the U.S. Environmental Protection Agency , in coordination with state governments. Its implementing regulations are codified at 40 C.F.R. Subchapters D, N, and O .

Exam Probability: **Medium**

1. *Answer choices:*

(see index for correct answer)

- a. Permanent water rights
- b. Water right
- c. Clean Water Act
- d. Return flow

Guidance: level 1

:: Agricultural labor ::

The _____ of America, or more commonly just _____ , is a labor union for farmworkers in the United States. It originated from the merger of two workers' rights organizations, the Agricultural Workers Organizing Committee led by organizer Larry Itliong, and the National Farm Workers Association led by César Chávez and Dolores Huerta. They became allied and transformed from workers' rights organizations into a union as a result of a series of strikes in 1965, when the mostly Filipino farmworkers of the AWOC in Delano, California initiated a grape strike, and the NFWA went on strike in support. As a result of the commonality in goals and methods, the NFWA and the AWOC formed the _____ Organizing Committee on August 22, 1966. This organization was accepted into the AFL-CIO in 1972 and changed its name to the _____ Union.

Exam Probability: **Medium**

2. *Answer choices:*

(see index for correct answer)

- a. Landwirtschaftliche Produktionsgenossenschaft
- b. State Agricultural Farm
- c. Kibbutz volunteer
- d. United Farm Workers

Guidance: level 1

:: ::

_____ ism is a form of government characterized by strong central power and limited political freedoms. Individual freedoms are subordinate to the state and there is no constitutional accountability and rule of law under an _____ regime. _____ regimes can be autocratic with power concentrated in one person or it can be more spread out between multiple officials and government institutions. Juan Linz`s influential 1964 description of _____ ism characterized _____ political systems by four qualities.

Exam Probability: **High**

3. *Answer choices:*

(see index for correct answer)

- a. deep-level diversity
- b. personal values
- c. hierarchical perspective
- d. Authoritarian

Guidance: level 1

:: ::

A _____ is a set of rules, often written, with regards to clothing. _____ s are created out of social perceptions and norms, and vary based on purpose, circumstances and occasions. Different societies and cultures are likely to have different _____ s.

4. *Answer choices:*

(see index for correct answer)

- a. personal values
- b. hierarchical
- c. Dress code
- d. surface-level diversity

Guidance: level 1

:: Confidence tricks ::

A _____ is a business model that recruits members via a promise of payments or services for enrolling others into the scheme, rather than supplying investments or sale of products. As recruiting multiplies, recruiting becomes quickly impossible, and most members are unable to profit; as such, _____ s are unsustainable and often illegal.

Exam Probability: **High**

5. *Answer choices:*

(see index for correct answer)

- a. Great Oil Sniffer Hoax
- b. Pyramid scheme

- c. Email fraud
- d. Mock auction

Guidance: level 1

:: ::

_____ is the collection of mechanisms, processes and relations by which corporations are controlled and operated. Governance structures and principles identify the distribution of rights and responsibilities among different participants in the corporation and include the rules and procedures for making decisions in corporate affairs. _____ is necessary because of the possibility of conflicts of interests between stakeholders, primarily between shareholders and upper management or among shareholders.

Exam Probability: **Low**

6. *Answer choices:*

(see index for correct answer)

- a. hierarchical
- b. open system
- c. Corporate governance
- d. levels of analysis

Guidance: level 1

:: Business ethics ::

A _____ is a person who exposes any kind of information or activity that is deemed illegal, unethical, or not correct within an organization that is either private or public. The information of alleged wrongdoing can be classified in many ways: violation of company policy/rules, law, regulation, or threat to public interest/national security, as well as fraud, and corruption. Those who become _____ s can choose to bring information or allegations to surface either internally or externally. Internally, a _____ can bring his/her accusations to the attention of other people within the accused organization such as an immediate supervisor. Externally, a _____ can bring allegations to light by contacting a third party outside of an accused organization such as the media, government, law enforcement, or those who are concerned. _____ s, however, take the risk of facing stiff reprisal and retaliation from those who are accused or alleged of wrongdoing.

Exam Probability: **High**

7. *Answer choices:*

(see index for correct answer)

- a. Corporate sustainability
- b. Centre for Research on Multinational Corporations
- c. Enron Code of Ethics
- d. Repugnant market

Guidance: level 1

:: ::

The _____ of 1973 serves as the enacting legislation to carry out the provisions outlined in The Convention on International Trade in Endangered Species of Wild Fauna and Flora . Designed to protect critically imperiled species from extinction as a "consequence of economic growth and development untempered by adequate concern and conservation", the ESA was signed into law by President Richard Nixon on December 28, 1973. The law requires federal agencies to consult with the Fish and Wildlife Service &/or the NOAA Fisheries Service to ensure their actions are not likely to jeopardize the continued existence of any listed species or result in the destruction or adverse modification of designated critical habitat of such species. The U.S. Supreme Court found that "the plain intent of Congress in enacting" the ESA "was to halt and reverse the trend toward species extinction, whatever the cost." The Act is administered by two federal agencies, the United States Fish and Wildlife Service and the National Marine Fisheries Service .

Exam Probability: **Medium**

8. *Answer choices:*

(see index for correct answer)

- a. levels of analysis
- b. imperative
- c. process perspective
- d. Endangered Species Act

Guidance: level 1

:: ::

_____ is the study and management of exchange relationships. _____ is the business process of creating relationships with and satisfying customers. With its focus on the customer, _____ is one of the premier components of business management.

Exam Probability: **High**

9. *Answer choices:*

(see index for correct answer)

- a. personal values
- b. corporate values
- c. information systems assessment
- d. hierarchical perspective

Guidance: level 1

:: Toxicology ::

_____ or lead-based paint is paint containing lead. As pigment, lead chromate , Lead oxide, , and lead carbonate are the most common forms. Lead is added to paint to accelerate drying, increase durability, maintain a fresh appearance, and resist moisture that causes corrosion. It is one of the main health and environmental hazards associated with paint. In some countries, lead continues to be added to paint intended for domestic use, whereas countries such as the U.S. and the UK have regulations prohibiting this, although _____ may still be found in older properties painted prior to the introduction of such regulations. Although lead has been banned from household paints in the United States since 1978, paint used in road markings may still contain it. Alternatives such as water-based, lead-free traffic paint are readily available, and many states and federal agencies have changed their purchasing contracts to buy these instead.

Exam Probability: **High**

10. *Answer choices:*

(see index for correct answer)

- a. Lead paint
- b. Pollutant
- c. Kombucha
- d. Evidence-based toxicology

Guidance: level 1

:: Mortgage ::

In finance, _____ means making loans to people who may have difficulty maintaining the repayment schedule, sometimes reflecting setbacks, such as unemployment, divorce, medical emergencies, etc. Historically, subprime borrowers were defined as having FICO scores below 600, although "this has varied over time and circumstances."

Exam Probability: **Low**

11. *Answer choices:*

(see index for correct answer)

- a. Foreclosure
- b. Mortgage analytics
- c. Foreclosure rescue scheme
- d. Subprime lending

Guidance: level 1

:: Reputation management ::

_____ or image of a social entity is an opinion about that entity, typically as a result of social evaluation on a set of criteria.

Exam Probability: **High**

12. *Answer choices:*

(see index for correct answer)

- a. Star
- b. Reputation
- c. personal brand
- d. The Economy of Esteem

Guidance: level 1

:: False advertising law ::

The Lanham Act is the primary federal trademark statute of law in the United States. The Act prohibits a number of activities, including trademark infringement, trademark dilution, and false advertising.

Exam Probability: **Medium**

13. *Answer choices:*

(see index for correct answer)

- a. Lanham Act
- b. POM Wonderful LLC v. Coca-Cola Co.

Guidance: level 1

:: ::

_____ is an eight-block-long street running roughly northwest to southeast from Broadway to South Street, at the East River, in the Financial District of Lower Manhattan in New York City. Over time, the term has become a metonym for the financial markets of the United States as a whole, the American financial services industry , or New York–based financial interests.

Exam Probability: **Low**

14. *Answer choices:*

(see index for correct answer)

- a. Character
- b. imperative
- c. surface-level diversity
- d. Wall Street

Guidance: level 1

:: Industrial ecology ::

_____ is a strategy for reducing the amount of waste created and released into the environment, particularly by industrial facilities, agriculture, or consumers. Many large corporations view P2 as a method of improving the efficiency and profitability of production processes by technology advancements. Legislative bodies have enacted P2 measures, such as the _____ Act of 1990 and the Clean Air Act Amendments of 1990 by the United States Congress.

Exam Probability: **Medium**

15. *Answer choices:*

(see index for correct answer)

- a. Pollution Prevention
- b. Best available technology
- c. Efficient energy use
- d. Material criticality

Guidance: level 1

:: Real estate ::

_____ s serve several societal needs – primarily as shelter from weather, security, living space, privacy, to store belongings, and to comfortably live and work. A _____ as a shelter represents a physical division of the human habitat and the outside .

Exam Probability: **Low**

16. *Answer choices:*

(see index for correct answer)

- a. Real-estate lock box
- b. Real estate pricing
- c. Property ladder

- d. Building

Guidance: level 1

:: ::

The _____ of 1906 was the first of a series of significant consumer protection laws which was enacted by Congress in the 20th century and led to the creation of the Food and Drug Administration. Its main purpose was to ban foreign and interstate traffic in adulterated or mislabeled food and drug products, and it directed the U.S. Bureau of Chemistry to inspect products and refer offenders to prosecutors. It required that active ingredients be placed on the label of a drug's packaging and that drugs could not fall below purity levels established by the United States Pharmacopeia or the National Formulary. The Jungle by Upton Sinclair with its graphic and revolting descriptions of unsanitary conditions and unscrupulous practices rampant in the meatpacking industry, was an inspirational piece that kept the public's attention on the important issue of unhygienic meat processing plants that later led to food inspection legislation. Sinclair quipped, "I aimed at the public's heart and by accident I hit it in the stomach," as outraged readers demanded and got the pure food law.

Exam Probability: **High**

17. *Answer choices:*

(see index for correct answer)

- a. empathy
- b. Character
- c. open system

- d. process perspective

Guidance: level 1

:: Leadership ::

_____ is a theory of leadership where a leader works with teams to identify needed change, creating a vision to guide the change through inspiration, and executing the change in tandem with committed members of a group; it is an integral part of the Full Range Leadership Model. _____ serves to enhance the motivation, morale, and job performance of followers through a variety of mechanisms; these include connecting the follower's sense of identity and self to a project and to the collective identity of the organization; being a role model for followers in order to inspire them and to raise their interest in the project; challenging followers to take greater ownership for their work, and understanding the strengths and weaknesses of followers, allowing the leader to align followers with tasks that enhance their performance.

Exam Probability: **Low**

18. *Answer choices:*

(see index for correct answer)

- a. Tribal Leadership
- b. The Leadership Council
- c. Ethical leadership
- d. Transformational leadership

Guidance: level 1

:: Offshoring ::

A _____ is the temporary suspension or permanent termination of employment of an employee or, more commonly, a group of employees for business reasons, such as personnel management or downsizing an organization. Originally, _____ referred exclusively to a temporary interruption in work, or employment but this has evolved to a permanent elimination of a position in both British and US English, requiring the addition of "temporary" to specify the original meaning of the word. A _____ is not to be confused with wrongful termination. Laid off workers or displaced workers are workers who have lost or left their jobs because their employer has closed or moved, there was insufficient work for them to do, or their position or shift was abolished . Downsizing in a company is defined to involve the reduction of employees in a workforce. Downsizing in companies became a popular practice in the 1980s and early 1990s as it was seen as a way to deliver better shareholder value as it helps to reduce the costs of employers . Indeed, recent research on downsizing in the U.S., UK, and Japan suggests that downsizing is being regarded by management as one of the preferred routes to help declining organizations, cutting unnecessary costs, and improve organizational performance. Usually a _____ occurs as a cost cutting measure.

Exam Probability: **Medium**

19. *Answer choices:*

(see index for correct answer)

- a. Advanced Contact Solutions
- b. Avasant
- c. Layoff
- d. TeleTech

:: Television terminology ::

A _____ organization , also known as a non-business entity, not-for-profit organization, or _____ institution, is dedicated to furthering a particular social cause or advocating for a shared point of view. In economic terms, it is an organization that uses its surplus of the revenues to further achieve its ultimate objective, rather than distributing its income to the organization's shareholders, leaders, or members. _____ s are tax exempt or charitable, meaning they do not pay income tax on the money that they receive for their organization. They can operate in religious, scientific, research, or educational settings.

Exam Probability: **Low**

20. *Answer choices:*

(see index for correct answer)

- a. distance learning
- b. multiplexing
- c. not-for-profit
- d. Satellite television

:: Statutory law ::

_____ or statute law is written law set down by a body of legislature or by a singular legislator . This is as opposed to oral or customary law; or regulatory law promulgated by the executive or common law of the judiciary. Statutes may originate with national, state legislatures or local municipalities.

Exam Probability: **Medium**

21. *Answer choices:*

(see index for correct answer)

- a. ratification
- b. Statutory law
- c. incorporation by reference
- d. Statute of repose

Guidance: level 1

:: Fraud ::

In law, _____ is intentional deception to secure unfair or unlawful gain, or to deprive a victim of a legal right. _____ can violate civil law , a criminal law , or it may cause no loss of money, property or legal right but still be an element of another civil or criminal wrong. The purpose of _____ may be monetary gain or other benefits, for example by obtaining a passport, travel document, or driver's license, or mortgage _____ : where the perpetrator may attempt to qualify for a mortgage by way of false statements.

22. *Answer choices:*

(see index for correct answer)

- a. Fraud
- b. Virginity fraud
- c. Cheat sheet
- d. Lottery scam

Guidance: level 1

:: United States federal trade legislation ::

The _____ of 1914 established the Federal Trade Commission. The Act, signed into law by Woodrow Wilson in 1914, outlaws unfair methods of competition and outlaws unfair acts or practices that affect commerce.

Exam Probability: **Low**

23. *Answer choices:*

(see index for correct answer)

- a. Tariff of 1883
- b. Tariff of Abominations
- c. Trade Act of 2002
- d. Federal Trade Commission Act

:: ::

> An _____ is the release of a liquid petroleum hydrocarbon into the environment, especially the marine ecosystem, due to human activity, and is a form of pollution. The term is usually given to marine _____ s, where oil is released into the ocean or coastal waters, but spills may also occur on land. _____ s may be due to releases of crude oil from tankers, offshore platforms, drilling rigs and wells, as well as spills of refined petroleum products and their by-products, heavier fuels used by large ships such as bunker fuel, or the spill of any oily refuse or waste oil.

Exam Probability: **Low**

24. *Answer choices:*

(see index for correct answer)

- a. information systems assessment
- b. Oil spill
- c. process perspective
- d. hierarchical perspective

Guidance: level 1

:: United States federal defense and national security legislation ::

The USA _____ is an Act of the U.S. Congress that was signed into law by President George W. Bush on October 26, 2001. The title of the Act is a contrived three letter initialism preceding a seven letter acronym , which in combination stand for Uniting and Strengthening America by Providing Appropriate Tools Required to Intercept and Obstruct Terrorism Act of 2001. The acronym was created by a 23 year old Congressional staffer, Chris Kyle.

Exam Probability: **High**

25. *Answer choices:*

(see index for correct answer)

- a. Export Administration Act
- b. Patriot Act

Guidance: level 1

:: ::

_____ Ltd. is the world`s 2nd largest offshore drilling contractor and is based in Vernier, Switzerland. The company has offices in 20 countries, including Switzerland, Canada, United States, Norway, Scotland, India, Brazil, Singapore, Indonesia and Malaysia.

Exam Probability: **High**

26. *Answer choices:*

- a. corporate values
- b. Transocean
- c. co-culture
- d. personal values

Guidance: level 1

:: Renewable energy ::

A _____ is a fuel that is produced through contemporary biological processes, such as agriculture and anaerobic digestion, rather than a fuel produced by geological processes such as those involved in the formation of fossil fuels, such as coal and petroleum, from prehistoric biological matter. If the source biomatter can regrow quickly, the resulting fuel is said to be a form of renewable energy.

Exam Probability: **Medium**

27. *Answer choices:*

- a. Wind power
- b. Biofuel
- c. Biomass
- d. Crosswind kite power

:: Corporate scandals ::

Exxon Mobil Corporation, doing business as _____ , is an American multinational oil and gas corporation headquartered in Irving, Texas. It is the largest direct descendant of John D. Rockefeller's Standard Oil Company, and was formed on November 30, 1999 by the merger of Exxon and Mobil . _____ 's primary brands are Exxon, Mobil, Esso, and _____ Chemical.

Exam Probability: **High**

28. *Answer choices:*

(see index for correct answer)

- a. ExxonMobil
- b. China Aviation Oil
- c. Great Phenol Plot
- d. Tunku Abdul Majid

:: ::

The _____ is an institution of the European Union, responsible for proposing legislation, implementing decisions, upholding the EU treaties and managing the day-to-day business of the EU. Commissioners swear an oath at the European Court of Justice in Luxembourg City, pledging to respect the treaties and to be completely independent in carrying out their duties during their mandate. Unlike in the Council of the European Union, where members are directly and indirectly elected, and the European Parliament, where members are directly elected, the Commissioners are proposed by the Council of the European Union, on the basis of suggestions made by the national governments, and then appointed by the European Council after the approval of the European Parliament.

29. *Answer choices:*

(see index for correct answer)

- a. imperative
- b. open system
- c. co-culture
- d. European Commission

Guidance: level 1

:: Progressive Era in the United States ::

The Clayton Antitrust Act of 1914 , was a part of United States antitrust law with the goal of adding further substance to the U.S. antitrust law regime; the _____ sought to prevent anticompetitive practices in their incipiency. That regime started with the Sherman Antitrust Act of 1890, the first Federal law outlawing practices considered harmful to consumers . The _____ specified particular prohibited conduct, the three-level enforcement scheme, the exemptions, and the remedial measures.

Exam Probability: **Low**

30. *Answer choices:*

(see index for correct answer)

- a. pragmatism
- b. Mann Act
- c. Clayton Act

Guidance: level 1

:: Minimum wage ::

The _____ are working people whose incomes fall below a given poverty line due to lack of work hours and/or low wages.Largely because they are earning such low wages, the _____ face numerous obstacles that make it difficult for many of them to find and keep a job, save up money, and maintain a sense of self-worth.

Exam Probability: **Low**

31. *Answer choices:*

(see index for correct answer)

- a. Minimum Wage Fairness Act
- b. Working poor
- c. Guaranteed minimum income
- d. Minimum wage

Guidance: level 1

:: Corporate governance ::

_____ refers to the practice of members of a corporate board of directors serving on the boards of multiple corporations. A person that sits on multiple boards is known as a multiple director. Two firms have a direct interlock if a director or executive of one firm is also a director of the other, and an indirect interlock if a director of each sits on the board of a third firm. This practice, although widespread and lawful, raises questions about the quality and independence of board decisions.

Exam Probability: **Low**

32. *Answer choices:*

(see index for correct answer)

- a. The Modern Corporation and Private Property
- b. Interlocking directorate
- c. Chief product officer

- d. AS 8015

Guidance: level 1

:: ::

A _____ is a proceeding by a party or parties against another in the civil court of law. The archaic term "suit in law" is found in only a small number of laws still in effect today. The term " _____ " is used in reference to a civil action brought in a court of law in which a plaintiff, a party who claims to have incurred loss as a result of a defendant's actions, demands a legal or equitable remedy. The defendant is required to respond to the plaintiff's complaint. If the plaintiff is successful, judgment is in the plaintiff's favor, and a variety of court orders may be issued to enforce a right, award damages, or impose a temporary or permanent injunction to prevent an act or compel an act. A declaratory judgment may be issued to prevent future legal disputes.

Exam Probability: **High**

33. *Answer choices:*

(see index for correct answer)

- a. personal values
- b. hierarchical perspective
- c. functional perspective
- d. surface-level diversity

Guidance: level 1

:: ::

_____ Corporation was an American energy, commodities, and services company based in Houston, Texas. It was founded in 1985 as a merger between Houston Natural Gas and InterNorth, both relatively small regional companies. Before its bankruptcy on December 3, 2001, _____ employed approximately 29,000 staff and was a major electricity, natural gas, communications and pulp and paper company, with claimed revenues of nearly $101 billion during 2000. Fortune named _____ "America's Most Innovative Company" for six consecutive years.

Exam Probability: **Medium**

34. *Answer choices:*

(see index for correct answer)

- a. similarity-attraction theory
- b. Enron
- c. Sarbanes-Oxley act of 2002
- d. surface-level diversity

Guidance: level 1

:: Monopoly (economics) ::

A _____ is a form of intellectual property that gives its owner the legal right to exclude others from making, using, selling, and importing an invention for a limited period of years, in exchange for publishing an enabling public disclosure of the invention. In most countries _____ rights fall under civil law and the _____ holder needs to sue someone infringing the _____ in order to enforce his or her rights. In some industries _____ s are an essential form of competitive advantage; in others they are irrelevant.

Exam Probability: **Low**

35. *Answer choices:*

(see index for correct answer)

- a. Municipalization
- b. Ramsey problem
- c. Eisenkammer Pirna
- d. Average cost pricing

Guidance: level 1

:: Writs ::

In common law, a writ of _____ is a writ whereby a private individual who assists a prosecution can receive all or part of any penalty imposed. Its name is an abbreviation of the Latin phrase _____ pro domino rege quam pro se ipso in hac parte sequitur, meaning "[he] who sues in this matter for the king as well as for himself."

36. *Answer choices:*

(see index for correct answer)

- a. Writ of execution
- b. Writ of assistance

Guidance: level 1

:: ::

A _____ is a form of business network, for example, a local organization of businesses whose goal is to further the interests of businesses. Business owners in towns and cities form these local societies to advocate on behalf of the business community. Local businesses are members, and they elect a board of directors or executive council to set policy for the chamber. The board or council then hires a President, CEO or Executive Director, plus staffing appropriate to size, to run the organization.

37. *Answer choices:*

(see index for correct answer)

- a. Chamber of Commerce
- b. co-culture
- c. surface-level diversity

- d. Sarbanes-Oxley act of 2002

Guidance: level 1

:: Auditing ::

_____ refers to the independence of the internal auditor or of the external auditor from parties that may have a financial interest in the business being audited. Independence requires integrity and an objective approach to the audit process. The concept requires the auditor to carry out his or her work freely and in an objective manner.

Exam Probability: **Low**

38. *Answer choices:*

(see index for correct answer)

- a. ISACA
- b. Continuous auditing
- c. Verified Audit Circulation
- d. Auditor independence

Guidance: level 1

:: Timber industry ::

The _____ is an international non-profit, multi-stakeholder organization established in 1993 to promote responsible management of the world's forests. The FSC does this by setting standards on forest products, along with certifying and labeling them as eco-friendly.

Exam Probability: **Low**

39. *Answer choices:*

(see index for correct answer)

- a. Forest Stewardship Council
- b. Lumber
- c. Ottawa River timber trade
- d. Planing mill

Guidance: level 1

:: Professional ethics ::

In the mental health field, a _____ is a situation where multiple roles exist between a therapist, or other mental health practitioner, and a client. _____ s are also referred to as multiple relationships, and these two terms are used interchangeably in the research literature. The American Psychological Association Ethical Principles of Psychologists and Code of Conduct is a resource that outlines ethical standards and principles to which practitioners are expected to adhere. Standard 3.05 of the APA ethics code outlines the definition of multiple relationships. Dual or multiple relationships occur when.

40. *Answer choices:*

(see index for correct answer)

- a. Continuous professional development
- b. Dual relationship
- c. ethical code

Guidance: level 1

:: Decentralization ::

_____ or sub _____ mainly refers to the unrestricted growth in many urban areas of housing, commercial development, and roads over large expanses of land, with little concern for urban planning. In addition to describing a particular form of urbanization, the term also relates to the social and environmental consequences associated with this development. In Continental Europe the term "peri-urbanisation" is often used to denote similar dynamics and phenomena, although the term _____ is currently being used by the European Environment Agency. There is widespread disagreement about what constitutes sprawl and how to quantify it. For example, some commentators measure sprawl only with the average number of residential units per acre in a given area. But others associate it with decentralization , discontinuity , segregation of uses, and so forth.

Exam Probability: **Medium**

41. *Answer choices:*

(see index for correct answer)

- a. Subsidiarity
- b. Local government in the Philippines
- c. District Rural Development Agencies
- d. Urban sprawl

Guidance: level 1

:: ::

A _____ is the ability to carry out a task with determined results often within a given amount of time, energy, or both. _____ s can often be divided into domain-general and domain-specific _____ s. For example, in the domain of work, some general _____ s would include time management, teamwork and leadership, self-motivation and others, whereas domain-specific _____ s would be used only for a certain job. _____ usually requires certain environmental stimuli and situations to assess the level of _____ being shown and used.

Exam Probability: **High**

42. *Answer choices:*

(see index for correct answer)

- a. hierarchical
- b. Character
- c. deep-level diversity
- d. Skill

:: ::

_____ is the introduction of contaminants into the natural environment that cause adverse change. _____ can take the form of chemical substances or energy, such as noise, heat or light. Pollutants, the components of _____ , can be either foreign substances/energies or naturally occurring contaminants. _____ is often classed as point source or nonpoint source _____ .In 2015, _____ killed 9 million people in the world.

Exam Probability: **Low**

43. *Answer choices:*

(see index for correct answer)

- a. similarity-attraction theory
- b. information systems assessment
- c. empathy
- d. imperative

Guidance: level 1

:: Trade unions ::

A _____ was a group formed of private citizens to administer law and order where they considered governmental structures to be inadequate. The term is commonly associated with the frontier areas of the American West in the mid-19th century, where groups attacked cattle rustlers and gangs, and people at gold mining claims. As non-state organizations no functioning checks existed to protect against excessive force or safeguard due process from the committees. In the years prior to the Civil War, some committees worked to free slaves and transport them to freedom.

Exam Probability: **Medium**

44. *Answer choices:*

(see index for correct answer)

- a. Vigilance committee
- b. Union dues
- c. Craft unionism
- d. Givebacks

Guidance: level 1

:: ::

A _____ is an astronomical body orbiting a star or stellar remnant that is massive enough to be rounded by its own gravity, is not massive enough to cause thermonuclear fusion, and has cleared its neighbouring region of _____ esimals.

45. *Answer choices:*

(see index for correct answer)

- a. Planet
- b. levels of analysis
- c. information systems assessment
- d. hierarchical perspective

Guidance: level 1

:: Monopoly (economics) ::

The _____ of 1890 was a United States antitrust law that regulates competition among enterprises, which was passed by Congress under the presidency of Benjamin Harrison.

Exam Probability: **Medium**

46. *Answer choices:*

(see index for correct answer)

- a. Practice of law
- b. Government-granted monopoly
- c. Network effect
- d. Sherman Antitrust Act

:: Ethically disputed business practices ::

_____ is the trading of a public company's stock or other securities by individuals with access to nonpublic information about the company. In various countries, some kinds of trading based on insider information is illegal. This is because it is seen as unfair to other investors who do not have access to the information, as the investor with insider information could potentially make larger profits than a typical investor could make. The rules governing _____ are complex and vary significantly from country to country. The extent of enforcement also varies from one country to another. The definition of insider in one jurisdiction can be broad, and may cover not only insiders themselves but also any persons related to them, such as brokers, associates and even family members. A person who becomes aware of non-public information and trades on that basis may be guilty of a crime.

Exam Probability: **High**

47. *Answer choices:*

(see index for correct answer)

- a. Intensive animal farming
- b. Insider trading
- c. Two sets of books
- d. Designer drug

:: Law ::

_____ is a body of law which defines the role, powers, and structure of different entities within a state, namely, the executive, the parliament or legislature, and the judiciary; as well as the basic rights of citizens and, in federal countries such as the United States and Canada, the relationship between the central government and state, provincial, or territorial governments.

Exam Probability: **High**

48. *Answer choices:*

(see index for correct answer)

- a. Constitutional law
- b. Comparative law

Guidance: level 1

:: ::

_____ is a product prepared from the leaves of the _____ plant by curing them. The plant is part of the genus Nicotiana and of the Solanaceae family. While more than 70 species of _____ are known, the chief commercial crop is N. tabacum. The more potent variant N. rustica is also used around the world.

Exam Probability: **Medium**

49. *Answer choices:*

(see index for correct answer)

- a. imperative
- b. similarity-attraction theory
- c. hierarchical perspective
- d. Sarbanes-Oxley act of 2002

Guidance: level 1

:: Private equity ::

In finance, a high-yield bond is a bond that is rated below investment grade. These bonds have a higher risk of default or other adverse credit events, but typically pay higher yields than better quality bonds in order to make them attractive to investors.

Exam Probability: **High**

50. *Answer choices:*

(see index for correct answer)

- a. Junk bond
- b. Firstpex
- c. Corporate synergy
- d. Corporate raid

:: ::

A _____ is an organization, usually a group of people or a company, authorized to act as a single entity and recognized as such in law. Early incorporated entities were established by charter . Most jurisdictions now allow the creation of new _____ s through registration.

Exam Probability: **Medium**

51. *Answer choices:*

(see index for correct answer)

- a. interpersonal communication
- b. information systems assessment
- c. Corporation
- d. hierarchical perspective

:: Labour law ::

An _____ is special or specified circumstances that partially or fully exempt a person or organization from performance of a legal obligation so as to avoid an unreasonable or disproportionate burden or obstacle.

Exam Probability: **Low**

52. *Answer choices:*

(see index for correct answer)

- a. New Hire Registry
- b. Undue hardship
- c. Work permit
- d. International Association of Labour Law Journals

Guidance: level 1

:: Hazard analysis ::

Broadly speaking, a _____ is the combined effort of 1. identifying and analyzing potential events that may negatively impact individuals, assets, and/or the environment ; and 2. making judgments "on the tolerability of the risk on the basis of a risk analysis" while considering influencing factors . Put in simpler terms, a _____ analyzes what can go wrong, how likely it is to happen, what the potential consequences are, and how tolerable the identified risk is. As part of this process, the resulting determination of risk may be expressed in a quantitative or qualitative fashion. The _____ is an inherent part of an overall risk management strategy, which attempts to, after a _____ , "introduce control measures to eliminate or reduce" any potential risk-related consequences.

53. *Answer choices:*

(see index for correct answer)

- a. Hazard
- b. Hazard identification
- c. Swiss cheese model
- d. Risk assessment

Guidance: level 1

:: ::

_____ or accountancy is the measurement, processing, and communication of financial information about economic entities such as businesses and corporations. The modern field was established by the Italian mathematician Luca Pacioli in 1494. _____ , which has been called the "language of business", measures the results of an organization's economic activities and conveys this information to a variety of users, including investors, creditors, management, and regulators. Practitioners of _____ are known as accountants. The terms " _____ " and "financial reporting" are often used as synonyms.

Exam Probability: **High**

54. *Answer choices:*

(see index for correct answer)

- a. Accounting
- b. deep-level diversity
- c. surface-level diversity
- d. Sarbanes-Oxley act of 2002

Guidance: level 1

:: Fraud ::

In the United States, _____ is the claiming of Medicare health care reimbursement to which the claimant is not entitled. There are many different types of _____ , all of which have the same goal: to collect money from the Medicare program illegitimately.

Exam Probability: **Medium**

55. *Answer choices:*

(see index for correct answer)

- a. Extrinsic fraud
- b. Medicare fraud
- c. misleading advertising
- d. Regummed stamp

Guidance: level 1

:: Ethical banking ::

A _____ or community development finance institution - abbreviated in both cases to CDFI - is a financial institution that provides credit and financial services to underserved markets and populations, primarily in the USA but also in the UK. A CDFI may be a community development bank, a community development credit union , a community development loan fund , a community development venture capital fund , a microenterprise development loan fund, or a community development corporation.

Exam Probability: **Medium**

56. *Answer choices:*

(see index for correct answer)

- a. Community development financial institution
- b. JAK Members Bank
- c. Institute for Social Banking
- d. GLS Bank

Guidance: level 1

:: ::

_____ is the means to see, hear, or become aware of something or someone through our fundamental senses. The term _____ derives from the Latin word perceptio, and is the organization, identification, and interpretation of sensory information in order to represent and understand the presented information, or the environment.

Exam Probability: **High**

57. *Answer choices:*

(see index for correct answer)

- a. cultural
- b. empathy
- c. interpersonal communication
- d. Perception

Guidance: level 1

:: ::

The American Recovery and Reinvestment Act of 2009 , nicknamed the _____ , was a stimulus package enacted by the 111th U.S. Congress and signed into law by President Barack Obama in February 2009. Developed in response to the Great Recession, the ARRA`s primary objective was to save existing jobs and create new ones as soon as possible. Other objectives were to provide temporary relief programs for those most affected by the recession and invest in infrastructure, education, health, and renewable energy.

58. *Answer choices:*

(see index for correct answer)

- a. information systems assessment
- b. similarity-attraction theory
- c. hierarchical
- d. interpersonal communication

Guidance: level 1

:: ::

_____ is "property consisting of land and the buildings on it, along with its natural resources such as crops, minerals or water; immovable property of this nature; an interest vested in this an item of real property, buildings or housing in general. Also: the business of _____ ; the profession of buying, selling, or renting land, buildings, or housing." It is a legal term used in jurisdictions whose legal system is derived from English common law, such as India, England, Wales, Northern Ireland, United States, Canada, Pakistan, Australia, and New Zealand.

Exam Probability: **Low**

59. *Answer choices:*

(see index for correct answer)

- a. open system
- b. interpersonal communication
- c. personal values
- d. Real estate

Guidance: level 1

Accounting

Accounting or accountancy is the measurement, processing, and communication of financial information about economic entities such as businesses and corporations. The modern field was established by the Italian mathematician Luca Pacioli in 1494. Accounting, which has been called the "language of business", measures the results of an organization's economic activities and conveys this information to a variety of users, including investors, creditors, management, and regulators.

:: Tax reform ::

_____ is the process of changing the way taxes are collected or managed by the government and is usually undertaken to improve tax administration or to provide economic or social benefits. _____ can include reducing the level of taxation of all people by the government, making the tax system more progressive or less progressive, or simplifying the tax system and making the system more understandable or more accountable.

Exam Probability: **Low**

1. *Answer choices:*

(see index for correct answer)

- a. Single tax
- b. Rational economic exchange
- c. Tax reform
- d. 2006 Puerto Rico budget crisis

Guidance: level 1

:: Marketing ::

_____ or stock is the goods and materials that a business holds for the ultimate goal of resale .

Exam Probability: **Medium**

2. *Answer choices:*

(see index for correct answer)

- a. Price on application
- b. Inventory
- c. Paddock girl
- d. Notability

Guidance: level 1

:: Business ::

The seller, or the provider of the goods or services, completes a sale in response to an acquisition, appropriation, requisition or a direct interaction with the buyer at the point of sale. There is a passing of title of the item, and the settlement of a price, in which agreement is reached on a price for which transfer of ownership of the item will occur. The seller, not the purchaser typically executes the sale and it may be completed prior to the obligation of payment. In the case of indirect interaction, a person who sells goods or service on behalf of the owner is known as a _____ man or _____ woman or _____ person, but this often refers to someone selling goods in a store/shop, in which case other terms are also common, including _____ clerk, shop assistant, and retail clerk.

Exam Probability: **Medium**

3. *Answer choices:*

(see index for correct answer)

- a. Free trade

- b. Business mileage reimbursement rate
- c. Sales
- d. Professional conference organiser

Guidance: level 1

:: ::

A _____ , in the word's original meaning, is a sheet of paper on which one performs work. They come in many forms, most commonly associated with children's school work assignments, tax forms, and accounting or other business environments. Software is increasingly taking over the paper-based _____ .

Exam Probability: **Low**

4. *Answer choices:*

(see index for correct answer)

- a. interpersonal communication
- b. Worksheet
- c. co-culture
- d. process perspective

Guidance: level 1

:: Generally Accepted Accounting Principles ::

In accounting, _____ is the income that a business have from its normal business activities, usually from the sale of goods and services to customers. _____ is also referred to as sales or turnover. Some companies receive _____ from interest, royalties, or other fees. _____ may refer to business income in general, or it may refer to the amount, in a monetary unit, earned during a period of time, as in "Last year, Company X had _____ of $42 million". Profits or net income generally imply total _____ minus total expenses in a given period. In accounting, in the balance statement it is a subsection of the Equity section and _____ increases equity, it is often referred to as the "top line" due to its position on the income statement at the very top. This is to be contrasted with the "bottom line" which denotes net income .

Exam Probability: **Low**

5. *Answer choices:*

(see index for correct answer)

- a. Insurance asset management
- b. Revenue
- c. Expense
- d. Management accounting principles

Guidance: level 1

:: Financial markets ::

_____ s are monetary contracts between parties. They can be created, traded, modified and settled. They can be cash , evidence of an ownership interest in an entity , or a contractual right to receive or deliver cash .

Exam Probability: **Low**

6. *Answer choices:*

(see index for correct answer)

- a. Earnings guidance
- b. Alternative public offering
- c. Time-weighted average price
- d. Long/short equity

Guidance: level 1

:: Generally Accepted Accounting Principles ::

_____ is, in accrual accounting, money received for goods or services which have not yet been delivered. According to the revenue recognition principle, it is recorded as a liability until delivery is made, at which time it is converted into revenue.

Exam Probability: **Low**

7. *Answer choices:*

(see index for correct answer)

- a. Liability
- b. Consolidation
- c. Provision
- d. Deferred income

Guidance: level 1

:: Generally Accepted Accounting Principles ::

In accrual accounting, the revenue recognition principle states that expenses should be recorded during the period in which they are incurred, regardless of when the transfer of cash occurs. Conversely, cash basis accounting calls for the recognition of an expense when the cash is paid, regardless of when the expense was actually incurred.

Exam Probability: **Medium**

8. *Answer choices:*

(see index for correct answer)

- a. Engagement letter
- b. Historical cost
- c. Construction in progress
- d. Matching principle

Guidance: level 1

:: Auditing ::

_____ , as defined by accounting and auditing, is a process for assuring of an organization's objectives in operational effectiveness and efficiency, reliable financial reporting, and compliance with laws, regulations and policies. A broad concept, _____ involves everything that controls risks to an organization.

Exam Probability: **High**

9. *Answer choices:*

(see index for correct answer)

- a. Certified Quality Auditor
- b. Event data
- c. Internal control
- d. Provided by client

Guidance: level 1

:: Finance ::

In accounting, _____ is the portion of a subsidiary corporation's stock that is not owned by the parent corporation. The magnitude of the _____ in the subsidiary company is generally less than 50% of outstanding shares, or the corporation would generally cease to be a subsidiary of the parent.

Exam Probability: **High**

10. *Answer choices:*

(see index for correct answer)

- a. Minimum lease payments
- b. trading volume
- c. Minority interest
- d. Spot date

Guidance: level 1

:: ::

From an accounting perspective, _____ is crucial because _____ and _____ taxes considerably affect the net income of most companies and because they are subject to laws and regulations .

Exam Probability: **High**

11. *Answer choices:*

(see index for correct answer)

- a. open system
- b. co-culture
- c. Payroll
- d. Sarbanes-Oxley act of 2002

Guidance: level 1

:: Inventory ::

Costs are associated with particular goods using one of the several formulas, including specific identification, first-in first-out , or average cost. Costs include all costs of purchase, costs of conversion and other costs that are incurred in bringing the inventories to their present location and condition. Costs of goods made by the businesses include material, labor, and allocated overhead. The costs of those goods which are not yet sold are deferred as costs of inventory until the inventory is sold or written down in value.

Exam Probability: **Medium**

12. *Answer choices:*
(see index for correct answer)

- a. Stock demands
- b. Order picking
- c. Specific identification
- d. Stock mix

:: Macroeconomics ::

_____ is a change in a price of a good or product, or especially of a currency, in which case it is specifically an official rise of the value of the currency in relation to a foreign currency in a fixed exchange rate system. Under floating exchange rates, by contrast, a rise in a currency's value is an appreciation. Altering the face value of a currency without changing its purchasing power is a redenomination, not a _____ .

Exam Probability: **Low**

13. *Answer choices:*

(see index for correct answer)

- a. Ricardian equivalence
- b. Hydraulic macroeconomics
- c. Robot economics
- d. Revaluation

:: Loans ::

In corporate finance, a _____ is a medium- to long-term debt instrument used by large companies to borrow money, at a fixed rate of interest. The legal term " _____ " originally referred to a document that either creates a debt or acknowledges it, but in some countries the term is now used interchangeably with bond, loan stock or note. A _____ is thus like a certificate of loan or a loan bond evidencing the fact that the company is liable to pay a specified amount with interest and although the money raised by the _____ s becomes a part of the company`s capital structure, it does not become share capital. Senior _____ s get paid before subordinate _____ s, and there are varying rates of risk and payoff for these categories.

Exam Probability: **Medium**

14. *Answer choices:*

(see index for correct answer)

- a. Interest-only loan
- b. Loan waiver
- c. Farm operating loans
- d. SGE Loans

Guidance: level 1

:: Accounting terminology ::

_____ is an accounting system for recording resources whose use has been limited by the donor, grant authority, governing agency, or other individuals or organisations or by law. It emphasizes accountability rather than profitability, and is used by Nonprofit organizations and by governments. In this method, a fund consists of a self-balancing set of accounts and each are reported as either unrestricted, temporarily restricted or permanently restricted based on the provider-imposed restrictions.

Exam Probability: **Medium**

15. *Answer choices:*

(see index for correct answer)

- a. Fund accounting
- b. Impairment cost
- c. Basis of accounting
- d. Mark-to-market

Guidance: level 1

:: Negotiable instrument law ::

_____ of a financial instrument, such as a cheque, is only a signature, not indicating the payee. The effect of this is that it is payable only to the bearer – legally, it transforms an order instrument into a bearer instrument. It is one of the types of endorsement of a negotiable instrument.

Exam Probability: **Low**

16. *Answer choices:*

(see index for correct answer)

- a. Gold v. Eddy
- b. Clearfield Trust Co. v. United States
- c. Blank endorsement
- d. holder in due course doctrine

Guidance: level 1

:: ::

A _____ is the period used by governments for accounting and budget purposes, which varies between countries. It is also used for financial reporting by business and other organizations. Laws in many jurisdictions require company financial reports to be prepared and published on an annual basis, but generally do not require the reporting period to align with the calendar year . Taxation laws generally require accounting records to be maintained and taxes calculated on an annual basis, which usually corresponds to the _____ used for government purposes. The calculation of tax on an annual basis is especially relevant for direct taxation, such as income tax. Many annual government fees—such as Council rates, licence fees, etc.—are also levied on a _____ basis, while others are charged on an anniversary basis.

Exam Probability: **Medium**

17. *Answer choices:*

(see index for correct answer)

- a. hierarchical
- b. imperative
- c. process perspective
- d. information systems assessment

:: Accounting software ::

_____ is an accounting software package developed and marketed by Intuit. _____ products are geared mainly toward small and medium-sized businesses and offer on-premises accounting applications as well as cloud-based versions that accept business payments, manage and pay bills, and payroll functions.

Exam Probability: **Low**

18. *Answer choices:*

(see index for correct answer)

- a. Microsoft Money
- b. Moneydance
- c. Sage 50 Accounting
- d. Procurify

:: Accounting systems ::

In bookkeeping, a _____ statement is a process that explains the difference on a specified date between the bank balance shown in an organization's bank statement, as supplied by the bank and the corresponding amount shown in the organization's own accounting records.

Exam Probability: **Medium**

19. *Answer choices:*

(see index for correct answer)

- a. Substance over form
- b. Inflation accounting
- c. Counting house
- d. Momentum accounting and triple-entry bookkeeping

Guidance: level 1

:: Accounting in the United States ::

The _____ is the source of generally accepted accounting principles used by state and local governments in the United States. As with most of the entities involved in creating GAAP in the United States, it is a private, non-governmental organization.

Exam Probability: **Low**

20. *Answer choices:*

(see index for correct answer)

- a. International Qualification Examination
- b. Governmental Accounting Standards Board
- c. Accounting Research Bulletins
- d. Adjusted basis

Guidance: level 1

:: Finance ::

A _____ , publicly-traded company, publicly-held company, publicly-listed company, or public limited company is a corporation whose ownership is dispersed among the general public in many shares of stock which are freely traded on a stock exchange or in over-the-counter markets. In some jurisdictions, public companies over a certain size must be listed on an exchange. A _____ can be listed or unlisted .

Exam Probability: **High**

21. *Answer choices:*

(see index for correct answer)

- a. Financial commons
- b. Portfolio optimization
- c. NOPAT
- d. Public company

:: Financial accounting ::

_____ is a financial metric which represents operating liquidity available to a business, organisation or other entity, including governmental entities. Along with fixed assets such as plant and equipment, _____ is considered a part of operating capital. Gross _____ is equal to current assets. _____ is calculated as current assets minus current liabilities. If current assets are less than current liabilities, an entity has a _____ deficiency, also called a _____ deficit.

Exam Probability: **High**

22. *Answer choices:*

(see index for correct answer)

- a. Tax amortization benefit
- b. Working capital
- c. Commuted cash value
- d. Holding gains

:: Marketing ::

_____ or stock control can be broadly defined as "the activity of checking a shop's stock." However, a more focused definition takes into account the more science-based, methodical practice of not only verifying a business' inventory but also focusing on the many related facets of inventory management "within an organisation to meet the demand placed upon that business economically." Other facets of _____ include supply chain management, production control, financial flexibility, and customer satisfaction. At the root of _____ , however, is the _____ problem, which involves determining when to order, how much to order, and the logistics of those decisions.

Exam Probability: **Low**

23. *Answer choices:*

(see index for correct answer)

- a. Mystery shopping
- b. Inventory control
- c. Exploratory research
- d. Pricing objectives

Guidance: level 1

:: Financial ratios ::

The _____ is a financial ratio indicating the relative proportion of shareholders' equity and debt used to finance a company's assets. Closely related to leveraging, the ratio is also known as risk, gearing or leverage. The two components are often taken from the firm's balance sheet or statement of financial position , but the ratio may also be calculated using market values for both, if the company's debt and equity are publicly traded, or using a combination of book value for debt and market value for equity financially.

Exam Probability: **Medium**

24. *Answer choices:*

(see index for correct answer)

- a. Debt-to-equity ratio
- b. Sales density
- c. Theoretical ex-rights price
- d. Information ratio

Guidance: level 1

:: Commercial crimes ::

_____ is the act of withholding assets for the purpose of conversion of such assets, by one or more persons to whom the assets were entrusted, either to be held or to be used for specific purposes. _____ is a type of financial fraud. For example, a lawyer might embezzle funds from the trust accounts of their clients; a financial advisor might embezzle the funds of investors; and a husband or a wife might embezzle funds from a bank account jointly held with the spouse.

25. *Answer choices:*

(see index for correct answer)

- a. Embezzlement
- b. Price gouging
- c. Cartel
- d. Offshore leaks

Guidance: level 1

:: Stock market ::

A _____ , equity market or share market is the aggregation of buyers and sellers of stocks , which represent ownership claims on businesses; these may include securities listed on a public stock exchange, as well as stock that is only traded privately. Examples of the latter include shares of private companies which are sold to investors through equity crowdfunding platforms. Stock exchanges list shares of common equity as well as other security types, e.g. corporate bonds and convertible bonds.

Exam Probability: **High**

26. *Answer choices:*

(see index for correct answer)

- a. Stock Market

- b. Common ordinary equity
- c. Ada TV
- d. China Concepts Stock

Guidance: level 1

:: Management accounting ::

A _____ is an organizational unit headed by a manager, who is responsible for its activities and results. In responsibility accounting, revenues and cost information are collected and reported on by _____ s.

Exam Probability: **Low**

27. *Answer choices:*

(see index for correct answer)

- a. Variance
- b. Construction accounting
- c. Responsibility center
- d. Management accounting in supply chains

Guidance: level 1

:: Management accounting ::

In economics, _____ s, indirect costs or overheads are business expenses that are not dependent on the level of goods or services produced by the business. They tend to be time-related, such as interest or rents being paid per month, and are often referred to as overhead costs. This is in contrast to variable costs, which are volume-related and unknown at the beginning of the accounting year. For a simple example, such as a bakery, the monthly rent for the baking facilities, and the monthly payments for the security system and basic phone line are _____ s, as they do not change according to how much bread the bakery produces and sells. On the other hand, the wage costs of the bakery are variable, as the bakery will have to hire more workers if the production of bread increases. Economists reckon _____ as a entry barrier for new entrepreneurs.

Exam Probability: **Medium**

28. *Answer choices:*

(see index for correct answer)

- a. Accounting management
- b. Fixed cost
- c. Cost accounting
- d. Average per-bit delivery cost

Guidance: level 1

:: Production and manufacturing ::

_____ consists of organization-wide efforts to "install and make permanent climate where employees continuously improve their ability to provide on demand products and services that customers will find of particular value." "Total" emphasizes that departments in addition to production are obligated to improve their operations; "management" emphasizes that executives are obligated to actively manage quality through funding, training, staffing, and goal setting. While there is no widely agreed-upon approach, TQM efforts typically draw heavily on the previously developed tools and techniques of quality control. TQM enjoyed widespread attention during the late 1980s and early 1990s before being overshadowed by ISO 9000, Lean manufacturing, and Six Sigma.

Exam Probability: **Low**

29. *Answer choices:*

(see index for correct answer)

- a. Mockup
- b. Hydrosila
- c. Total quality management
- d. Common Industrial Protocol

Guidance: level 1

:: Accounting terminology ::

Accounts are typically defined by an identifier and a caption or header and are coded by account type. In computerized accounting systems with computable quantity accounting, the accounts can have a quantity measure definition.

30. *Answer choices:*

(see index for correct answer)

- a. revenue recognition principle
- b. Chart of accounts
- c. Accounts receivable
- d. Accrued liabilities

Guidance: level 1

:: Quality control tools ::

A _____ is a type of diagram that represents an algorithm, workflow or process. _____ can also be defined as a diagramatic representation of an algorithm .

Exam Probability: **Medium**

31. *Answer choices:*

(see index for correct answer)

- a. P-chart
- b. Seven Basic Tools of Quality
- c. Flowchart
- d. Scatter plot

:: Taxation ::

_____ refers to the base upon which an income tax system imposes tax. Generally, it includes some or all items of income and is reduced by expenses and other deductions. The amounts included as income, expenses, and other deductions vary by country or system. Many systems provide that some types of income are not taxable and some expenditures not deductible in computing _____ . Some systems base tax on _____ of the current period, and some on prior periods. _____ may refer to the income of any taxpayer, including individuals and corporations, as well as entities that themselves do not pay tax, such as partnerships, in which case it may be called "net profit".

Exam Probability: **Medium**

32. *Answer choices:*

(see index for correct answer)

- a. Taxable income
- b. Tolerance tax
- c. Fiscal burden of government
- d. Severance tax

:: Pharmaceutical industry ::

A _____ is a document in which data collected for a clinical trial is first recorded. This data is usually later entered in the case report form. The International Conference on Harmonisation of Technical Requirements for Registration of Pharmaceuticals for Human Use guidelines define _____ s as "original documents, data, and records." _____ s contain source data, which is defined as "all information in original records and certified copies of original records of clinical findings, observations, or other activities in a clinical trial necessary for the reconstruction and evaluation of the trial."

Exam Probability: **High**

33. *Answer choices:*

(see index for correct answer)

- a. Access to Medicine Index
- b. Big Pharma conspiracy theory
- c. Insulated shipping container
- d. Source document

Guidance: level 1

:: Business ethics ::

In accounting and in most Schools of economic thought, _____ is a rational and unbiased estimate of the potential market price of a good, service, or asset. It takes into account such objectivity factors as.

Exam Probability: **High**

34. *Answer choices:*

(see index for correct answer)

- a. Jewish business ethics
- b. Conspiracy of Fools
- c. Fair value
- d. Center for Adult Development

Guidance: level 1

:: Fundamental analysis ::

_____ is the monetary value of earnings per outstanding share of common stock for a company.

Exam Probability: **Medium**

35. *Answer choices:*

(see index for correct answer)

- a. Enterprise value
- b. Restricted stock
- c. Earnings per share
- d. Growth stock

Guidance: level 1

:: Pricing ::

_____ is a pricing strategy in which the selling price is determined by adding a specific amount markup to a product's unit cost. An alternative pricing method is value-based pricing.

Exam Probability: **Medium**

36. *Answer choices:*

(see index for correct answer)

- a. Cost-plus pricing
- b. private valuation
- c. Express pricing
- d. Flooding the market

Guidance: level 1

:: Foreign exchange market ::

A currency , in the most specific sense is money in any form when in use or circulation as a medium of exchange, especially circulating banknotes and coins. A more general definition is that a currency is a system of money in common use, especially for people in a nation. Under this definition, US dollars , pounds sterling , Australian dollars , European euros , Russian rubles and Indian Rupees are examples of currencies. These various currencies are recognized as stores of value and are traded between nations in foreign exchange markets, which determine the relative values of the different currencies. Currencies in this sense are defined by governments, and each type has limited boundaries of acceptance.

Exam Probability: **High**

37. *Answer choices:*

(see index for correct answer)

- a. VND Index
- b. Monetary unit
- c. Managed float regime
- d. Exchange-rate regime

Guidance: level 1

:: Generally Accepted Accounting Principles ::

_____ is a small amount of discretionary funds in the form of cash used for expenditures where it is not sensible to make any disbursement by cheque, because of the inconvenience and costs of writing, signing, and then cashing the cheque.

Exam Probability: **Medium**

38. *Answer choices:*

(see index for correct answer)

- a. Closing entries
- b. Petty cash
- c. Net profit
- d. Goodwill

Guidance: level 1

:: Taxation ::

A _____ is a person or organization subject to pay a tax. _____ s have an Identification Number, a reference number issued by a government to its citizens.

Exam Probability: **Low**

39. *Answer choices:*

(see index for correct answer)

- a. Back taxes
- b. Value capture
- c. Energy tax
- d. Taxpayer

:: Real property law ::

A _____ or millage rate is an ad valorem tax on the value of a property, usually levied on real estate. The tax is levied by the governing authority of the jurisdiction in which the property is located. This can be a national government, a federated state, a county or geographical region or a municipality. Multiple jurisdictions may tax the same property. This tax can be contrasted to a rent tax which is based on rental income or imputed rent, and a land value tax, which is a levy on the value of land, excluding the value of buildings and other improvements.

Exam Probability: **Medium**

40. *Answer choices:*
(see index for correct answer)

- a. Public land
- b. Property tax
- c. Servient estate
- d. Disseisor

:: Accounting source documents ::

_____ is a letter sent by a customer to a supplier to inform the supplier that their invoice has been paid. If the customer is paying by cheque, the _____ often accompanies the cheque. The advice may consist of a literal letter or of a voucher attached to the side or top of the cheque.

Exam Probability: **High**

41. *Answer choices:*

(see index for correct answer)

- a. Remittance advice
- b. Bank statement
- c. Air waybill
- d. Credit memorandum

Guidance: level 1

:: SEC filings ::

_____ is a prescribed regulation under the US Securities Act of 1933 that lays out reporting requirements for various SEC filings used by public companies. Companies are also often called issuers , filers or registrants .

Exam Probability: **High**

42. *Answer choices:*

(see index for correct answer)

- a. Form 20-F
- b. Form 144
- c. Regulation S-K
- d. Form D

Guidance: level 1

:: Business economics ::

_____ is one of the constituents of a leasing calculus or operation. It describes the future value of a good in terms of absolute value in monetary terms and it is sometimes abbreviated into a percentage of the initial price when the item was new.

Exam Probability: **Low**

43. *Answer choices:*

(see index for correct answer)

- a. Average daily rate
- b. Disclosed fees
- c. Peer group analysis
- d. Lateral expansion

Guidance: level 1

:: Legal terms ::

A _____ is a gathering of people who have been invited by a host for the purposes of socializing, conversation, recreation, or as part of a festival or other commemoration of a special occasion. A _____ will typically feature food and beverages, and often music and dancing or other forms of entertainment. In many Western countries, parties for teens and adults are associated with drinking alcohol such as beer, wine, or distilled spirits.

Exam Probability: **High**

44. *Answer choices:*

(see index for correct answer)

- a. Police caution
- b. Informed refusal
- c. Party
- d. Assisting Offender

Guidance: level 1

:: Financial ratios ::

In finance, the _____ , also known as the acid-test ratio   is a type
of liquidity ratio which measures the ability of a company to use its near
cash or quick assets to extinguish or retire its current liabilities
immediately. Quick assets include those current assets that presumably can be
quickly converted to cash at close to their book values. It is the ratio
between quickly available or liquid assets and current liabilities.

Exam Probability: **Low**

45. *Answer choices:*

(see index for correct answer)

- a. Net interest spread
- b. Cash flow return on investment
- c. Return on event
- d. Quick ratio

Guidance: level 1

:: Accounting software ::

_____ is any item or verifiable record that is generally accepted as
payment for goods and services and repayment of debts, such as taxes, in a
particular country or socio-economic context. The main functions of _____
are distinguished as: a medium of exchange, a unit of account, a store of value
and sometimes, a standard of deferred payment. Any item or verifiable record
that fulfils these functions can be considered as _____ .

46. *Answer choices:*

(see index for correct answer)

- a. You Need a Budget
- b. Chrysler Comprehensive Compensation System
- c. Kerridge Commercial Systems
- d. Comparison of accounting software

Guidance: level 1

:: Financial accounting ::

In accounting, _____ is the value of an asset according to its balance sheet account balance. For assets, the value is based on the original cost of the asset less any depreciation, amortization or impairment costs made against the asset. Traditionally, a company's _____ is its total assets minus intangible assets and liabilities. However, in practice, depending on the source of the calculation, _____ may variably include goodwill, intangible assets, or both. The value inherent in its workforce, part of the intellectual capital of a company, is always ignored. When intangible assets and goodwill are explicitly excluded, the metric is often specified to be "tangible _____".

Exam Probability: **Medium**

47. *Answer choices:*

(see index for correct answer)

- a. Controlling interest
- b. Working capital
- c. Book value
- d. Floating capital

Guidance: level 1

:: Business law ::

A _____ is a business entity created by two or more parties, generally characterized by shared ownership, shared returns and risks, and shared governance. Companies typically pursue _____ s for one of four reasons: to access a new market, particularly emerging markets; to gain scale efficiencies by combining assets and operations; to share risk for major investments or projects; or to access skills and capabilities.

Exam Probability: **High**

48. *Answer choices:*

(see index for correct answer)

- a. Joint venture
- b. Statutory liability
- c. Bulk transfer
- d. Closed shop

Guidance: level 1

:: Fraud ::

In law, _____ is intentional deception to secure unfair or unlawful gain, or to deprive a victim of a legal right. _____ can violate civil law , a criminal law , or it may cause no loss of money, property or legal right but still be an element of another civil or criminal wrong. The purpose of _____ may be monetary gain or other benefits, for example by obtaining a passport, travel document, or driver's license, or mortgage _____ , where the perpetrator may attempt to qualify for a mortgage by way of false statements.

Exam Probability: **Low**

49. *Answer choices:*

(see index for correct answer)

- a. Claims Conference
- b. Corporate scandal
- c. Extrinsic fraud
- d. Address fraud

Guidance: level 1

:: Management accounting ::

_____ , or dollar contribution per unit, is the selling price per unit minus the variable cost per unit. "Contribution" represents the portion of sales revenue that is not consumed by variable costs and so contributes to the coverage of fixed costs. This concept is one of the key building blocks of break-even analysis.

Exam Probability: **High**

50. *Answer choices:*

(see index for correct answer)

- a. Management control system
- b. Contribution margin
- c. Resource consumption accounting
- d. Net present value

Guidance: level 1

:: Generally Accepted Accounting Principles ::

Expenditure is an outflow of money to another person or group to pay for an item or service, or for a category of costs. For a tenant, rent is an _____ . For students or parents, tuition is an _____ . Buying food, clothing, furniture or an automobile is often referred to as an _____ . An _____ is a cost that is "paid" or "remitted", usually in exchange for something of value. Something that seems to cost a great deal is "expensive". Something that seems to cost little is "inexpensive". " _____ s of the table" are _____ s of dining, refreshments, a feast, etc.

51. *Answer choices:*

(see index for correct answer)

- a. Gross profit
- b. Expense
- c. Standard Business Reporting
- d. Depreciation

Guidance: level 1

:: Organizational structure ::

An _____ defines how activities such as task allocation, coordination, and supervision are directed toward the achievement of organizational aims.

Exam Probability: **Low**

52. *Answer choices:*

(see index for correct answer)

- a. Unorganisation
- b. Organizational structure
- c. Organization of the New York City Police Department
- d. Automated Bureaucracy

:: Internal Revenue Code ::

The _____ , formally the _____ of 1986, is the domestic portion of federal statutory tax law in the United States, published in various volumes of the United States Statutes at Large, and separately as Title 26 of the United States Code . It is organized topically, into subtitles and sections, covering income tax , payroll taxes, estate taxes, gift taxes, and excise taxes; as well as procedure and administration. Its implementing agency is the Internal Revenue Service.

Exam Probability: **Low**

53. *Answer choices:*

(see index for correct answer)

- a. Internal Revenue Code section 132
- b. Internal Revenue Code
- c. 527 organization
- d. Casualty loss

:: United States Generally Accepted Accounting Principles ::

In a companies' financial reporting, _____ "includes all changes in equity during a period except those resulting from investments by owners and distributions to owners". Because that use excludes the effects of changing ownership interest, an economic measure of _____ is necessary for financial analysis from the shareholders' point of view

Exam Probability: **High**

54. *Answer choices:*

(see index for correct answer)

- a. Single Audit
- b. Comprehensive income
- c. Permanent fund
- d. Comprehensive annual financial report

Guidance: level 1

:: Taxation in the United States ::

Basis , as used in United States tax law, is the original cost of property, adjusted for factors such as depreciation. When property is sold, the taxpayer pays/ taxes on a capital gain/ that equals the amount realized on the sale minus the sold property's basis.

Exam Probability: **High**

55. *Answer choices:*

(see index for correct answer)

- a. Voluntary disclosure agreement
- b. Half-year convention
- c. Tax Day
- d. Income tax audit

Guidance: level 1

:: Land value taxation ::

_____ , sometimes referred to as dry _____ , is the solid surface of Earth that is not permanently covered by water. The vast majority of human activity throughout history has occurred in _____ areas that support agriculture, habitat, and various natural resources. Some life forms have developed from predecessor species that lived in bodies of water.

Exam Probability: **Low**

56. *Answer choices:*

(see index for correct answer)

- a. Prosper Australia
- b. Land
- c. Land value tax
- d. Lands Valuation Appeal Court

:: Management ::

The _____ is a strategy performance management tool – a semi-standard structured report, that can be used by managers to keep track of the execution of activities by the staff within their control and to monitor the consequences arising from these actions.

Exam Probability: **High**

57. *Answer choices:*

(see index for correct answer)

- a. Power structure
- b. Operations research
- c. Overtime rate
- d. Management styles

:: Accounting terminology ::

_____ or capital expense is the money a company spends to buy, maintain, or improve its fixed assets, such as buildings, vehicles, equipment, or land. It is considered a _____ when the asset is newly purchased or when money is used towards extending the useful life of an existing asset, such as repairing the roof.

Exam Probability: **High**

58. *Answer choices:*

(see index for correct answer)

- a. Impairment cost
- b. Capital expenditure
- c. Accounts receivable
- d. Accounts payable

Guidance: level 1

:: Manufacturing ::

_____ s are goods that have completed the manufacturing process but have not yet been sold or distributed to the end user.

Exam Probability: **Low**

59. *Answer choices:*

(see index for correct answer)

- a. Useful art
- b. Finished good
- c. Boutique manufacturing
- d. fixed position

Guidance: level 1

INDEX: Correct Answers

Foundations of Business

1. a: Risk management

2. a: Credit card

3. d: Bias

4. d: Corporate governance

5. a: Business

6. c: Venture capital

7. : Life

8. d: Best practice

9. a: Organizational culture

10. : Restructuring

11. a: Committee

12. a: Social responsibility

13. : Quality control

14. d: Project management

15. c: Law

16. a: ITeM

17. c: Subsidiary

18. : Joint venture

19. d: Evaluation

20. c: Free trade

21. d: Information systems

22. d: Exchange rate

23. d: Manufacturing

24. d: Strategic alliance

25. : Income statement

26. b: Partnership

27. c: Document

28. b: Chart

29. : Capital market

30. b: Franchising

31. b: Expense

32. b: Stock market

33. a: Policy

34. c: Perception

35. a: Trade

36. a: Sony

37. d: Preference

38. d: Commerce

39. d: Sales

40. b: Gross domestic product

41. d: Question

42. a: Frequency

43. : Innovation

44. a: Protection

45. a: Property rights

46. b: Security

47. c: Employment

48. d: Integrity

49. c: Dividend

50. : Trade agreement

51. c: Consumer Protection

52. c: Training

53. b: Political risk

54. a: Capitalism

55. a: Cooperation

56. : Shareholders

57. c: Buyer

58. : Exercise

59. c: Patent

Management

1. b: Fixed cost

2. a: Benchmarking

3. a: Expert

4. : Dilemma

5. : Size

6. : Synergy

7. d: Utility

8. d: Justice

9. : Information

10. c: Self-assessment

11. b: Income

12. b: Case study

13. a: Question

14. a: Negotiation

15. b: Goal setting

16. d: Schedule

17. b: Resource

18. c: Organizational structure

19. : Project

20. c: Analysis

21. b: Business model

22. b: Job rotation

23. b: Statistic

24. a: Problem

25. : Ownership

26. d: Performance

27. d: Industrial Revolution

28. a: Transactional leadership

29. a: Reputation

30. d: Training

31. : Political risk

32. a: Sexual harassment

33. a: Restructuring

34. : Board of directors

35. : Best practice

36. d: Perception

37. b: Quality control

38. a: Time management

39. a: Stereotype

40. : Knowledge management

41. b: Assessment center

42. : Market share

43. c: Collective bargaining

44. : Ratio

45. : Change management

46. d: Total quality management

47. a: Chief executive officer

48. d: Inventory control

49. c: Checklist

50. c: Pension

51. d: SWOT analysis

52. b: Enron

53. : General manager

54. a: Affirmative action

55. : Warehouse

56. b: Integrity

57. a: Virtual team

58. c: Mission statement

59. : Cost

Business law

1. d: Standing

2. c: Trial

3. a: Statute of frauds

4. d: Cooperative

5. d: Purchasing

6. b: Amendment

7. b: Security interest

8. d: Output contract

9. c: Criminal law

10. b: Economic espionage

11. b: Social responsibility

12. c: Specific performance

13. b: Environmental Protection

14. c: Contract law

15. : Sherman Act

16. b: Asset

17. b: Corporate governance

18. : Regulation

19. : Liquidated damages

20. d: Promissory note

21. c: Writ

22. d: Consumer protection

23. b: Inventory

24. d: Public policy

25. d: Lease

26. : Restraint of trade

27. a: Bailee

28. c: Firm

29. a: Option contract

30. c: Corporation

31. a: Disparagement

32. c: Real property

33. a: Corruption

34. : Foreign Corrupt Practices Act

35. b: Buyer

36. a: Eminent domain

37. a: Damages

38. b: Impossibility

39. : Acceleration clause

40. c: Tort

41. c: Constitutional law

42. b: Good faith

43. : Liquidation

44. d: Parol evidence

45. d: Insolvency

46. c: Economic Espionage Act

47. : Requirements contract

48. a: Revocation

49. b: Arbitration

50. d: Breach of contract

51. b: World Trade Organization

52. d: Market value

53. a: Mediation

54. c: Procedural law

55. b: Employment discrimination

56. a: Bill of lading

57. c: Advertising

58. c: Warranty

59. : Securities and Exchange Commission

Finance

1. a: Stockholder

2. c: Interest rate risk

3. d: Merchandising

4. c: Commercial bank

5. c: Ledger

6. : Internal control

7. a: Bank reconciliation

8. d: Rate of return

9. : Revenue

10. a: Operating expense

11. d: Security

12. b: Chart of accounts

13. : Mutual fund

14. : Managerial accounting

15. a: Financial instrument

16. a: Risk assessment

17. : Insurance

18. b: Capital asset

19. : Capital expenditure

20. : Rate risk

21. : Limited liability

22. b: WorldCom

23. d: Yield curve

24. b: Value Line

25. d: Historical cost

26. : Compound interest

27. : Treasury stock

28. : Fair value

29. b: Competition

30. a: Normal balance

31. a: Saving

32. b: Cost accounting

33. : Financial accounting

34. a: Shareholder

35. b: Conservatism

36. b: Accelerated depreciation

37. a: General journal

38. d: Market price

39. a: Debt ratio

40. d: Factory

41. d: Revenue recognition

42. b: Commercial paper

43. b: Liquidation

44. c: Accrued interest

45. d: Pension fund

46. c: International Financial Reporting Standards

47. a: Inventory

48. c: Long-term liabilities

49. : Securities and Exchange Commission

50. b: Futures contract

51. c: Advertising

52. c: Accounts payable

53. a: Exchange rate

54. d: Income tax

55. : Risk premium

56. b: Tax expense

57. b: Cost object

58. d: Indenture

59. a: Capital lease

Human resource management

1. c: Performance improvement

2. d: Ricci v. DeStefano

3. c: Committee

4. d: Job enrichment

5. b: Job description

6. : Compa-ratio

7. d: Industrial relations

8. a: Learning organization

9. c: Business model

10. a: Evaluation

11. a: Test validity

12. c: Assessment center

13. : Employee stock

14. b: Disability insurance

15. d: Pregnancy discrimination

16. a: Performance management

17. d: Sweatshop

18. d: Unemployment insurance

19. d: Free Trade

20. : Pattern bargaining

21. b: E-HRM

22. c: Outsourcing

23. a: Control group

24. c: Locus of control

25. c: Training

26. d: Nepotism

27. : Employee Polygraph Protection Act

28. a: Service Employees International Union

29. a: Case interview

30. b: Right to work

31. a: Whistleblower

32. b: Knowledge worker

33. : Workplace bullying

34. a: Organizational structure

35. : Realistic job preview

36. c: Schedule

37. c: Collective bargaining

38. c: Overlearning

39. c: Pension

40. b: Census

41. b: Asset

42. d: Recession

43. b: Cost of living

44. : Content validity

45. c: Coaching

46. c: Exit interview

47. d: Wage

48. d: Employee handbook

49. b: Affirmative action

50. d: Cost leadership

51. : Needs assessment

52. c: Wage curve

53. b: Human resource management

54. : Vertical integration

55. b: Fair Labor Standards Act

56. c: Piece rate

57. : Family violence

58. c: Self-actualization

59. b: Behavior modification

Information systems

1. b: Enterprise application

2. d: Information ethics

3. d: Operational system

4. a: Click-through

5. a: Read-only memory

6. c: Decision support system

7. a: Global Positioning System

8. b: Google

9. b: Business rule

10. : Disaster recovery plan

11. d: Interactivity

12. : Information governance

13. c: Identity theft

14. a: Privacy policy

15. c: Payment system

16. d: Backbone network

17. d: Data cleansing

18. a: Spyware

19. b: Acceptable use policy

20. a: Drill down

21. d: Digital rights management

22. : Downtime

23. : Supply chain

24. c: Electronic data interchange

25. a: Questionnaire

26. b: Second Life

27. c: Fault tolerance

28. b: Password

29. b: ICANN

30. b: Common Criteria

31. b: Database

32. : Dashboard

33. : Knowledge management

34. d: Personalization

35. : System

36. c: Resource management

37. b: Craigslist

38. c: Byte

39. b: Consumerization

40. : Enterprise resource planning

41. c: Encryption

42. a: Random access

43. a: Data aggregator

44. a: Data analysis

45. a: Picasa

46. a: Computer fraud

47. : Data dictionary

48. c: Government-to-business

49. : Groupware

50. a: Word

51. d: Click fraud

52. b: Data warehouse

53. b: Infrastructure

54. a: Payment Card Industry Data Security Standard

55. c: Copyright

56. b: Government-to-citizen

57. b: Galileo

58. c: Service level agreement

59. : Automation

Marketing

1. a: Direct marketing

2. a: Marketing strategy

3. c: Retail

4. a: Performance

5. d: Qualitative research

6. a: Utility

7. c: Cognitive dissonance

8. b: Marketing plan

9. a: Retailing

10. c: Perception

11. b: Franchising

12. : Infomercial

13. : Partnership

14. b: Productivity

15. c: Competitive advantage

16. : Data analysis

17. d: Star

18. c: Investment

19. : Frequency

20. c: Brand awareness

21. b: General Motors

22. b: Quantitative research

23. : Electronic data interchange

24. d: Brand extension

25. a: Advertising agency

26. b: Reinforcement

27. c: Creativity

28. : Hearing

29. b: Information system

30. : Complaint

31. b: Brand equity

32. c: Empowerment

33. a: Economies of scale

34. c: Expense

35. b: Cost-plus pricing

36. : Exploratory research

37. b: Stock

38. d: Subsidiary

39. a: Monopoly

40. b: Social media

41. d: Communication

42. c: Testimonial

43. b: Telemarketing

44. : Creative brief

45. : Warranty

46. : Buyer

47. b: Interview

48. c: Market share

49. : Questionnaire

50. a: Customer value

51. a: Business marketing

52. b: Manufacturing

53. a: Mass customization

54. : Business Week

55. a: Target market

56. : Credit

57. c: Google

58. : Loyalty

59. : Health

Manufacturing

1. c: Obsolescence

2. d: New product development

3. b: Glass

4. a: Credit

5. : Elastomer

6. d: Ball

7. b: Reorder point

8. d: Heat transfer

9. c: Cost driver

10. d: Root cause

11. a: Cash register

12. b: Statistical process control

13. : Joint Commission

14. d: Workflow

15. b: Project manager

16. a: Sensitivity analysis

17. b: Good

18. c: Resource

19. a: Steel

20. : Quality Engineering

21. b: Project

22. a: Heat treating

23. d: Tool

24. a: Procurement

25. c: Vendor relationship management

26. : Sequence

27. c: Service quality

28. b: Scheduling

29. d: Transaction cost

30. : Expediting

31. a: Rolling Wave planning

32. : Chemical industry

33. : Chemical reaction

34. c: Strategic planning

35. b: EFQM

36. : Reverse auction

37. b: Value engineering

38. a: Sharing

39. c: Accreditation

40. a: Quality costs

41. c: Volume

42. a: Customer

43. b: Process capital

44. : METRIC

45. b: Stakeholder management

46. b: Perfect competition

47. b: Gantt chart

48. d: Project management

49. b: Sales

50. b: Indirect costs

51. d: Process capability

52. c: Quality management

53. a: ROOT

54. c: Asset

55. a: Supply chain network

56. c: Downtime

57. a: Change management

58. c: Kanban

59. b: Supplier relationship management

Commerce

1. a: Chief executive officer

2. a: Inventory control

3. b: Initiative

4. : Good

5. b: Authentication

6. b: Board of directors

7. b: Wall Street Journal

8. b: Antitrust

9. b: Bank

10. a: Liquidation

11. : E-commerce

12. : Cost structure

13. a: Economy

14. a: Trial

15. c: Insurance

16. d: Case study

17. b: Land

18. : Industry

19. : Appeal

20. : Procurement

21. : Product line

22. c: Long run

23. b: Social shopping

24. a: Information system

25. a: Commerce

26. d: Financial services

27. c: Automation

28. a: Logistics Management

29. a: Management

30. a: Contribution margin

31. : Pension

32. : Human resources

33. d: Customs

34. : Overhead cost

35. : Graduation

36. b: Excite

37. c: Customer satisfaction

38. : Payment card

39. b: Contract

40. b: Microsoft

41. c: Committee

42. c: Security

43. b: Cooperative

44. b: Merchant

45. : Building

46. d: Lease

47. a: Optimum

48. b: Wholesale

49. b: Encryption

50. c: Stock

51. : Complaint

52. : Organizational structure

53. d: Standing

54. b: Organization chart

55. d: Economic regulation

56. : Bottom line

57. a: Standardization

58. d: Public relations

59. a: Total revenue

Business ethics

1. c: Clean Water Act

2. d: United Farm Workers

3. d: Authoritarian

4. c: Dress code

5. b: Pyramid scheme

6. c: Corporate governance

7. : Whistleblower

8. d: Endangered Species Act

9. : Marketing

10. a: Lead paint

11. d: Subprime lending

12. b: Reputation

13. a: Lanham Act

14. d: Wall Street

15. a: Pollution Prevention

16. d: Building

17. : Pure Food and Drug Act

18. d: Transformational leadership

19. c: Layoff

20. : Nonprofit

21. b: Statutory law

22. a: Fraud

23. d: Federal Trade Commission Act

24. b: Oil spill

25. b: Patriot Act

26. b: Transocean

27. b: Biofuel

28. a: ExxonMobil

29. d: European Commission

30. c: Clayton Act

31. b: Working poor

32. b: Interlocking directorate

33. : Lawsuit

34. b: Enron

35. : Patent

36. c: Qui tam

37. a: Chamber of Commerce

38. d: Auditor independence

39. a: Forest Stewardship Council

40. b: Dual relationship

41. d: Urban sprawl

42. d: Skill

43. : Pollution

44. a: Vigilance committee

45. a: Planet

46. d: Sherman Antitrust Act

47. b: Insider trading

48. a: Constitutional law

49. : Tobacco

50. a: Junk bond

51. c: Corporation

52. b: Undue hardship

53. d: Risk assessment

54. a: Accounting

55. b: Medicare fraud

56. a: Community development financial institution

57. d: Perception

58. : Recovery Act

59. d: Real estate

Accounting

1. c: Tax reform

2. b: Inventory

3. c: Sales

4. b: Worksheet

5. b: Revenue

6. : Financial instrument

7. d: Deferred income

8. d: Matching principle

9. c: Internal control

10. c: Minority interest

11. c: Payroll

12. : Cost of goods sold

13. d: Revaluation

14. : Debenture

15. a: Fund accounting

16. c: Blank endorsement

17. : Fiscal year

18. : QuickBooks

19. : Bank reconciliation

20. b: Governmental Accounting Standards Board

21. d: Public company

22. b: Working capital

23. b: Inventory control

24. a: Debt-to-equity ratio

25. a: Embezzlement

26. a: Stock Market

27. c: Responsibility center

28. b: Fixed cost

29. c: Total quality management

30. b: Chart of accounts

31. c: Flowchart

32. a: Taxable income

33. d: Source document

34. c: Fair value

35. c: Earnings per share

36. a: Cost-plus pricing

37. b: Monetary unit

38. b: Petty cash

39. d: Taxpayer

40. b: Property tax

41. a: Remittance advice

42. c: Regulation S-K

43. : Residual value

44. c: Party

45. d: Quick ratio

46. : Money

47. c: Book value

48. a: Joint venture

49. : Fraud

50. b: Contribution margin

51. b: Expense

52. b: Organizational structure

53. b: Internal Revenue Code

54. b: Comprehensive income

55. : Cost basis

56. b: Land

57. : Balanced scorecard

58. b: Capital expenditure

59. b: Finished good